THE EMPLOYMENT CONTRACT

THE EMPLOYMENT CONTRACT

Rights and Duties of Employers and Employees

WARREN FREEDMAN

Q Quorum Books

New York · Westport, Connecticut · London

Library of Congress Cataloging-in-Publication Data

Freedman, Warren.
   The employment contract : rights and duties of employers and
employees / Warren Freedman.
      p. cm.
   Includes index.
   ISBN 0–89930–376–5 (alk. paper)
    1. Labor laws and legislation—United States. 2. Labor contract—
United States. I. Title.
KF3319.F74   1989
344.73'01—dc19
[347.3041]   89–3783

British Library Cataloguing in Publication Data is available.

Library of Congress Catalog Card Number: 89–3783
ISBN: 0–89930–376–5

First published in 1989 by Quorum Books

Greenwood Press, Inc.
88 Post Road West, Westport, Connecticut 06881

Printed in the United States of America

The paper used in this book complies with the
Permanent Paper Standard issued by the National
Information Standards Organization (Z39.48–1984).

10 9 8 7 6 5 4 3 2 1

Contents

1

Introduction to the Employment Relationship

1.1 HISTORICAL BACKGROUND

It is said that, before the Industrial Revolution in England (1750 to 1850), employment relations were of minor importance in the law. Most economic activity was carried on by individual agricultural and commercial units composed of the entrepreneur, his family, and perhaps a few servants.[1] The master-servant relationship was one of status; that is, the master took care of all the physical, food, and shelter needs of the servant, while the servant had the duty to obey and work for the master.[2] The relationship of master and servant was obviously not a matter of contract; yet the obligations of both the master and servant were imposed by the English common law as a matter of public policy.[3] At the end of the eighteenth century the great legal scholar Blackstone delineated that relationship in these words:

The . . . great relations in private life are, (1) that of master and servant, which is founded in convenience, whereby a man is directed to call in the assistance of others, where his own skill and labor will not be sufficient to answer the cares incumbent upon him. . . . The first sort of servants therefore, acknowledged by the laws of England, are menial servants; so called from being intra moenia, or domestics. The contract between them and their masters arises upon the hiring. If the hiring be general without any particular time limited, the law construes it to be a hiring for a year; upon a principle of natural equity, that the servant shall serve, and the master maintain him, throughout all the revolutions of the respective seasons; as well when there is work to be done, as when there is not.

One of the great shortcomings of that master-servant relationship was the legal restriction on termination of the working relationship. Parliament, for example, enacted statutes from time to time prohibiting servants from terminating their relationships with masters.[5] There was civil liability upon third parties who lured a servant away from the master; such conduct was deemed an unwanted interference with the master-servant relationship.[6]

Historically, the Industrial Revolution in England brought about the decline of the master-servant relationship, and the immediate recognition of a new relationship between worker or employee and entrepreneur or employer. The contract, oral or written, became the vehicle for employment, and the relationship between employer and employee took on the mantle of "agency." In brief, the relationship of employer and employee is said to exist when, pursuant to an express or implied agreement of the parties, one person, the employee, undertakes to perform services or do work under the direction and control of the other, the employer. Obviously, the employee was no longer a servant without rights,[7] for the employer-employee relationship was now dependent upon the consent of both parties. Historically, wages constituted the sole reward for labor, but, in present day employment, employee benefits gained by individual bargaining, by union recognition, or by federal or state statutes are taken for granted.

1.2 THE CONCEPT OF PROTECTION OF EMPLOYEE RIGHTS

Employment security protection, developed through the English common law, commenced under contract theories and later under tort theories for wrongful dismissal. Compensation for the employee was governed by the same set of principles that apply to the compensation of an agent; upon discharge or dismissal from employment, the employee is entitled to wages down to the expiration of the last pay period, in the absence of an agreement to the contrary. It is a breach of the employment contract for the employer to withhold wages.

Recovery for wrongful dismissal of an employee was recognized as a cause of action under contract principles in Petermann v. Teamsters,[8] where the California appellate court found a violation of public policy when the employee refused to commit the crime of perjury on behalf of the defendant, and therefore he was wrongfully discharged. This implied breach of the employment contract due to wrongful discharge also encompassed the "bad faith" dismissal, as illustrated in Monge v. Beebe Rubber Co.,[9] where the New Hampshire Supreme Court balanced the employee's interest in continued employment with the employer's interest in operating his own business. And the Supreme Court of Michigan in 1980 opined that the legitimate employee expectation of employment was protectible where the employer issued policy statements and published handbooks on the integrity of the employment contract and the disavowal of precipitous employee dismissals.[10]

Tortious recovery for wrongful dismissal of an employee is illustrated in Nees v. Hocks,[11] where the Oregon court awarded the plaintiff not only compensatory damages for the employer's tortious act but also punitive damages; all that the employee had done to merit dismissal was to request jury duty over his employer's objections. The court found that the employer's willful violation of public policy in favor of jury service gave rise to tort liability. But the New York Court of Appeals' decision in Murphy v. American Home Products, Inc.[12] constituted a refusal to recognize a tort cause of action for wrongful dismissal; the court believed that public policy judgments are not for the courts nor for the employee to decide, but only for the state legislatures.

Individual rights of employees, are recognized today, particularly in corporate employment, whether the employee is in production or clerical, whether the employee is a professional, middle manager, or executive. Basically, such employee rights involve the definition and observance of rights to liberty and to due process on the job and to freedom from reprisals at work for the exercise of individual rights off the job.[13] Balanced here are employer prerogatives, such as the right to determine personnel policies, against employee protections; yet the law does not guarantee anyone a right to work or to be retained in a job once hired.[14] The law does, however, protect employees from mistreatment or exploitation, and from unlimited or unrestricted employer prerogatives.[15] Labor laws specify minimum wages and maximum hours and also protect the right of employees to advocate joining and to join unions.[16] The employee rights to be protected have been delineated under such categories as the right of expression and dissent, the right of employee privacy, the right of fair procedure and due process, the right of participation, and the right to information.[17] As Professor Alan F. Westin pointed out in 1978,[18] the category of expression and dissent, for example, encompassed a recognition that employees are not supposed to execute employer policies that are illegal or unethical, like knowingly marketing defective products or furthering violation of state or federal laws on sanitation. "Whistle-blowers"[19] are expected to keep employers on their toes! Employee privacy must be respected.[20] An employer must have a fair procedure and due process of law to handle complaints and grievances. Employees should have the right to feel a sense of participation in the business as well as a right to know more about the present and future conduct of the business in which they are employed.[21]

1.3   UNIQUE ASPECTS OF THE EMPLOYMENT RELATIONSHIP

The employment relationship has given rise to many unique and challenging situations, such as that illustrated in Corporation of the Presiding Bishop of the Church of Jesus Christ of Latter Day Saints v. Amos,[22] decided by the U.S. Supreme Court on June 25, 1988. Here the highest court gave its blessing to the Mormon Church in firing employees who are not church members in good standing. The ruling gave religious groups operating non-profit businesses wide authority to hire only members of their own faith and to fire those church members who backslide. According to the court, "a law is not unconstitutional simply because it allows churches to advance religion, which is their very purpose." Here seven employees of the church-owned Beehive Clothing Mills, which manufactures church garments, and of the church-owned Deseret Gymnasium, which operates an exercise building open to all Utah citizens, were fired when they did not receive a Mormon "temple recommend" certification which, inter alia, required the employee to pay a tithe of 10 percent of pretax income to the Mormon Church. Seeking to put some limits on the 5–4 ruling of the court, the four dissenters suggested that the majority opinion should be restricted to non-profit operations that are more clearly religious activities: "Sensitivity to individual religious freedom dictates that religious discrimination be permitted only with respect to employment in religious activities. . . . Because of the nature of non-profit activities . . . a categorical exemption for such enterprises appropriately balances these competing concerns."[23]

The case of the Easter Seal Society v. Playboy Enterprises[24] prompted the Fifth U.S. Court of Appeals to answer the question whether independent contractors could be statutory employees under the Copyright Act. The court analyzed the work-for-hire provision of the act, and in particular Section 201, which provides that copyright in a work vests initially in the author of the work and that, in the case of a work made for hire, the employer or other person for whom the work was prepared is considered the author; and, unless the parties have agreed otherwise in a written agreement signed by them, the employer owns all of the rights composing the copyright. The court concluded that a work is "made for hire" within the meaning of the act if and only if the seller is an employee within the meaning of agency law. The term "scope of employment" is virtually a term of art in agency law; only works by actual employees and independent contractors who fulfill the requisites of Section 101(2) of the Copyright Act can be "for hire" under the act. Copyright "employees" are those persons called "employees" or "servants" for purposes of agency law, according to the court. The court ruled that the plaintiff was not the statutory "author" of the videotapes here, and that the use of the videotapes did not infringe on plaintiff's rights.[25]

In Felton v. Equal Employment Opportunity Commission[26] a federal employee was suspended from her job for 30 days for allegedly allowing a clerical employee to use a government-owned automobile for unofficial purposes. But the federal court reversed, holding that there was no finding that she knew or should have known of the unofficial purpose to which the car was put or that she acted in reckless disregard of the possibility that the car would be used for unofficial purposes.

AIDS (acquired immune deficiency syndrome) in the workplace is a dilemma for employers if they are to avoid discrimination while addressing workers' fears.[27] Some workers simply do not want to work with people infected with the AIDS virus; yet AIDS is considered a handicap under both federal and state laws prohibiting discrimination against the handicapped. As of August 1, 1988, more than 69,000 cases of AIDS have been reported and 39,000 victims have died; it is estimated that 365,000 people will have contracted the disease by the year 1992.[28]

In U.S. Equal Employment Opportunity Commission v. Townley Engineering and Manufacturing Co.[29] the Ninth U.S. Court of Appeals was faced with a situation in which workers at defendant's Christian-operated Arizona plant were required to attend "nondenominational" prayer service during work hours once per week. Although one dissenting judge opined that the defendant employer had done enough by allowing employees to wear ear plugs and read newspapers while attending the religious services, the court majority struck down the employer practice: "Where the practices of the employer and employee conflict . . . it is not inappropriate to require the employer, who structures the workplace to a substantial degree, to travel the extra mile . . . to accomodate the employee's rights." The federal appellate court pointed out that the defendant employer could not show that it would suffer "undue hardship" by allowing an employee to refuse to participate in the prayer services. No economic effect was claimed, and the employer cannot assert "spiritual hardship." Above all, "an employee's right to be free from forced observance of the religion of his employer" must be respected.[30]

Richard Becker, a disgruntled employee, brought 17 lawsuits in the federal District Court for the Southern District of New York and filed 124 age discrimination actions with the New York office of the U.S. Equal Employment Opportunity Commission. Finally, in Becker v. Dunkin' Donuts of America, Inc.,[31] the federal court, acting under its inherent power, entered an injunction against the pro se litigant, regulating the circumstances under which plaintiff Becker could commence future litigation in that district.[32] Becker was enjoined from filing further complaints other than "actions including allegations of judicial misconduct" unless he also filed with the complaint an affidavit (a) setting forth the evidence supporting his claim; (b) identifying the names and addresses of every witness he intends to call; (c) listing all other actions he has brought against the defendant being sued; and (d) providing notice of the existence of the special limitations placed upon him as a litigant. Becker's complaint must also be approved by a judge in the district before the claim can go forward. Furthermore, the court enjoined plaintiff from applying for any position of employment with defendant.

And in Weiner v. McGraw-Hill, Inc.[33] the New York Court of Appeals identified the following factors as presenting a triable issue as to the existence of an employment contract: (a) whether the employee was induced to leave his former employment by assurances that employees are not discharged by defendant without cause; (b) whether the employee handbook and its various job assurances were incorporated in the employment application; (c) whether the employee rejected other job offers in reliance upon the employer's job security assurances; and (d) whether instructions were given to the employee by the employer to follow the handbook's procedures in dismissing his own subordinates in order to avoid legal action.

Must an injured employee be compelled to seek compensation exclusively under workers' compensation? This query was answered in the negative by the Michigan appellate court in Panagos v. North Detroit General Hospital.[34] Here the plaintiff hospital employee, while eating lunch in the hospital cafeteria, cut her mouth on a foreign particle contained in a piece of pie. She sued her hospital employer for damages, and the defendant employer moved to dismiss her claim on the grounds that any claim for compensation can be asserted only under workers' compensation. But the court ruled that her cause of action was not based upon the fact that she was employed by the defendant hospital; her case was based

entirely upon the fact that there was deleterious material in a piece of pie she had purchased in her employer's cafeteria. . . . Plaintiff's present case is based on the vendor-vendee relationship. The whole theory of the cause of action has nothing to do with the fact that plaintiff also happened to be employed by the defendant. We see no need for plaintiff to first seek relief from the Workmen's Compensation Department when it is clear that employer–employee relationship is unrelated to the cause of action.

On the other hand, in Herman v. Theis[35] the same court just three years earlier had found that plaintiff's injuries sustained when he fell asleep while driving home from work were properly a matter for his employer's workers' compensation.

Termination of employment as a teacher due to a physical disability was upheld in Fisher v. Church of St. Mary,[36] because the Wyoming appellate court could not say "as a matter of law that the trial court was wrong in treating an absence of 4 months and 18 days a sufficient portion of the 10-month contract to materially inconvenience and injure the school and to justify termination."

1.4 SCOPE OF EMPLOYMENT LITIGATION

Employee litigation runs the gamut of contract and tort litigation and encounters situations far beyond mere termination or dismissal.[37] For example, there are claims by employees for failure of employers to promote and for objections to demotion;[38] there are claims regarding sexual harassment.[39] Discrimination based upon religion, national origin, age, sex, or race is a dramatic and ever-popular law suit.[40] Claims for invasion of privacy,[41] for an employee's right to know,[42] for restraints placed by the employer upon the employee's practice of a trade or profession,[43] or for no workers' compensation program[44] are subject to litigation almost daily. Immigration is another issue litigated between employees and governments, with the employer also a part of the muddle.[45] Employees and employers are in battle under union contracts,[46] and arbitration looms on the horizon in many instances as an alternative to judicial decision on the employee-employer relationship. Pre-employment drug testing[47] as well as employment drug testing[48] are paramount issues of the day, locally and nationally.

It should be observed that employee litigation is not limited to corporate employers but encompasses individual employers and even law firm partnerships, as illustrated in Hishon v. King & Spaulding,[49] where the U.S. Supreme Court ruled that a former female associate of the law firm had a cause of action under Title VII of the Civil Rights Act[50] against the law firm partnership's alleged sex-based discrimination in not granting plaintiff lawyer partner status.

NOTES

1. See generally Perritt, Employee Dismissal Law and Practice 1.2 (1984).

2. See generally Mantoux, The Industrial Revolution in the 18th Century 47–86 (1961).

3. Note Selznick, Law, Society and Industrial Justice 123–124 (1969).

4. See Blackstone, Commentaries 422–425 (12th ed., 1793).

5. Supra note 3 at p. 126, citing the 1563 Statute of Artificers, inter alia.

6. See generally 93 Harv L Rev 1514 (1980); see Lumley v. Gye, 118 Eng. Rep. 749 (Q.B.,1853), decided at the advent of the Industrial Revolution in England.

7. Note Frank Horton & Co., Inc. v. Diggs, 544 S.W.2d 313 (Mo. Ct. App. 1976).

8. 344 P.2d 25 (Cal. App. 1959).

9. 316 A.2d 549 (N.H. 1974).

10. See Toussaint v. Blue Cross & Blue Shield, 292 N.W.2d 880 (1980); see also Perritt, Employee Dismissal Law and Practice 10–11 (1984).

11. 536 P.2d 512 (Or. 1975).

12. 448 N.E.2d 86 (N.Y. 1983).

13. See generally Westin and Salisbury, Individual Rights in the Corporation: A Reader on Employee Rights, at xi (1980).

14. Id. at xii.

15. Note chapter 4 on discrimination.

16. Note chapter 11 on unions.

17. Supra note 10, Perritt, at Introduction, xiii to xx.

18. Id.

19. See chapter 4 on discrimination.

20. See chapter 2.

21. Supra note 17.

22. ———U.S.———(1988). See New York Times, June 25, 1988, at B15.

23. The dissent of Justice William J. Brennan.

24. ———F.2d———(5th Cir. 1987).

25. See N.Y.L.J. at 1 et seq. May 29, 1987.

26. ———F.R.D.———(D.C. 1988).

27. See A.B.A.J. 24 (October 1, 1988).

28. Id.

29. ———F.2d———(9th Cir. September 19, 1988); lower court opinion at 675 F. Supp 566, (Ariz. 1987).

30. See also New York Times, September 21, 1988, at A10.

31. 665 F. Supp 211 (S.D.N.Y. 1987).

32. Becker was subjected to a similar discipline by the federal District Court for the Eastern District of New York, and also fined $660.65 for prior conduct of the same litigation.

33. 443 N.E.2d 441 (N.Y. 1982).

34. 192 N.W.2d 542 (Mich. App. 1971).

35. 160 N.W.2d 365 (Mich. App. 1968).

36. 497 P.2d 882 (Wyo. 1972).

37. See chapter 3.

38. See chapters 4 through 6.

39. See chapter 6.

40. See chapter 4.

41. See chapter 2 and note Warren Freedman, The Right of Privacy in the Computer Age (1987).

42. Id. See also chapter 9.

43. See chapter 10.

44. See chapter 8.

45. See chapter 12.

46. See chapter 11.

47. See chapter 2.

48. See chapter 2.

49. 467 U.S. 69 (1984).

50. See chapter 4.

2

The Employer and the Employee Generally

2.1 THE EMPLOYEE DEFINED

The recent New York decision of Frigerio v. LML Cafe, Inc.[1] illustrates the troublesome issue involved when a person advances money to his prospective employer, and the employer deems the money an investment incidental to the employment and repayable, if at all, only upon the sale of the business. On the other hand, the disgruntled employee seeks immediate repayment of his loan to his corporate employer. Here the employee was given a promissory note for $20,000 for monies loaned to the corporate employer. The note was undated and was silent as to the date of maturity, but these omissions, according to the court, did not make the transaction anything less than an outright loan by a prospective employee to his corporate employer. Plaintiff's role as an employee was fully protected here. In Plumley v. U.S. Bureau of Prisons[2] a federal prisoner who was dismissed from a prison clerical job for complaining of exposure to hazardous fumes won lost pay and privileges in a settlement agreement with defendant federal agency, on the ground that he was an "employee" for the purposes of environmental protection laws.[3] Plaintiff, who was serving a 12-year sentence for bank robbery at a high-security federal penitentiary, was thus accorded the status of "employee" and, like ordinary citizens, given the same rights in enforcing workplace health standards and protection against employer recrimination as a "whistle-blower."[4]

Employees have been uniquely and successfully "leased" like a chattel or other property; for a fee ranging from 4 percent to 16 percent of the payroll, employee leasing companies take over the role of personnel and payroll departments of the employer.[5] "Employee leasing" reduces costs because employees are not needed to handle those administrative functions. But "leasing" does not shift the responsibility of employers for their employees.

Still another interesting aspect of the definition of "employee" arose in Vomvas v. Clarendon, Ltd.,[6] where the prime issue was the alleged breach of an oral employment contract relating to serverance pay. Defendant employer sought letters rogatory to take the depositions of certain former officers and employees who were then residents of Switzerland. (In fact, these alleged former employees had "fled the United States for Switzerland in 1983 to avoid prosecution on criminal charges.") The New York court observed that the testimony of these would-be deponents was "material and necessary to the defense against the complaint," and thereupon the court ordered the letters rogatory to be taken. The fact that the deponents were no longer officers and employees of defendant was beside the point, since they were third-party witnesses whose testimony was "material and necessary."

An employee is readily distinguished from an agent who is authorized to act under the control of and for another, the principal.[7] But an employee may be an agent also, as where he is the driver of a milk delivery truck and is both an agent of the employer for collection of monies and an employee with respect to physically delivering milk. A person who appears to be an independent contractor may in fact be so controlled by the other party that such a contractor is regarded as an agent or even an employee of the controlling person, as shown in Hill v. Newman.[8] Here plaintiff purchased furniture from Grant, and when she complained about the damaged furniture, Grant sent defendant, an independent contractor, to fix it. Unfortunately, defendant lacquered the furniture and it exploded, causing serious fire injury to plaintiff. In affirming judgment for the plaintiff against both Grant and defendant, the New Jersey court rejected defendant Grant's astute argument that defendant was an independent contractor and Grant therefore could not be vicariously liable for defendant's negligence. Here the court found that defendant was allowed to become "the apparent agent of the employer" Grant: "One who employs an independent contractor to perform services for another which are accepted in the reasonable belief that the services are being rendered by the employer or by his servants, is subject to liability for physical harm caused by the negligence of the contractor in supplying such services, to the same extent as though the employer were supplying them himself or by his servants." But mere inspection of the work done does not make the independent contractor an employee of the company servicing the plaintiff.[9] An employer who handles applications for group insurance for his employees may be an agent of the insurance company.[10]

The mere fact that a tort or a crime is committed by an employee does not necessarily impose vicarious liability upon the employer. If the employee was acting within the scope of authority or in the course of his employment, the employer may be liable. In Gandy v. Cole[11] plaintiff alleged that she was defrauded by Webb, an agent of defendant; defendant contended that no fraud was committed within the scope of Webb's authority and therefore defendant was not liable. Plaintiff's husband had subscribed to defendant's services to gas station operators; when the husband died, defendant took an active part in the management of plaintiff's finances. Webb, defendant's agent, subsequently squandered plaintiff's monies, and plaintiff argued that defendant had placed Webb in a position where he could defraud her, but the court disagreed because Webb, as defendant's agent, had gone far beyond the services ordinarily provided by defendant. Plaintiff had placed her reliance not on defendant but on Webb; plaintiff had no contact with defendant and did not pay defendant a fee for the services: "Webb did not deal with the plaintiff as an agent of Cole, but rather acted in his personal capacity. Since Webb was not acting or professedly acting on Cole's account, Cole cannot be held to have ratified Webb's acts." The strong dissenting opinion observed that

when, as in this case, a principal permits an agent to present to potential customers a business card proclaiming to all and sundry that he, the principal, is a "business counsellor" and that the card bearer is his representative, the principal had better make it his business to know what "counseling" is done, particularly when the counseling results in doing a customer of the principal out of some $15,000. . . . A faultless principal has no defense against dishonesty, but it does not follow that this accords a principal the right to limitless gullibility. . . . There was an obligation upon the principal to inform himself of his agent's doings.

However, in International Distributing Co. v. American District Telegraph Co.[12] it was held that the employer is not liable where the employee steals property from a customer of his employer, even though it was the work of the employer that put the dishonest employee on the customer's premises and in a position to steal the property. The better view is exemplified in Price v. Ford Motor Credit Co.,[13] where the finance company itself was held liable for punitive damages where its agents wrongfully repossessed plaintiff's automobile. And in Gilmore v. Constitution Life Insurance Co.[14] the Tenth U.S. Court of Appeals ruled that the employer is liable simply because it was an employee who did the wrong!

2.2 NEGLIGENT HIRING OF EMPLOYEES

It should be obvious that every employer has a duty to exercise reasonable care in the selection and retention of employees. Section 213(b) of the *Restatement (Second) of Agency* provides that "a person conducting an activity through servants or other agents is subject to liability for harm resulting from his conduct if he is negligent or reckless . . . in the employment of improper persons or instrumentalities in work involving risk of harm to others." As stated in Ponticas v. K.M.S. Investments[15] by the Minnesota court, "employers have a duty to exercise reasonable care in view of all the circumstances in hiring individuals, who, because of the employment, may pose a threat of injury to members of the public.'' This is the doctrine of negligent hiring, and it states that employees need not be acting within the scope of employment in order to render their employers liable.[16]

A real estate agent misrepresented the truth and "duped" the plaintiff into paying off a $158,000 loan; the realty company apparently knew that its agent had a history of forged documents and had been convicted of passing bad checks. The court readily found defendant liable to the tune of $158,000 plus $25,000 in punitive damages against the realty company for the tort of negligent hiring.[17] Several jurisdictions recognize the tort theory of negligent hiring to impose liability directly on the employers even for the intentional acts of negligently hired employees.[18] In essence, the business tort of negligent hiring places a duty on employers not to hire employees whom they knew, or in the exercise of reasonable care should have known, were potentially the creators of liability, perhaps liability based upon misrepresentation, deceit, or fraud.[19]

Employer liability for the acts of negligently hired employees undoubtedly evolved from the common law "fellow servant rule," which imposed a duty upon employers to provide their employees with a safe workplace.[20] Employers were required to exercise reasonable care to select reputable employees,[21] and third parties injured by the acts of such employees were able to sue upon the basis of the employer's negligence in hiring the unfit or incompetent employee.[22] Employers have a duty to conduct a reasonable investigation into a prospective employee's background to ascertain the employee's qualifications and suitability for the intended position.[23]

Liability for negligent hiring is predicated upon proof that the employer possessed knowledge of the employee's potential for misconduct or even mischief, and the act of hiring the employee was the proximate cause of plaintiff's injury, damage, or loss.[24] However, it has been held that an employer who diligently investigates the background of the employee is not liable when the employee lies about his personal qualifications.[25] Yet negligent hiring claims persist against employers for rapes,[26] murders,[27] sexual assaults,[28] and physical assaults,[29] inter alia, allegedly committed by employees allegedly unfit for the employment.

In summary, since recruitment is the first step toward employment, it is obvious that recruitment must also comply with antidiscrimination laws. The application should contain questions that aid in hiring the most qualified applicant according to the job specification. Questions on the application that cannot prove to be job related are suspect of discriminatory motives. In Gregory v. Litton Systems, Inc.,[30] questions about prior arrests were absolutely barred. Questions as to height and weight can be construed as screening out females and persons of Asian and Spanish descent.[31] It is wrong to ask marital status of women only, but where the employer has a "no spouse" hiring rule, the question can be relevant and allowable.[32] In Laffey v. Northwest Airlines[33] it was held unlawful to require that females not wear glasses while males could, although their jobs were similar.

2.3 THE EMPLOYMENT-AT-WILL DOCTRINE

Traditionally, employment-at-will meant that both employer and employee were free to terminate an employment relationship for any reason and at any time.[34] The New York Court of Appeals in its 1983 decision in Murphy v. American Home Products Corp.[35] spelled out the particulars: "Our long-settled rule is that where an employment is for an indefinite term, it is presumed to be a hiring at will which may be freely terminated by either party at any time for any reason or even for no reason." The Industrial Revolution in England had focused, inter alia, on the duration of employment, noting particularly that employment depended upon the demand for the product, and that it was not prudent to impose an obligation upon employers to continue employment when market demand for the product fell off.[36] Employees, on the other hand, regretting the lack of security inherent in the doctrine of employment-at-will, nevertheless were unhappy with the presumed one-year employment situation that tied them to one employer. Employee interests sought shorter and shorter employment contracts[37] in the belief that striking employees could avoid the civil and criminal penalties for breaching much longer employment contracts.[38]

The employment-at-will doctrine obviously provided little or no job security for the employee; and with the rapid growth of the U.S. economy at the end of the nineteenth century and the legal recognition of labor unions,[39] augmented by substantial public criticism and, in particular, legislative revision of the employment-at-will rule or doctrine, restrictions or limitations and changes were placed on the rule or doctrine.[40] These changes encompassed, inter alia, (a) revised contract theories, (b) revised tort theories, and (c) federal and state statutory restrictions, as we will discuss.

Such changes were first reflected in the concept of "freedom of contract" that evolved from the laissez-faire economic policy of the earlier centuries.[41] Maximization of wealth required that producers be free to contract for labor based on the value of the product in the marketplace. And so "freedom of contract" implied that the terms of the employment relationship, like those of any other economic relationship, should be determined entirely by the parties to the contract without interference from state or federal government.[42] While freedom of contract became a slogan for opposing labor protective legislation, the concept also meant that employment-at-will and the presumed one-year duration of the contractual commitment were at an end.[43] Courts took up the cudgel and called upon many judicial tools to preclude enforcement of indefinite employment contracts.[44] Social and economic pressures led to further legal developments protecting the economic welfare of workers; collective bargaining and unionization of employees[45] hastened the change and the erosion of the employment-at-will doctrine.[46] Also, the shift of American labor law in the late 1940s from protection of collective employee rights to the protection of individual employee rights in certain areas further eroded the bare bones of employment-at-will.[47]

Before reviewing in detail the revised contract theories, the revised tort theories, and the federal and state statutory restrictions that have somewhat emasculated the employment-at-will doctrine, it is well to examine some specific instances and specific court decisions that today still cling to this archaic doctrine. In Carroll v. Leeds[48] the New York court viewed the claim of a physician who sued the hospital after her employment was terminated. Since her employment was not for a specific length of time under any written contract or under the bylaws of the hospital, she was an employee-at-will and therefore could be dismissed at any time and without cause. The New York court pointed out that the physician's cause of action simply did not fall within the exception enunciated in the New York Court of Appeals decision in Weiner v. McGraw-Hill, Inc.[49] because "there is no allegation of an express limitation on the employer's right of discharge in an individual contract of employment, and there is no allegation as to the existence of a personnel policy or procedure handbook which gave assurance that plaintiff would not be discharged without just cause."

In another 1988 decision, Block v. Grindberg,[50] the New York court dismissed the complaint of a man who had quit his job and come to New York pursuant to an oral contract with defendants by which plaintiff would work for an unspecified period of time. Without a time specification in the contract, the man was employed merely at will, and defendants could terminate his employment "at any time." In Sabetay v. Sterling Drug Co.,[51] the New York Court of Appeals in 1987 sharply limited the right of at-will employees to challenge the termination of their employment. Here plaintiff was director of financial projects for a subsidiary of defendant corporation, and he was terminated when his job was eliminated. Plaintiff contended that the real reason for his discharge was his refusal to participate in defendant's illegal financial schemes (tax avoidance and maintenance of slush funds). Plaintiff had no written employment contract, and so the highest New York court held that he had "failed to demonstrate a limitation by express agreement on his employer's unfettered right to terminate at will." In still another New York case, Buchwalter v. Dayton Management Corp.,[52] the employee was fired after she took a day off to appear in court in response to a subpoena; she argued that under Section 215.14 of the New York Penal Law her employer was prohibited, under pain of criminal sanctions, from penalizing her for a compulsory appearance in court. But the court pointed out that she had not notified her employer in advance as to why she would be absent from work, and therefore her termination as an at-will employee was justified.

The Missouri Supreme Court in Johnson v. McDonnell Douglas Corp.[53] similarly upheld the severity of the employment-at-will doctrine by stating that there was no "handbook exception" in Missouri because the company handbook was not part of the employment contract. But the Kansas Supreme Court in Morriss v. Coleman Co., Inc.[54] unanimously declared that in an employment-at-will case the jury should decide whether the firing of a married man and an unmarried woman who took a business trip together was justified. According to the court, "Although no court has entirely abolished the employ-ment-at-will doctrine in court decisions, the cases throughout the United States indicate a trend to avoid the injustice of the rule. . . . State courts have rec-ognized causes of action based on the theories of wrongful discharge, violation of public policy, and breach of contract." The Kansas court opined that the two fired employees had an implied contract that would make it necessary for the employer to justify the firing. The employee manual and personnel bulletin had stated that employees would be fired only for just cause.

According to Professor Perritt in his *Employee Dismissal Law and Practice* (1984), "about half of American jurisdictions now have abandoned the Em-ployment-at-Will Rule as a strict substantive formulation. Some means of re-covery in tort or contract for wrongful dismissal have been recognized in the States of Alaska, California, Colorado, Connecticut, Florida, Hawaii, Idaho, Illinois, Indiana, Kansas, Kentucky, Maryland, Massachusetts, Michigan, Min-nesota, Missouri, Montana, Nevada, New Hampshire, New Jersey, New York, Oklahoma, Oregon, Pennsylvania, South Dakota, Virginia, Washington, West Virginia, and Wisconsin."[55]

To overcome the strictures of the employment-at-will doctrine, many state courts have revised contract theories to include "good faith and fair dealing," as illustrated in such cases as Fortune v. National Cash Register Co.,[56] where the Massachusetts court castigated the employer for discharging an employee with 25 years of employment in order to avoid paying a $92,000 sales bonus. In a California case[57] the discharge of a corporate vice president after 32 years of service was held to violate the implied covenant not to discharge, absent a valid and meaningful cause. In Section 205 of the *Restatement (Second) of Contracts* there is a covenant of good faith and fair dealing, and vindictive retaliation by an employer is improper.

Another method to overcome the impediments of the employment-at-will doctrine is the prominence accorded to employee handbooks and other written personnel policies of the employer, as seen in Weiner v. McGraw-Hill, Inc.,[58] where the New York Court of Appeals ruled that the presumption of freely terminable employment-at-will was rebuttable by reference to the parties' course of conduct and to written materials such as employee handbooks, employment application forms, and personnel policies. Another exception to the rigidity of the at-will rule is seen in Sides v. Duke University,[59] where a nurse was in-duced to move from Michigan to North Carolina in reliance upon the employ-er's representation that she could be terminated only for cause; the North Car-olina court ruled that these facts could overcome the presumption of an at-will contract of employment.

In revising tort theories of recovery, several courts have recognized the tor-tious act of threats, as shown in U.S. Fidelity & Guarantee Co. v. Millonas.[60] Here the plaintiff employee filed a claim with the defendant insurer of his employer for compensation for an injury he had suffered in the course of em-ployment. The insurer told him that he would lose his job if he persisted in his claim; and by threatening cancellation of the employer's policy, the defendant insurer procured the discharge of the injured employee. The defendant insurer argued that no cause of action could arise from its threatening to cancel the employer's policy, since it had the right to cancel. But the Alabama court rejected defendant's contention and ruled that the plaintiff's discharge was not procured as "the consequence of the exercise of a lawful right, but of the unlawful use of that lawful right by the defendant."[61] Intentional torts such as intentional infliction of emotional distress upon a discharged employee might also overcome the at-will freedom to discharge.[62]

Numerous federal and state statutes[63] limit the employer's prerogative to discharge or dismiss an employee-at-will. Title VII of the Civil Rights Act of 1964[64] and the Age Discrimination in Employment Act of 1967[65] are but two examples; these and other statutes are delineated at length in this book.[66] The employer's freedom has long been limited by child labor laws, by the legally protected status of labor unions, and by the growing body of laws prohibiting discrimination in employment.[67]

2.4   THE RIGHT OF PRIVACY IN THE EMPLOYMENT RELATIONSHIP

The right of privacy in the employment relationship is a veritable Pandora's Box in that there are innumerable situations giving rise to infringement upon employee privacy.[68] It has been said that the United States today is a surveillance society; the offender in the employment relationship can be either the employer or the employee, or both. In Bratt v. IBM,[69] the plaintiff employee alleged that his employer, the defendant, had breached his statutory right of privacy in allowing an IBM-retained physician to disclose and discuss his paranoid condition with IBM managerial employees without his consent. The breach of privacy claim pivoted on documentary evidence that such distressing disclosures not only breached the physician's duty of confidentiality and constituted an offensive invasion of his privacy, but also violated IBM's own internal regulations against disclosure of medical information by the medical staff to IBM management. The First U.S. Court of Appeals, in applying Massachusetts law, had received a prior certification from the Massachusetts Supreme Judicial Court that to determine whether communication of personal information about an employee by an employer violates the statutory right of privacy requires a balancing of the "employer's legitimate business interest in obtaining and publishing the information against the substantiality of the intrusion on the employee's privacy resulting from the disclosure."[70] The federal appellate court ruled that since the disclosures of the physician to management personnel violated IBM's own internal regulations, the employee's right of privacy was invaded; furthermore, IBM did not sustain the heavy burden of showing that its business interests in obtaining that information about the plaintiff employee warranted a violation of its own rules.

And in Dickson v. Office of Personnel Management,[71] the federal court up-held the suit against the defendant employer by an employee who claimed that the employer's file on him during his attempts to obtain federal civil service employment contained false, derogatory, and prejudicial information. The court found that the defendant employer was maintaining an employment record that violated the standard of fairness mandated by the Privacy Act,[72] one of the three major pieces of recent federal legislation designed to protect the individual in our informational society. The Right to Financial Privacy Act of 1978, or RFPA,[73] and the Fair Credit Reporting Act of 1970, or FCRA,[74] are of equal importance.

The FCRA was the first legislative assault upon private informational activities that can violate privacy.[75] Since 1971, actions for libel and for invasion of privacy were supplemented by FCRA's insistence that consumer reporting agencies[76] adopt reasonable procedures to provide credit information in a fair and equitable manner and with full regard to "the confidentiality, accuracy, relevancy and proper utilization of the information."[77] The individual, not the business entity, is protected, according to FCRA. When adverse action is taken on an application for credit, insurance, or employment, for example, and the adverse action is based wholly or in part on information in a consumer report, FCRA requires that the user advise the consumer of the adverse action and supply the name and address of the consumer reporting agency.[78] A user may violate FCRA if it waits for a request for the adverse information from the consumer before making the required disclosure. Civil and criminal liability is prescribed by FCRA.[79]

The Privacy Act of 1974, or PA, is directed at the *public* sector, and governs the collection, maintenance, use, and disclosure of *federal* governmental records on individuals. Only "relevant and necessary" data may be gathered by the federal government in the first place. Under PA the individual may gain access to his or her records kept by the government. It is a misdemeanor for a government employee[80] to knowingly and willfully make an unauthorized disclosure of a person's records, or to maintain records that do not meet the requirement of annual notice in the *Federal Register*. Briefly, the Privacy Act of 1974 requires federal agencies to disclose annually what records they keep, limits disclosure by federal agencies of personal data from agency records (including interagency disclosures), and affords individuals a limited right of access to, and opportunity to correct, agency records.

RFPA was passed on October 14, 1978, as Title XI of the Financial Institutions Regulatory and Interest Rate Control Act of 1978 and was signed into law on November 10, 1978, to be effective on March 10, 1979. RFPA limits the federal government's access to individual records held by banks and financial institutions. RFPA requires the federal government to pay for records (for example, IRS pays five dollars per hour or any portion of an hour of search time; other federal government agencies pay ten dollars per hour). RFPA also imposes rigid recordkeeping requirements. Unwarranted governmental intrusion into an individual's financial affairs is barred.[81] But a financial institution is protected from liability under Section 1103(b) if it acts in good faith. Section 1102 provides that no government authority may have access to information in the financial records of any "customer"[82] (i.e., individuals and partnerships of five or fewer individuals) of a financial institution, except through one of five disclosure mechanisms: (1) customer authorization, (2) search warrant, (3) administrative subpoena,[83] (4) judicial subpoena, or (5) formal written request. In all instances except the search warrant, the government must give the "customer" notice of its application to look at records and an opportunity to challenge. The act does not apply to grand jury subpoenas except for the payment provisions; and one further provision—rather interesting—that records obtained pursuant to a grand jury subpoena "shall be returned and actually presented to the grand jury." How all of these safeguards to the right of privacy work out in practice, only time will tell. One exception already permits the government to seek "name, address, account number, and type of account."[84]

In late 1980, the U.S. House of Representatives passed the Protection of Privacy Act of 1980 (PPA), and on October 14, 1980, President Carter signed it into law.[85] The new legislation accorded special protection against searches and seizures of materials in the possession of the media and their representatives by federal, state, and local law enforcement agencies.[86] Materials are subject to seizure by law enforcement agencies only if the custodian of the materials is suspected of criminal activity, or to prevent death, serious bodily harm, or destruction of evidence. Reporters and other protected people who believe their rights of privacy have been violated may sue for damages; the minimum award is $5,000.[87] In addition, the law directs the attorney general to issue guidelines, within six months of the effective date of the law, for the procedure to obtain materials in the possession of "an innocent person."[88] These guidelines require special scrutiny by the public and Congress, in light of the insensitivity to the principles of a free press that the U.S. Justice Department has sometimes displayed.[89] Unfortunately, PPA affords no protection for other innocent third parties like lawyers. Law office searches by state and local law enforcement authorities since 1978 have given rise to a concern among lawyers that client records will not be protected from random searches. Indeed, the inaccessibility of a lawyer's file is a small price to pay for protecting both the right of privacy and the right to counsel!

The insurance industry of the United States is doing a great job in protecting *consumer* privacy, according to a recent survey by Professor David Linowes, former chairman of the United States Privacy Protection Commission of 1977, and now professor of political economy and public policy at the University of Illinois.[90] Professor Linowes based his findings on survey responses from 19 of the largest insurance companies, representing a total of more than 98 million life insurance policyholders and more than 11 million property and casualty policyholders. The survey found that 60 percent of the insurance companies obtain written authorization from applicants to gather information within a specified time period; most require information about previous decisions by other companies against covering an applicant, but only 21 percent base their coverage decisions on that information; 93 percent notify applicants about supplemental background checks; 58 percent obtain authorization to disclose information to third parties; 83 percent give customers access to their records; and 82 percent regularly evaluate recordkeeping systems to assess privacy safeguards. It is obvious that insurance companies in the United States have learned that stronger privacy protection measures do not seriously burden their operations or increase their costs.

Another federal statute that is relevant to the delineation of the American *constitutional* right of privacy is the Freedom of Information Act of 1966 (FOIA), which gives every person the right to look at government records.[91] Many people have successfully explored the possibility of using the FOIA to obtain information about their business competitors or litigation adversaries,[92] either because an agency of the federal government has compiled relevant records or because a competitor or an adversary has submitted records or information to an agency in compliance with federal law.[93] Note that the federal government has the burden of proof to show why individual records should be kept secret!

The "right to know" doctrine prevails in behalf of the public, and unfair disclosure of personal data and information has indeed become a problem.[94] A government official who arbitrarily or unreasonably withholds such records is subject to disciplinary action. Key records and important documents that have been held disclosable by the courts include witnesses' sworn statements taken by the government in investigating an unfair labor practice;[95] an abstract of individual offers actually accepted by the Internal Revenue Service;[96] and a government investigatory accident report based upon hearsay.[97] Interestingly, although FOIA does not define "records," the legislative intent is clearly to include everything that is written or transcribed or electronically recorded, such as computer printouts and tape recordings.

On the other hand, there are nine exemptions or exceptions permitting the federal government to withhold information or data: (1) documents classified by executive order concerning national defense or foreign policy; (2) internal personnel rules and practices of a government agency; (3) documents exempt under other federal statutes, such as income tax returns and patent applications; (4) trade secrets and commercial and financial information obtained and classified as privileged or confidential; (5) interagency or intraagency memoranda or letters; (6) individual personnel and medical files; (7) investigatory records compiled for law enforcement purposes; (8) reports of agencies responsible for regulation or supervision of financial institutions; and (9) geological and geophysical data including location of oil wells, for example.

Item (6) (individual personnel and medical files) poses a grave threat to the right of privacy, for these are the records that concern the private lives of individuals. While *in theory* there is a stated exemption, actual practice has resulted in disclosures that have caused irreparable harm to individuals. Some courts have permitted disclosure of individual personnel and medical files by simply balancing the public's right to know and the individual's right to privacy.[98] Actually it is the clear-cut policy of most government agencies to disclose *exempt* materials unless there is a compelling reason not to do so. These disclosures constitute unwarranted invasions of personal privacy and should be closely monitored.[99]

The privacy of medical records, computerized or not, has not been adequately protected in the United States, despite legislative efforts.[100] The Hippocratic oath (which is part of the professional code in every state) simply imposes upon physicians a *moral* obligation: "Whatever in connection with my professional practice, or not in connection with it, I see or hear, in the life of men, which ought not to be spoken abroad, I will not divulge, as reckoning that all such should be kept secret." Some states have privacy laws that cover medical records, but only the records of physicians, not the records of health care providers.[101] And few courts have upheld the right of a patient or his physician to insist upon the confidentiality of medical records.[102] Consent forms freely signed by patients, for example, readily permit access to medical information by any third person, firm, or corporation with an interest in the data. The U.S. Privacy Protection Study Commission in 1974 concluded: "The outward flow of medical data . . . has enormous impact on people's lives. It affects decisions on whether they are hired or fired; whether they can secure business licenses and life insurance; whether they are permitted to drive cars; whether they are placed under police surveillance or labeled a security risk; or even whether they can get nominated for and elected to political office."[103]

One different area in privacy of medical or health-related records is the patient's own right to inspect and copy his or her records. In general, "upon request, an individual who is the subject of a medical record maintained by a medical care provider, or another responsible person designated by the individual, [should] be allowed to have access to that medical record, including an opportunity to see and copy it. The medical-care provider should be able to charge a reasonable fee (not to exceed the amount charged to third parties) for preparing and copying the record."[104] But the U.S. Privacy Protection Study Commission emphasized that this right of the patient is not an absolute guarantee because there may be instances when it would be prudent not to give the information to the patient but rather to give it to a third person designated by the patient. Direct access to the data by the patient could be harmful to the patient or to another person. On the other hand, there is little disagreement with the right of the patient to *correct* his or her medical or health-related records.

Note that an employee's right of privacy may be protected by state law, as in California where Section 1198.5 of the California Labor Code mandates that a private employer permit employees to inspect certain of the employer's records and personnel files. Access is given to the employee so that he or she may determine qualifications for employment, promotion, additional compensation, or termination or other disciplinary action. Among the excluded records are letters of reference and investigatory records of possible criminal offenses. It would appear that California's privacy legislation goes well beyond the federal laws protecting privacy.

2.5   COMPENSATION AND OTHER PAYMENTS TO THE EMPLOYEE

In Khalfan v. Khalfan,[105] the defendant employer allegedly induced plaintiff to give up a job and a business in Tanzania with the promise of lifetime employment with defendant. Plaintiff accepted the employment offer, although his contract of employment was not put in writing; the salary was believed to be a 50 percent interest in the business. After five years of employment, plaintiff was discharged, allegedly without cause. He sought to recover $95,500 in compensation for services rendered to the date of dismissal and $465,000 as additional compensation for services to be rendered over his life span. The New York court rejected defendant's argument that the contract of employment was unenforceable by reason of the Statute of Frauds: "There may still be recovery of the reasonable value of the services rendered." But the court denied compensation for services that "would have been performed under the alleged oral lifetime contract" because "an oral lifetime contract of employment is unenforceable."

In Rochlin v. Silverman & Weinraub[106] plaintiff attorney with defendant law firm was fired after 13 years when he suffered a stroke; the law firm paid his salary for six months thereafter. Plaintiff alleged discrimination in violation of the New York Human Rights Law,[107] since he was disabled by the stroke. But the New York court pointed out that his disability did not prevent him "from performing in a reasonable manner the activities involved in the job or occupation sought or held"[108] on the very date that he was fired. Accordingly, "even though plaintiff may have been able to perform certain select assignments, his condition prevented him from performing his normal employment duties and, therefore, he was not 'disabled' within the purview of the Human Rights Law." But the court refused to refund defendant law firm the six-month post-stroke salary because there was some merit to plaintiff's claim that the law firm was paying him because they valued his legal services.

In 1987 the U.S. Supreme Court upheld 5–4 a Maine statute requiring employers to pay "severance benefits" to workers laid off in plant closings.[109] The federal Employee Retirement Income Security Act of 1974 (ERISA) and the National Labor Relations Act (NLRB) did not preempt state regulation because "severance pay," unlike pension and health care and other employee benefit plans, was a lump sum payment that did not involve administration of "an employee welfare benefit plan or employer payments of ongoing benefits on a continuous basis."

Employees may qualify as a class in a contract suit against an employer, and thereby compound the compensatory payments to be made by the employer, according to Colin v. CBS, Inc.[110] Suit was brought for the employer's failure to pay certain employees under its employee incentive plan. The New York court found that plaintiffs had met the numerous criteria required to maintain a class action.[111]

And in Morales v. Cadena,[112] punitive damages were awarded the plaintiff who was not hired by the employer because the employer had violated plaintiff's right to free speech. Plaintiff had applied for the post of migrant inspector with the Wisconsin Migrant Bureau; he had scored the highest of 62 applicants on a bilingual language skills test, but he had a history of supporting aggressive enforcement of labor laws and was perhaps an anathema to his prospective employer. Failure to hire resulted in the award of both compensatory and punitive damages.

2.6 DRUG TESTING OF EMPLOYEES

The scourge of drugs and drug abuse has plagued the employment field, and the emotional issue of drug testing of employees has been voiced throughout the United States. On one side, the employer has a right and a duty to maintain a healthy and safe workplace; on the other hand, the employee has certain rights, like privacy and civil liberty interests, that must not be violated.[113] The Fourth Amendment to the U.S. Constitution bans unreasonable searches and seizures, and therefore the Constitution places an important limitation on drug testing of employees. However, Presidential Executive Order 12564, dated September 15, 1986, authorizes mandatory drug testing of federal employees in "sensitive" positions, such as in law enforcement, public health, or national security.

A public school system in Jones v. McKenzie[114] was permitted to test its employees for drugs where the evidence showed that employees' duties directly affected the physical safety of young school children. However, the drug testing had to be part of a routine, reasonably required medical examination. The New York Court of Appeals in Patchogue-Medford Congress of Teachers v. Board of Education[115] ruled that both the federal and New York constitutions afforded state employees the right *not* to be required to submit to drug testing, except where the state or employer had reasonable suspicion of individualized drug use. In short, compulsory urinalysis of probationary public school teachers to detect illegal drug use, in the absence of reasonable suspicion of individualized drug use, constitutes an unlawful and unreasonable search and seizure. New York's highest court rejected the squeamish argument that constitutional protection does not attach because urine is a waste product periodically eliminated from the body and obtainable without invading the body. According to the court, "random searches conducted by the State without reasonable suspicion are closely scrutinized, and generally only permitted when the privacy interests implicated are minimal, the government's interest is substantial and safeguards are provided to insure that the individual's reasonable expectation of privacy is not subjected to unregulated discretion."[116]

The Fifth U.S. Court of Appeals in National Treasury Employees Union v. Von Raab[117] upheld drug testing of job applicants for sensitive positions in the U.S. Customs Service; there were "strong governmental interests in employing individuals for key positions in drug enforcement who themselves are not drug users and the limited intrusiveness of this particular program." The Third U.S. Court of Appeals in Shoemaker v. Handel[118] approved regulations of the New Jersey Racing Commission that permitted drug and alcohol testing for racing officials, jockeys, trainers, and grooms, because such a requisite was appropriate for an already well regulated industry. And the Eighth U.S. Court of Appeals upheld drug testing of employees at correctional institutions because security interests are paramount, and therefore drug testing may be performed without individualized suspicion either "uniformly or by systematic random selection."[119]

Pre-employment drug testing was blocked by a California court in Smith v. Matthew Bender & Co.[120] Here a class action lawsuit had been brought on behalf of three plaintiff employees who refused to take the employer's drug test as a condition for being hired in editorial positions with the defendant law book publisher. The Alameda County Superior Court found that pre-employment drug testing does not act as a deterrent to drug abuse nor does it accurately predict whether an employee will be a risk in the workplace. In issuing a preliminary injunction against the employer, the court held that the drug testing policy of the employer violated the privacy provision of the California Constitution.[121]

A review of recent court decisions on drug testing of employees points up the overall confusion, not only with respect to the nature of mandatory testing, but also as to the grounds for rejecting drug testing of employees.

1. *Patchogue-Medford Congress of Teachers v. Board of Education*:[122] Mandatory urine testing of probationary school teachers for drug use before they are permanently appointed was deemed by the New York Court of Appeals in 1987 to be an illegal search and seizure in violation of the Fourth Amendment and an invasion of privacy.[123] The New York Appellate Division, Second Department, had in 1986 stated, "balancing a board of education's interest in ensuring that its employees are fit to perform their jobs against the teacher's reasonable expectation of privacy, we hold that the reasonable suspicion standard is the appropriate basis for constitutionally compelling a public school teacher to submit to a urine test for the purposes of detecting the use of controlled substances." The appellate court (whose decision was affirmed by New York's highest court) opined that as to privacy rights, "intense governmental scrutiny" is not controlling for teachers, since teachers are not in the same category as such "pervasively regulated" fields as liquor, firearms, casino gambling, and horse racing, where employees have "a significantly diminished expectation of privacy."

2. *Smith v. Houston Belt & Terminal Railway*:[124] A railway employee was

tested for drugs after fainting on the job when he accidentally cut his face, and the test revealed traces of the drug methadone. But a follow-up drug test showed evidence of a normal compound whose characteristics resembled methadone.[125] Nevertheless, the employee was fired on the pretext that he failed to report his accident to his employer on time. The Texas appellate court affirmed awards in compensatory and punitive damages for the discharged employee, because "the jury was entitled to conclude from the evidence that . . . the employers made false statements in writing that he was a narcotics user when they knew better."

3. *Allen v. City of Marietta*:[126] Six workers were fired after they all tested positive for the presence of marijuana in their bodies. It appeared that these workers had been asked to submit to urinalysis after an informer of the employer observed some of them smoking marijuana at work. The federal district court held that the urinalysis here was not a Fourth Amendment unlawful search and seizure because the city as employer had used the drug testing for work-related reasons and not as part of any present or future criminal investigation. The city has the same right to maintain a safe, productive, and drug-free environment as does the private employer. The court concluded that the need for a safe environment around such "extremely hazardous work" and the employer's right to maintain a drug-free work force outweighed the employees' expectation of privacy.

4. *McDonnell v. Hunter*:[127] A corrections officer was asked to submit to urinalysis after his superiors had received confidential information that he was seen off duty with persons under scrutiny by law enforcement officials investigating drug-related activities. After refusing to undergo urinalysis, he was fired, but the federal district court found such drug testing to be an unreasonable search and seizure because there was an almost total lack of standards for authorizing a drug test of the employee. Furthermore, the remote possibility of identifying employee drug users and those likely to smuggle drugs into the correctional institution was "far too attenuated to make seizures of body fluids constitutionally reasonable." The court concluded that the Fourth Amendment allowed the governmental employer "to demand of an employee a urine, blood, or breath specimen for chemical analysis only on the basis of a reasonable suspicion, based on specific objective facts in light of experience, that the employee is then under the influence of alcoholic beverages or controlled substances." But the Eighth U.S. Court of Appeals subsequently reversed and upheld the drug testing on the grounds that security interests are paramount.[128]

5. *Shoemaker v. Handel*:[129] Random drug testing of the horse racing business was upheld on the ground that horse racing is one of a special class of industries accustomed to heavy state regulation, and the need to promote safety and honesty outweighs the interests of jockeys, trainers, racing officials, and grooms, all of whom have "significantly diminished expectations of privacy."

6. *National Treasury Employees Union v. Von Raab*:[130] The Fifth U.S. Court of Appeals reinstated the U.S. Customs Service drug testing program on

the basis that (a) drug screening by urinalysis is not a significant intrusion on an employee's reasonable expectation of privacy, and (b) the validity of the reasonable search and seizure was "assessed by balancing the social and government need for it against the risk that the search will itself undermine the social order by unduly invading the personal rights of privacy." The court considered such factors as the scope of the intrusion, the manner in which the intrusion is conducted, the justification for the intrusion, the place where the intrusion is conducted, the effectiveness of the intrusion in achieving its purposes, the voluntariness of the person to be tested, the employment relationship of the parties, the administrative purpose of the search, the extent of government regulation of the industry, and the availability of less intrusive measures.[131]

7. *Turner v. Fraternal Order of Police*:[132] The court upheld a police department regulation that officers must submit to urinalysis on suspicion of drug abuse, but required a reasonable and objective basis for that suspicion that urinalysis would produce evidence of drug abuse by the police officer.[133]

8. *Burnley v. Railway Labor Executives' Association*:[134] The Ninth U.S. Court of Appeals viewed regulations of the Federal Railway Administration that required blood and urine tests to be conducted on all crew members of trains involved in accidents that cause death, major injury, property damage, or release of a hazardous substance. The regulations were declared unconstitutional in February 1988 because they were not grounded on a "particularized suspicion" of drug use by an individual train crew member: "Accidents, incidents, or rule violations, by themselves, do not create reasonable grounds for suspecting that testing will demonstrate alcohol or drug impairment in any one railroad employee, much less an entire train crew. . . . We think when testing is undertaken to detect drug or alcohol abuse as a means of improving the safe operation of a railroad, it poses no insurmountable burden on the government to require individualized suspicion."

9. *Jones v. McKenzie*:[135] The court stated that in the absence of probable cause the public school system could administer drug tests to bus attendants who are responsible for supervising, attending, and carrying handicapped children only if the drug testing is capable of showing "on the job" drug use.

10. *O'Connor v. Ortega*:[136] The U.S. Supreme Court declared that an employer need not have probable cause to conduct a search of a public employee's desk but merely a "reasonable ground for suspecting that the search will turn up evidence that the employee is guilty of misconduct or that the search is necessary for a non-investigatory purpose. . . . "

11. *Schmerber v. California*:[137] The highest court ruled that California or any state may require a blood test of an individual suspected of drunken driving without violating the person's right of privacy because drawing a small amount of blood for testing purposes is a "minor intrusion" justified by the value of the evidence to be obtained.

12. *Matter of Caruso v. Ward*:[138] The New York court struck down a New

York City order that would require current and future members of the police department's Organized Crime Control Bureau to consent and submit to random drug testing. The court found that the employer's reasons for such a standardless testing policy (deterrence, drug-free work force, and so on) did not justify a random drug testing policy.

An interesting aspect of this problem of drug testing of employees is the possible negligence of the person or persons administering the drug test.[139] In Otis Engineering Corp. v. Clark,[140] two husbands whose wives were killed in an automobile accident caused by an intoxicated employee sued the driver's employer for the wrongful deaths of their spouses. On the night of the fatal accident, the employee was intoxicated at work and his supervisor told him to drive home from work. The Texas court upheld the claim against the employer for the supervisor's negligence in letting the intoxicated employee drive home: "When, because of an employee's incapacity, an employer exercises control over the employee, the employer has a duty to take such action as a reasonably prudent employer under the same or similar circumstances would take to prevent the employee from causing an unreasonable risk of harm to others."

NOTES

1. —N.Y.S.2d—(New York County, 1988).
2. —F.R.D.—(D.C. 1987).
3. See New York Times, June 25, 1987, at 10.
4. See chapter 8.
5. See A.B.A.J. (December 1, 1987) at 24.
6. —N.Y.S.2d—(New York County, July 14, 1988).
7. Note Section 1 of Restatement (SECOND) on Agency, and see Rule v. Jones, 40 N.W.2d 580 (Wis. 1949).
8. 316 A.2d 8 (N.J., 1973).
9. Note Lipka v. United States, 369 F.2d 288 (2nd Cir. 1966).
10. See Weeks v. Pilot Life Insurance Co., 180 S.E.2d 875 (S.C. 1971).
11. 193 N.W.2d 58 (Mich. App. 1971).
12. 385 F. Supp. 871 (D.C. 1974).
13. 530 S.W.2d 249 (Mo. App. 1975).
14. 502 F.2d 1344 (10th Cir. 1974).
15. 331 N.W.2d 907 (Minn. 1983).
16. See Dieter v. Baker Service Tools, Inc., 739 S.W.2d 405 (Tex. Civ. App. 1987) and Cosgrove v. Lawrence, 520 A.2d 844 (N.J. 1986).
17. Pruitt v. Pavelin, 685 P.2d 1347 (Cal. 1984).
18. See generally 19 Suffolk L Rev 371 (1985).
19. See DiCosala v. Kay, 450 A.2d 508 (N.J. 1982) and Evans v. Morsell, 395 A.2d 480 (Md. 1978).
20. Note Ponticas v. KMS Investments, Inc., 331 N.W.2d 907 (Minn. 1983).
21. See generally 10 New Mex L Rev 491 (1980).
22. See Plains Resources, Inc. v. Gable, 682 P.2d 653 (Kan. 1984) and also Gregor v. Kleiser, 443 N.E.2d 1162 (Ill. App. 1983).

23. Note Estate of Arrington v. Fields, 578 S.W.2d 173 (Tex. Civ. App. 1979).

24. See Gaines v. Monsanto Co., 655 S.W.2d 568 (Mo. App. 1983). See also A.B.A.J. (May 1, 1987) at 72 et seq.

25. See Edwards v. Robinson-Humphrey Co., 298 S.E.2d 600 (Ga. App. 1982).

26. See Cramer v. Housing Opportunities Commission, 501 A.2d 35 (Md. 1985).

27. See Giles v. Shell Oil Corp., 487 A.2d 610 (D.C. 1985).

28. See Henley v. Prince George's County, 503 A.2d 1333 (Md. 1986).

29. See Easley v. Appolo Detective Agency, Inc., 387 N.E.2d 1241 (Ill. App. 1979).

30. 472 F.2d 671 (9th Cir. 1972).

31. See Dothard v. Rawlinson, 433 U.S. 321 (1977).

32. See Harper v. TWA, 525 F.2d 409 (8th Cir. 1975).

33. 567 F.2d 429 (D.C. Cir. 1976).

34. See generally Landes and Vittor, "Employee Litigation: Recent Developments," N.Y.L.J. 3 (October 8, 1987).

35. 448 N.E.2d 86 (N.Y. 1983).

36. See Selznick, Law, Society and Industrial Justice 135–136 (1980).

37. Note Feinman, "The Development of the Employment at Will Rule," 20 Am. J. Leg. Hist. 118, 121–122 (1976); also see Perritt, Employee Dismissal Law and Practice §1.3 (1984).

38. Id.

39. See chapter 9.

40. Supra note 34.

41. Note, Hurst, Law and Markets in United States History 23 (1982).

42. Interestingly, in this period, as shown in Adair v. United States, 208 U.S. 161 (1908), governments simply were not permitted by the courts to regulate employment relationships. Here the U.S. Supreme Court had held that federal legislation outlawing "yellow dog contracts" in the railroad industry was unconstitutional.

43. For historical background, see Wood, A Treatise on the Law of Master and Servant (1877), and note Martin v. New York Life Insurance Co., 148 N.Y. 117, 121 (1895).

44. For example, see Adolph v. Cookware Company of America, 278 N.W. 687 (Mich. 1938).

45. Supra note 36 at p. 138.

46. Civil service protection for federal employees as set forth in the Lloyd-La-Follette Act of 1912 was a paramount factor, as historically recounted in Bush v. Lucas, 103 S. Ct. 2404 (1983).

47. See Perritt, Employee Dismissal Law and Practice §1.9 (1984); also see Wellington, Labor and the Legal Process (1968).

48. —N.Y.S.2d—(New York County, July 11, 1988).

49. 457 N.Y.S.2d 193 (1982), aff. 443 N.E.2d 441 (N.Y. 1982).

50. —N.Y.S.2d—(1988).

51. 69 N.Y.2d 329, —N.E.2d— (1987).

52. 526 N.Y.S.2d 900 (1988).

53. —S.W.2d—(Mo. 1988).

54. —P.2d—(Kan. 1988).

55. Professor Perritt (supra note 47) cites the following cases in support of his conclusion that 29 states have overcome the strictures of the employment-at-will doc-

trine: "Eales v. Tanana Valley Medical-Surgical Group, Inc., 663 P.2d 958 (Alaska 1983) (recovery on implied contract theory permitted); Tameny v. Atlantic Richfield Co., 27 Cal.3d 167, 164 Cal. Rptr. 839, 610 P.2d 1330 (1980) (discharge for refusal to participate in price fixing plan actionable in tort); Pugh v. See's Candies, Inc., 116 Cal. App.3d 311, 171 Cal. Rptr. 917 (1981) (implied promise to terminate for good cause only); Brooks v. Trans World Airlines, —F. Supp.—, 114 L.R.R.M. 3136 (D. Colo. 1983) (handbook can be enforceable under Colorado law on unilateral contract theory); Lampe v. Presbyterian Medical Center, 41 Colo. App. 465, 590 P.2d 513 (1978) (at-will doctrine outweighs general statutory pronouncement that nurses who act improperly will not be relicensed); Sheets v. Teddy's Frosted Foods, Inc., 179 Conn. 471, 427 A.2d 385 (1980) (cause of action stated by quality control supervisor discharged for insistence on compliance with food and drug act); Smith v. Piezo Technology & Prof. Adm'rs, 427 So.2d 182 (Fla. 1983) (limited recovery for discharge under workers' compensation statute); *but see* Muller v. Stromberg Carlson Corp., 427 So. 2d 266 (Fla. App. 1983) (employer policy not enforceable); Parnar v. Americana Hotels, Inc., 65 Hawaii 370, 652 P.2d 625 (1982) (tort; summary judgment for employer reversed); Jackson v. Minidoka Irrig. Dist., 98 Idaho 330, 563 P.2d 54 (1977) (exception to at-will rule where proof of motive offending public policy, but not in this case); Kelsay v. Motorola, Inc., 74 Ill.2d 172, 384 N.E.2d 353 (1978) (tort recovery permitted for firing in retaliation for workers' compensation claim); Palmateer v. International Harvester Co., 85 Ill.2d 124, 421 N.E.2d 876 (1981) (public policy of reporting thefts); Frampton v. Central Indiana Gas Co., 260 Ind. 249, 297 N.E.2d 425 (1973); *but see* Campbell v. Eli Lilly & Co., —Ind.—, 421 N.E.2d 1099 (1981); Johnson v. National Beef Packing Co., 220 Kan. 52, 551 P.2d 779 (1976) (refusal to find contract from handbook but not rejecting tort theory); *compare* Higdon Food Serv. Inc., v. Walker, 641 S.W.2d 750 (Ky. 1982) (promise to limit reasons for discharge might be enforceable) *with* Scroghan v. Kraftco Corp., 551 S.W.2d 811 (Ky. App. 1977) (no tort action for dismissal caused by plans to attend law school); Adler v. American Std. Corp., 291 Md. 31. 432 A.2d 464 (1981) (tort cause of action exists); Maddaloni v. Western Mass. Bus Lines, 386 Mass. 877, 438 N.E.2d 351 (1982) (covenant of good faith; jury verdict for plaintiff affirmed); Sucholdowski v. Consolidated Gas Co., 412 Mich. 692, 316 N.W.2d 710 (1982); Toussaint v. Blue Cross & Blue Shield, 408 Mich. 579, 292 N.W.2d 880 (1980) (employment tenure implied from handbook); Pine River State Bank v. Mettille, 333 N.W.2d 622 (Minn. 1983) (implied contract recovery permitted); Arie v. Intertherm, 648 S.W.2d 142, 153 (Mo. App. 1983) (contract can be implied from handbook); Nye v. Dept. of Livestock, —Mont.—, 639 P.2d 498 (1982) (tort recognized); Gates v. Life of Montana Ins. Co., —Mont.—, 638 P.2d 1063 (1982)(covenant of good faith recognized); Southwest Gas Corp. v. Ahmad, —Nev.—, 668 S.W.2d 261 (1983) (accepting implied contract theory); Cloutier v. Great Atl. & Pac. Tea Co., 121 N.H. 915, 436 A.2d 1140 (1981) (judgment for plaintiff in tort affirmed); Pierce v. Ortho Pharmaceutical Corp., 84 N.J. 58, 417 A.2d 505 (1980) (tort theory recognized); Weiner v. McGraw-Hill, Inc., 57 N.Y.2d 458, 457 N.Y.S.2d 193, 443 N.E.2d 441 (1982) (implied contract theory recognized); Murphy v. American Home Prods., 58 N.Y.2d 293, 461 N.Y.S.2d 232, 448 N.E.2d 86 (1983) (no *abusive discharge* tort); Langdon v. Saga Corp., 569 P.2d 524 (Okla. App. 1977) (plaintiff recovery of severance pay under personnel manual implies wrongful discharge action might succeed); Nees v. Hocks, 272 Or. 210, 536 P.2d 512 (1975) (tort action permitted for discharge caused by jury service); Geary v. United States Steel Corp., 456 Pa. 171, 319 A.2d

174 (1974) (suggesting tort action on other facts); Forman v. BRI Corp., 532 F.Supp. 49 (E.D. Pa. 1982) (implied contract); Osterkamp v. Alkota Mfg., Inc., 332 N.W.2d 275 (S.D. 1983) (failure to follow policy manual supports breach of contract action); *compare* Frazier v. Colonial Williamsburg, —F. Supp.—, 114 L.R.R.M. 3130 (E.D. Va. 1983) (implied contract claim for unfair dismissal goes to jury under Virginia law) and Sea-Land Service v. O'Neal, 224 Va. 343, 297 S.E.2d 647 (1982) (resignation from one position provided consideration to make promise of another position enforceable), *with* Griffith v. Electrolux Corp., 454 F.Supp. 29 (E.D. Va. 1978) (reason for termination immaterial); Roberts v. Atlantic Richfield Co., 88 Wash.2d 887, 568 P.2d 764 (1977) (recognizing tort cause of action when based on statutory right of refusal to engage in criminal activity); Harless v. First Nat'l Bank, 246 S.E.2d 270 (W.Va. 1978) (retaliatory discharge action is tort); Brockmeyer v. Dun & Bradstreet, Inc., 113 Wis.2d 343, 335 N.W.2d 834 (1983) (well-defined public policy overrides at-will rule; contract but not tort action is appropriate).''

56. 364 N.E.2d 1251 (Mass. 1977).

57. Rulon-Miller v. IBM, 208 Cal. Rptr. 524 (1984).

58. Infra note 55.

59. 328 S.E.2d 818 (N.C. 1985).

60. 89 So. 732 (Ala. 1921).

61. Id. at 735.

62. Cf. Murphy v. American Home Products Co., 448 N.E.2d 86 (N.Y. 1983).

63. See chapter 8.

64. 42 U.S.C. 2000e et seq.

65. 29 U.S.C. 621 et seq.

66. Supra note 63.

67. See Note, 67 Colum. L. Rev. (1967).

68. See Warren Freedman, The Right of Privacy in the Computer Age §2.10, 4.9 (1987).

69. 785 F.2d 352 (1st Cir. 1986).

70. 467 N.E.2d 126 (Mass. 1984); also note 29 ATLA L. Rep. 155 (May 1986).

71. —F.2d—(D.C. Cir. 1988).

72. 5 U.S.C. 522(a).

73. 12 U.S.C. 3401 to 3422.

74. 15 U.S.C. 1681 to 1681t.

75. It is of interest to note that consumer credit reports are deemed ''commercial speech'' *outside* the protection of the First Amendment; Millstone v. O'Hanlon Reports, Inc., 528 F.2d 829 (6th Cir. 1976).

76. The U.S. Congress intended to prevent unreasonable or careless invasion of consumer privacy, not to preclude dissemination of critical credit information; *In Re TRW Inc.*, 460 F. Supp. 1007 (D.C. Mich. 1978).

77. ''Consumer reporting agency'' under Section 1681a of FCRA is defined as including an agency that acts for monetary fees or dues, or on a cooperative non-profit basis, and regularly engages in whole or in part in gathering or evaluating information on consumers in order to distribute such information to third parties engaged in commerce. See Porter v. Talbot Perkins Children's Services, 355 F. Supp. 174 (D.C. N.Y. 1973).

78. Under Section 1681(4) of FCRA, the emphasis is placed upon ''respect for the consumer's right to privacy.''

79. But the onus is not upon the credit reporting agency to inform consumers who

dispute information contained in their credit files; Roseman v. Retail Credit Co., 428 F. Supp. 643 (D.C. Pa. 1977), and Middlebrooks v. Retail Credit Co., 416 F. Supp. 1013 (D.C. Ga. 1976).

80. See Section 1681n on civil liability for *willful* noncompliance. See Thornton v. Equifax, Inc., 467 F. Supp. 1008 (D.C. Ark. 1979) and Millstone v. O'Hanlon Reports, Inc., *supra* note 76. See also Section 1681o on civil liability for *negligent* noncompliance. See Wood v. Holiday Inns, Inc., 508 F.2d 167 (C.A. Ala. 1975).

81. In Wolman v. United States, decided by the U.S. District Court for the District of Columbia on November 24, 1980, it was held that the Selective Service System's requirement that draft registrants supply Social Security numbers violated Section 7 of PA, which provided that the federal government shall not deny any "right, benefit or privilege" because the individual refused to disclose his Social Security number. Indeed, the purpose of Section 7 was to block any further expansion of the use of Social Security numbers as a universal identifier! But Social Security numbers may be required where specifically directed by statute, or where disclosure was already required by statute or regulation under a system of records in existence and operating prior to 1975. Judge Gesell enjoined the Selective Service System from mandatorily requiring Social Security numbers in subsequent regulation, and authorized withdrawal of Social Security numbers by the plaintiff and others of the same mind.
Earlier on July 17, 1980, in Albright v. United States, 732 F.2d 181 (1980), the U.S. Circuit Court for the District of Columbia had ruled that PA forbade any federal agency that "maintains a system of records" from "maintaining, collecting, using or disseminating" any record of an individual's exercise of First Amendment rights, such as video tape records.

82. Yet in Smiertka v. U.S. Dept. of Treasury, 447 F. Supp. 221 (D.C. 1978), it was held that only federal agencies, not the individual agency officials, are proper party defendants.
In late 1980, the Veterans Administration complained that its records were too open to the public. It reported that investigations conducted by the office of inspector general were seriously hampered when the person who was the subject of investigation requested and received under the PA access to all information that the inspector general had found. The Veterans Administration in 45 Fed. Reg. 77050 (Nov. 21, 1980) proposed regulations to exempt certain materials under the PA. The exemptions, if permitted under the law, would enable the agency to withhold documents that reveal confidential sources, criminal investigative techniques, and reports compiled following an arrest through disposition.

83. In 1979, Congress amended Section 1104 of Public Law 95-630, Title IX, relieving financial institutions of the onus of notifying their customers of their rights under this law, and placing the burden upon the Board of Governors of the Federal Reserve System.

84. See Suburban Trust Co. v. Waller, 44 Md. App. 335, 408 A.2d 758 (1979) *re* a bank's disclosure of a depositor's account.

85. See McGloshen v. U.S. Dept. of Agriculture, 480 F. Supp. 247 (D.C. Ky. 1979).

86. Other federal enactments involving the right of privacy include the Family Educational Rights & Privacy Act of 1974 [20 U.S.C.A. 1232(g)], and the Omnibus Crime Control & Safe Streets Act of 1968 (47 U.S.C.§§5, 15, 18, 28, 42, and 47), which dealt with willful interception of any wire or oral communication.

87. The new law, which the House approved by a vote of 357–2, substantially

contradicted the 1978 U.S. Supreme Court decision in Zurcher v. Stanford Daily, 434 U.S. 547, 98 S. Ct. 1970 (1978), which upheld as not in violation of the First Amendment a police search of the newsroom of Stanford University's student newspaper. That decision, according to President Carter, "raised the concern that law enforcement authorities could conduct unannounced searches of reporters' notes and files to seek evidence. Such a practice could have a chilling effect on the ability of reporters to develop sources and pursue stories."

88. In most cases, the new law requires federal, state, and local law enforcement authorities wishing to examine a reporter's notes, films, tapes, files, or other documentary records to do one of two things: they may request voluntary cooperation in turning over the material; and if they do not request such compliance, they must give advance notice that certain records will be subpoenaed and that a court hearing may be requested to contest the subpoena. These provisions also apply to authors and scholars writing for publication. Exceptions to the ban on surprise searches are permitted only in four special cases: (1) if the reporter or author can reasonably be suspected of having committed the crime being investigated; (2) if serious injury or death will result if the materials are not immediately seized; (3) if the materials would be destroyed or altered were advance notice of a subpoena given; or (4) if an individual failed to turn over materials that had already been legally subpoenaed.

89. The new law does not prohibit surprise searches of innocent third parties who are not members of the press or writing for publication. When documentary evidence is being sought from such individuals, unannounced searches may be made.
On January 2, 1981, the U.S. Department of Justice published guidelines restricting the use of search warrants by federal investigators seeking documents, tape recordings, or similar materials from journalists, lawyers, physicians, and clergy who are not suspected of any crime. Search warrants are not to be used when materials held by a "disinterested third party" could be obtained by subpoena, by a summons, or by a simple request. The guidelines say that subpoenas are preferable to search warrants except where subpoenas might delay an investigation or lead to the destruction of evidence. A subpoena provides advance notice of the request for specific documents and an opportunity to contest the request in court. A search warrant allows a search with no advance warning. The guidelines, it should be noted, do not cover contraband or material related to the commission of a crime.

90. One of the difficult court decisions on the recognition of the right of privacy was the 1976 case of U.S. v. Miller, 425 U.S. 435, 96 S. Ct. 1619, involving an unregistered or unlicensed still. Prior to trial, Miller's attorney moved to suppress copies of checks that government agents had obtained without Miller's knowledge from two banks. Miller argued that his Fourth Amendment right against unreasonable search and seizure was violated when the government (1) required the banks to copy all his personal checks or records under the Bank Security Act; and (2) required the banks to produce those individual records at his trial. The lower federal court and the U.S. Court of Appeals agreed, but the U.S. Supreme Court reversed upon the ground that Miller had no "legitimate expectation of privacy": "Even if we direct our attention to the original checks and deposit slips rather than to the microfilm copies actually viewed and obtained by means of the subpoena, we perceive no legitimate 'expectation of privacy' in their contents . . . the depositor takes the risk, in revealing his affairs to another, that the information will be conveyed by that person to the Government." (425 U.S. at 442–43). The Court ruled that the checks were not confidential communications entitled to privacy protection, and that the account record was the property of the bank and not the

plaintiff's property. This death blow to the right of privacy [the State of California in Burrows v. Superior Court, 529 F.2d 590 (1974) had upheld the right of privacy in a similar situation] was corrected by the U.S. Congress, which inserted into the Tax Reform Act of 1976 the requirement that the government must give notice to the tax-payer when it serves a summons from the Internal Revenue Service. In State ex rel Tarver v. Smith (78 Wash. 152, 470 P.3d 172, 1971; *cert. den.* 402 U.S. 1001), a "welfare mother" became ill and was hospitalized. The Juvenile Court of the State of Washington placed her children in the custody of the Washington Department of Public Assistance after reviewing a case worker's report that described "child neglect." Subsequently Mrs. Tarver was exonerated of the charge of "child neglect" and her children were returned to her. Thereupon she endeavored unsuccessfully to expunge from the court record the charge of "child neglect." Her grievance, according to the Court, was not directly related to her eligibility for public assistance, and so her privacy could not be protected under these circumstances.

91. A.B.A.J. (March 1981) at "LawScope."

92. 5 U.S.C. 522 (1966).

In December 1980, a study by the evaluation staff of the U.S. Department of Justice Management Division revealed that the Justice Department itself violated its own rules by failing to give people effective guidance in using the Privacy Act of 1974 and the Freedom of Information Act of 1966. The study found that the Department had inadequate reading rooms for the public to see and copy documents made public, and had widely varied policies for charging fees for reproducing documents. Three separate offices handled various coordination aspects of the work generated by 65,000 annual requests for files. The study found that reorganizations designed to improve release of information "have instead caused internal confusion by failing to clearly delineate organizational responsibilities." The study said that fee policies were being set by 28 Justice Department units. It reported that six units charged for searching for documents but only one had a system for recording search time. Several units never waived fees for the poor or for disclosures in the public interest as the rules authorized.

93. Congress did not intend to permit litigants to use the FOIA instead of the discovery mechanism provided by the Federal Rules of Civil Procedure. Congress did not desire to give participants in litigation "any earlier or greater access" under FOIA than they would receive through normal discovery procedures when the act was first passed (HR Rep. No. 1497, 89th Cong., 2nd Sess., 1966). When the FOIA was amended in 1974 to change the limits of exemption 7 (investigatory records compiled for law enforcement purposes), members of Congress were careful to state that they did not desire to permit increased access to investigation files in lieu of discovery. [See *120 Cong. Rec.* 170333 (May 30, 1974)]

94. See Moore-McCormack Lines, Inc. v. ITO Corp., 508 F.2d 945 (4th Cir. 1974). This ability on the part of third parties to obtain information submitted to the government under the expectation of continued confidentiality was highlighted by Chrysler Corp. v. Brown, 441 U.S. 285 (1979). See 36 BUS. LAW 57–78 (November 1980). The United States Supreme Court sanctioned the "reverse-FOIA suit" as an established landmark on the landscape of American litigation. To maintain confidentiality was held to be summum bonum; enjoining disclosure of information was proper. Also, note 78 herein.

95. As the result of a 1974 amendment, the FOIA requires the government to pub-

lish comprehensive indexes of records so people would know where to direct their requests for information. Administratively, the processing of such requests has been speeded
up, particularly with respect to the litigation needs of individuals requesting the information.

96. Temple-Eastex, Inc. v. NLRB, 410 F. Supp. 183 (1976).

97. Robins & Weill, Inc. v. U.S., 63 F.R.D. 73 (1974).

98. Moore-McCormack Lines, Inc. v. ITO Corp., supra note 94.

99. See Common Cause v. Ruff, 467 F. Supp. 941 (1979).

100. Individuals who have supplied information to the government and who object
to the release of that information to other parties have no greater rights than the parties
requesting the information. The U.S. Supreme Court in Chrysler Corp. v. Brown (441
U.S. 281, 1979), supra note 94, held that a party submitting documents to a federal
agency does not have a private right of action under FOIA to enjoin subsequent disclosure. That party's interest in confidentiality is limited to the extent that it is endorsed
by the agency holding the records. The Court unanimously rejected the theory that FOIA
exemptions were intended to be mandatory bars to disclosure. The Court referred to the
legislative history indicating that exemptions were intended merely to permit an agency
to withhold certain information. In addition, the Court interpreted FOIA as purely a
disclosure statute because the act confers jurisdiction on federal courts to enjoin with-
holding records but not to prohibit disclosure. The Court also placed significant limitations on the use of Section 1905 of the Trade Secrets Act (18 U.S.C. 1905) as a vehicle
for a "reverse FOIA suit." The Court held that Section 1905 does not create a private
right of action to enjoin disclosure. The Court refused, however, to permit the government to ignore the impediment to disclosure imposed by the Trade Secrets Act. The
Court remanded to the Third U.S. Court of Appeals for consideration of whether the
contemplated disclosures would violate the prohibition of Section 1905. The Court confirmed that violations of the Trade Secrets Act were subject to judicial review under the
provisions of Section 10 of the Administrative Procedure Act (5 U.S.C. 702). But Chrysler,
although an "adversely affected person" under the statute, was entitled only to review
of the administrative board, not de novo consideration by the district court. In remand-
ing, the Court cautioned that it had not attempted to determine the relative "ambits" of
Exemption 4 and Section 1905, or to determine whether Section 1905 is an exemption
statute within the terms of Exemption 3 of FOIA. The Court acknowledged the theoret-
ical possibility that material might be outside Exemption 4 yet within Section 1905, and
thus FOIA might be considered "authorization by law" for purposes of Section 1905.
See 41 C.F.R. § 105.60 (1979). Also, Soucie v. David, 448 F.2d 1067 (1971).

101. See Assn. of the Bar of the City of New York, Committee Reports, Privacy of
Medical Records 488–514 (1980).

102. There is in some states a privilege prohibiting a physician from disclosing information without the patient's consent; but the privilege does not apply to hospitals,
only to physicians, and there is no reported case in which a hospital or physician had
to compensate a patient for a breach of the privilege. But see Hawaii Psychiatric Assn.
v. Ariyoshi, Cv. 79–0113 (D.C. Hawaii, October 22, 1979).

103. The enormity of data about an individual found in medical and health records
has been delineated by Privacy Protection Study Commission, "Personal Privacy in an
Information Society,"282 (July 1974): "The physician-patient relationship is an inherently intrusive one in that the patient who wants and needs medical care must grant the
doctor virtually unconstrained discretion to delve into the details of his life and his

person. As a practical matter, because so much information may be necessary for proper diagnosis and treatment, no area of inquiry is excluded. In addition to describing the details of his symptoms, the patient may be asked to reveal what he eats, how much he drinks or smokes, whether he uses drugs, how often he has sexual relations and with whom, whether he is depressed or anxious, where and how long he has worked, and perhaps what he does for recreation. Moreover, he is expected to submit to as much direct observation and recording of what is observed as his condition suggests and as the confines of the medical-care setting permit.''

104. Access by government officials to individual medical and health related records has been controversial; their needs for individually identifiable records may include investigation and prosecution of such criminal acts as (1) inflated charges for services by health care institutions, or charges for services not rendered at all, which result in over-reimbursement of the institution under Medicare or Medicaid programs; (2) illicit drug prescriptions written by health professionals; (3) violations of health and safety laws, such as improper exposure to toxic substances; (4) fraudulent schemes involving sales of worthless products; (5) homicide, where the killer may be a doctor; (6) charges defended on the basis of insanity; (7) child abuse; (8) tax evasion through invalid medical deductions; and (9) acts of a foreign agent or of terrorists or fugitives. Or the following additional uses of medical records: (1) identification of an assailant in rape cases, by determining blood types, through a chemical analysis of semen deposits, or by isolating unusual physical characteristics such as a scar; (2) analysis of blood alcohol contents in vehicular homicide cases, including hit and run cases; (3) analysis of injuries where the suspect claims he acted in self-defense; (4) analysis of injuries to a victim who refuses to cooperate with the authorities; (5) emergency situations such as kidnapping, hostage-taking, and mass murder where it may be necessary to "talk down" the suspect. But these clearly legitimate uses by government officials must be subject to the constitutional protection of a lawful process, i.e., subpoena or summons. A court can judge the need of the government official for access to the individual record. Perhaps the individual whose privacy is affected can be notified and given the opportunity to challenge the scope and relevance of the subpoena or summons.

105. —N.Y.S.2d—(Queens County, August 22, 1988).

106. —N.Y.S.2d—(New York County, 1987).

107. Section 296(1)(a) provides: "It shall be an unlawful discriminatory practice: (a) For an employer . . . because of the . . . disability . . . of any individual, to refuse to hire or employ or to bar or to discharge from employment such individual or to discriminate against such individual in compensation or in terms, conditions or privileges of employment.''

108. Note Section 292(21) of the New York Executive Law.

109. Fort Halifax Packing Company v. Coyne, 107 S. Ct. 221 (1987). Also note New York Times, June 2, 1987, at 1.

110. —N.Y.S.2d—(New York County, August 26, 1988).

111. The 5 requisites of a class action are set forth in CPLR 901 and reads as follows:

a. One or more members of a class may sue or be sued as representative parties on behalf of all if:

1. The class is so numerous that joinder of all members, whether otherwise required or permitted, is impracticable;

2. there are questions of law or fact common to the class which predominate over any questions affecting only individual members;

3. the claims or defenses of the representative parties are typical of the claims or defenses of the class;

4. the representative parties will fairly and adequately protect the interest of the class; and

5. a class action is superior to other available methods for the fair and efficient adjudication of the controversy.

112. 825 F.2d 1095 (7th Cir. 1987).

113. See Payson and Rosen, "Substance Abuse: A Crisis in the Workplace," Trial Magazine 25 et seq. (July 1987).

114. —F.2d—(D.C. Cir. 1987); lower court opinion at 628 F. Supp. 1500 (D.C. 1986).

115. 70 N.Y.2d 57,—N.E.2d—(1987).

116.

The act of discharging urine is a private, indeed intimate, one and the product may contain revealing information concerning an individual's personal life and habits for those capable of analyzing it. . . . Requiring a person to urinate in the presence of a government official or agent, as is sometimes required in these cases is at least as intrusive as a strip search. Even when the individual is permitted to perform the act in private, at the command and supervision of a person designated by the State, privacy interests are implicated. Ordering a person to empty his or her bladder and produce the urine in a container for inspection and analysis by public officials is no less offensive to personal dignity than requiring an individual to empty his pockets and produce a report containing the results of a urinalysis examination. 70 N.Y.2d at 67–68 (citations omitted).

117. 816 F.2d 170 (5th Cir. 1987).

118. 795 F.2d 1136 (3rd Cir. 1986).

119. See McDonnell v. Hunter, 809 F.2d 1302 (8th Cir. 1987). Also see Neal, "Mandatory Drug Testing: Court Weighs Civil Liberties Objections," A.B.A.J. 58 (October 1, 1988).

120. —Cal. Rptr.—(June 10, 1988).

121. See New York Times, June 11, 1988, at 39.

122. Supra note 115.

123. See Fox, "Testing Teachers for Drugs Ruled Invasion of Privacy," N.Y.L.J. 1 et seq. (August 12, 1986).

124. 548 S.W.2d 743 (Tex. Civ. App. 1977).

125. See Trial Magazine 93 (September 1986).

126. 601 F. Supp 482 (N.D. Ga. 1985).

127. 612 F. Supp 1122 (S.D. Iowa 1985); see reversal by eighth U.S. Court of Appeals, 809 F.2d 1302 (8th Cir. 1987).

128. Supra note 127.

129. Supra note 118.

130. Supra note 117.

131. Supra note 113 at p. 26.

132. 500 A.2d 1005 (D.C. 1985).

133. Supra note 113 at p. 28.

134. 839 F.2d 575 (9th Cir. 1988).

135. 833 F.2d 335 (D.C. Cir. 1987).

136. 107 S.Ct. 1492 (1987).

137. 384 U.S. 757 (1966).

138. 520 N.Y.S.2d 551 (1986); also 131 A.D.2d 214 (1986).

139. See generally Herman & Bernholz, "Negligence in Employee Drug Testing," Case & Comment 3 et seq. (July–August 1987).

140. 668 S.W.2d 307 (Tex. 1983).

3

Termination of Employment Contracts and Dismissal of Employees

3.1 INTRODUCTION TO TERMINATION AND DISMISSAL OF EMPLOYEES

At common law the employer's freedom to terminate the employment relationship or to dismiss the employee was absolute.[1] But over the centuries since those early days in England the employer's right of termination or discharge has been increasingly restricted by court decisions, by state and federal statutes, and by collective bargaining agreements with unions and their members and employers. Yet in the final analysis the basic principle of the employer's right to terminate or discharge remains unimpaired.

In National Labor Relations Board v. Local Union No. 1229[2] the U.S. Supreme Court in 1953 held that the discharge of striking employees of a television station because of their attack on the television station for its poor programming and inadequate public service did not constitute an "unfair labor practice" under the National Labor Relations Act. The effort of the employees to discredit the employer's business was deemed to be "detrimental disloyalty," which constituted "just cause" for discharge or termination of their employment: "There is no more elemental cause for discharge of an employee than disloyalty to his employer." Accordingly, the employer's right to discharge or terminate for "insubordination, disobedience, or disloyalty" was sanctioned by the highest court! As one attorney expressed it, employment policies of employers should "obviously go far beyond the legal issues."[3] Still another attorney has observed that employees seeking compensation for termination or discharge should show that they gave up something tangible, particularly if they were thinking about the employer's promise when they gave that something up![4]

The 1987 Nevada decision in K Mart Corporation v. Ponsock[5] illustrates a growing recognition that many discharges and terminations are in bad faith and may even involve infringement of the employee's civil rights. Here Ponsock, age 43, was hired in 1972 as a forklift driver, after leaving his job as a coin counter at a Nevada casino. His work as a forklift driver was ranked as excellent by his immediate supervisor; after $9\frac{1}{2}$ years he was approximately six months away from 100 percent vesting of his retirement benefits when he was fired upon the specious grounds that without authorization from his employer he had applied gray paint to the battery cover of the forklift. The Nevada Supreme Court, in approving a jury verdict for compensatory and punitive damages, observed: "K Mart's explanation of the reasons for firing Ponsock does not hold together very well. Ponsock was only six months away from retirement. That K Mart fired Ponsock, an admittedly excellent, long-term employee, over the trivial paint episode may very well have been rejected by the jury. K Mart's characterization of Ponsock as a thief also was likely to have done very little to the company's credibility in this lawsuit. All in all, it is likely rather than merely possible that the jury saw K Mart's true motive as being to divest Ponsock of his retirement rights." The court concluded that the employer was guilty of much more flagrant conduct than mere breach of the employment contract: the jury could properly find that the employer fired him "for the very unworthy motive of evading its duty to pay retirement benefits." The tort of bad faith here amounted to malicious conduct on the part of the employer! The employment relationship delineates an employer's commitment to a dependent employee for extended employment and subsequent retirement benefits, and a breach of that employment relationship gives the aggrieved employee a tort remedy for the employer's bad faith in evading the employee's retirement rights.

3.2 "GOOD CAUSE" FOR TERMINATION OR DISCHARGE OF EMPLOYEES

"Good cause" as the basis for termination or discharge of employees will undoubtedly vary with the beholder, and the courts may find "good cause" in many situations where other persons or entities would not find "good cause." For example, in the California case of Clutterham v. Coachman Industries, Inc.[6] the plaintiff had been employed by defendant as its West Coast representative for seven years when the parties entered into a written contract, which included a termination clause that allowed either party to terminate on 30 days' written notice. Several months later plaintiff was fired on the grounds that the market for recreational vehicles had declined and defendant had decided to consolidate its operations elsewhere. The California trial court granted defendant summary judgment, finding that there was "good cause" for termination because of the depressed industry conditions and the need for relocation of corporate operations.[7] The appellate court in affirming declared that "courts must take care not to interfere with a legitimate exercise of managerial discretion. . . . [Nothing] suggests that in making the business judgment to reorganize its marketing operations respondent had a duty to consider appellant's economic interest and try to preserve his job if possible.''

A similar approach is found in another California case[8] where the federal district court granted summary judgment against an employee who claimed that his layoff following defendant's business decision to streamline operations violated an implied contract not to lay him off. The court stated that the employer was under no obligation to consider the plaintiff's seniority in deciding whom to lay off, because courts should not interfere in legitimate, nonpretextual exercises of managerial discretion.[9] Thus the court found "good cause" for the employer's termination or discharge of the employee.

The New York Appellate Division, First Department, in Mandelblatt v. Devon Stores, Inc.,[10] faced a disgruntled employee consultant whose contract of employment had been terminated, although the contract had provided in paragraph 7 that he might "be discharged as a consultant without any breach of this Agreement," i.e., "upon expiration of the contract, upon respondent's death, in the event of respondent's incapacity due to illness, or for cause." The agreement defined "cause" as "the willful and continued failure by Mandelblatt to substantially provide the services" called for after a demand for performance had been delivered by the directors of the company, or "the willful engaging by Mandelblatt, in his capacity as consultant, in gross misconduct materially injurious to Pantry Pride monetarily or otherwise," or respondent's conviction of a felony under federal or state law.

Plaintiff was discharged for "cause" for his "threats to fail to perform" his duties unless he received "a new and more lucrative contract" and for his "lack of cooperation with and discouragement of prospective purchasers of Devon Stores, Inc." after his demand for a new contract was rejected by appellants. Thereafter, appellants tendered him $714,785 "as required by the contract, conditioned upon his return of the company car and the execution of a release absolving appellant of all liability under the contract," according to the court. Respondent rejected the payment tendered, refused to execute the release, and retained the automobile valued at $25,000.

In reversing the partial summary judgment for the employee, the New York court here observed that the trial court had erred "in determining, as a matter of law, the intention of the parties." Paragraph 7 was ambiguous because it did not identify the person or entity that could terminate the contract of employment![11] However, appellant employer was permitted to "amend the answer to assert counterclaims for breach of contract, breach of fiduciary duty, and intentional interference with prospective economic advantage."

In a 1988 New York case the court ruled that the discharged employee, a housing police officer, had offered no proof that she had been terminated for "cause" or in bad faith.[12] One interesting aspect of that case was the court's remonstrance that "a termination of employment for 'unsatisfactory services' is not considered stigmatic. . . . When Lucy Serra was terminated from employment, there was no public disclosure of this fact or the reasons for dismissal. Since there was no public disclosure, petitioner cannot argue that her name and reputation was impaired."

"Good cause" as a justification for termination or discharge of an employee was explained in the California decision of Crosier v. United Parcel Service, Inc.:[13] "The court must balance the employer's interest in operating his business efficiently and profitably with the interest of the employee in maintaining his employment and the interest of the public in maintaining a proper balance between the two." But the employer does not have exclusive discretion to terminate or discharge an employee: "If we were to adopt such a rule, an employer could implement a patently absurd business policy" without regard to judicial inquiry. In the Connecticut case of Owens v. American National Red Cross[14] the employee had apparently been discharged for taking half a personal day to attend the unemployment hearing of a former employee of defendant; she had also falsely identified herself at the hearing as a representative of her employer. The court agreed that defendant employer "may have been unfair," but that act of termination or discharge was simply "not enough" to rebut the "good cause" firing of plaintiff employee; she had left her work without permission and had misrepresented her status.

On the other hand, in the following cases the courts determined that there was an utter lack of "good cause" for the termination or discharge of the employee:

1. *Teaman v. ASI Market Research, Inc.*:[15] Plaintiff, a market research specialist, sold his company to defendant and the parties negotiated a three-year employment contract, which provided, inter alia, that plaintiff would not compete, consult, or invest in market research, that plaintiff would be discharged only for "good cause" and with reasons supplied to him, and that plaintiff would not be entitled to further pay if discharged. About a year and a half later defendant asked plaintiff to resign, but plaintiff refused and so defendant fired him without stating the reasons for the firing. The parties agreed to stay the action pending arbitration, and the award found that defendant had indeed breached the contract without "good cause."

2. *Cohen v. Fox-Knapp, Inc.*:[16] Plaintiff president of the defendant company won summary judgment that defendant had breached the employment agreement by discontinuing payment following his medical disability and inability to work. Defendant employer contended that it never intended to make payments in the plaintiff's absence from work, and that there was "good cause" for its termination or discharge of plaintiff employee. But the court disagreed with defendant's contention, and added: "Having determined that the plaintiff's wages due under the employment agreement were improperly withheld, plaintiff is also entitled to reasonable attorneys fees."

3. *Huber v. Standard Insurance Co.*:[17] The Ninth U.S. Court of Appeals, applying California law, stated that once an employee establishes a prima facie case for tortious breach of an employment contract, the burden of proof switches

to the employer to show "good cause" for the termination or discharge. Plaintiff employee was fired after nine years of employment without the 30-day notice (he was given four days notice) and without being given the option to choose a demotion in order to work enough time for pension benefits to vest. The court found lack of "good cause" and furthermore recognized that there is an implied covenant of good faith and fair dealing in all contracts of employment.

4. *Phipps v. Clark Oil & Refining Corp.*:[18] Plaintiff was fired from his job in a gasoline filling station for refusing to put leaded gasoline into a car that was supposed to be filled only with unleaded gasoline. The Minnesota Supreme Court found lack of "good cause" for the firing, since the firing was motivated by his good faith refusal to violate the law.

5. *Bell v. Sandford-Corbitt-Bruker, Inc.*:[19] Here plaintiff had been an insurance policy rate clerk for 12 years when her employer fired her; she had miscalculated rates, alienated clients, and frequently missed work. Four years later defendant employer lost money when a former partner filed for bankruptcy, and defendant employer thereupon told all employees that anyone who filed for bankruptcy would be fired. It was then that plaintiff was fired when she filed for personal bankruptcy under Chapter 13; but under 11 USC 525(b) and 11 USC 101 et seq. "no private employer may terminate the employment of . . . an individual . . . solely because such debtor or bankrupt . . . is or has been a debtor under this title. . . . " The federal district court found an absence of "good cause" for the firing based upon plaintiff's bankruptcy.

6. *DiCocco v. Capital Area Community Health Plan, Inc.*:[20] Plaintiff nurse had been placed on probation after complaints about her performance were registered; she then took seven sick days' leave and was discharged for misuse of sick leave. Defendant employer's personnel manual had authorized twelve days' leave. The New York court found that this writing limited her employer's right to fire her without cause, and that she had relied upon that provision in the personnel manual at the time she accepted employment.

7. *Dowd v. Ward*:[21] The petitioner sought to annul the police department's termination of her probationary appointment as a police officer. She had apparently been dismissed for failing to appear for a urine analysis, but she claimed that at the time of the urine analysis she had been on sick leave due to a line-of-duty injury. The New York court found that her claim was insufficient to establish "bad faith" termination, even though the police department gave no reason for ending her career as a police officer: "It is well settled that a probationary employee may be discharged without a hearing and without a statement of reasons in the absence of any demonstration that dismissal was for a constitutionally impermissible purpose or in violation of statutory or decisional law. [citation omitted]"

It should be clear that courts are unwilling to overrule the discretionary action of public officials, particularly with regard to appointment, promotion, or termination of public employees.[22] However, in Bellman v. McGuire[23] the New

York Appellate Division observed a young probationary police officer who had been severely injured and disabled in the line of duty while attempting to remove a drunk driver from an automobile; he was summarily dismissed and denied a pension. The court reinstated him after denying him the same relief just four years earlier![24] Yet under Section 63 of the New York Civil Service Law and under Section 14–109b of the New York City Administrative Code a probationary police officer can be dismissed at any time during the probationary period at the discretion of the police commissioner, who need offer no reason for doing so.

One aspect of the need for "good cause" for discharge or termination of employment is seen in the category of "retaliatory" discharge or termination. In Herbster v. North American Company for Life and Health Insurance[25] plaintiff was the defendant's chief legal officer when he was fired, allegedly for refusing to destroy or hide discovery documents, although the defendant pointed to plaintiff's poor job performance as the basis for firing. The Illinois court granted summary judgment for the employer, stating that there is no cause of action for "retaliatory discharge" by an attorney whose employment is terminated by the client. The court favored the confidentiality privilege above the right of a discharged attorney to have a remedy for "retaliatory discharge." Obviously the court was mistaken, for plaintiff, while an attorney, was fundamentally an employee of the defendant employer.[26] The Fifth U.S. Court of Appeals in Doe v. A Corporation,[27] on the other hand, upheld the right of an attorney to pursue a cause of action on his own behalf against his corporate employer for discharge or termination of the employment contract without "good cause." In short, "the client does not gain the right to cheat the lawyer by imparting confidences to him." Note that the suit here was filed using fictitious names of the parties in order to preserve the confidentiality of secrets learned by the attorney-employee in the employment relationship!

3.3   FEDERAL STATUTES ON RETALIATORY DISCHARGE AND "WHISTLE-BLOWING"

Numerous federal statutes protect employee conduct against retaliatory discharge. One example is the Occupational Safety and Health Act of 1970 (OSHA),[28] which under Section 11(c) prohibits employers from discharging employees who file OSHA complaints against them or otherwise exercise rights afforded by the act against employers. Specific instances of employee conduct are informing OSHA of unsafe conditions or requesting a federal inspection of the workplace or assisting OSHA inspectors or seeking injunctive relief against the employers.[29] Where an employee refuses to work or perform hazardous job activities in certain circumstances, the U.S. Supreme Court has upheld the reasonable right of the employee to refuse to work and not be fired. Furthermore, the employer cannot discriminate against such an employee, although the employer may refuse to pay the employee for work not performed.[30] But a discharged employee has no private right of action against the employer based on Section 11(c) of OSHA.[31]

There is an antiretaliation provision in the National Labor Relations Act of 1935,[32] as amended in 1947 and 1959, which defines as an "unfair labor practice" on the part of the employer the act of retaliating against employees who file charges under the act or who give testimony in an NLRB hearing.[33] The Age Discrimination in Employment Act also has an antiretaliation provision.[34]

Section 10 of the Federal Employers Liability Act[35] prohibits contracts of employment containing provisions preventing employees from furnishing a person in interest with facts incident to an injury or death of any employee. It is a crime punishable by a fine and imprisonment to threaten, intimidate, or discharge an employee for furnishing such information. The discharged employee may bring suit for an injunction precluding his or her unwarranted discharge under the act.[36]

Section 212 of the Federal Railroad Safety Act[37] prohibits the railroad carrier from discharging an employee because the employee filed a complaint under the act or testified in proceedings under the act. The Ninth U.S. Court of Appeals in Burke v. Compania Mexicana de Aviacion, S.A.[38] held that the affected employee under the Railway Labor Act had a private right of action: "The only remedies adequate fully to effectuate congressional purpose in this case are those requested by Burke—damages and reinstatement." The same court 12 years later in Ostrofe v. Crocker Co.[39] held that the congressional purpose was served by permitting such an action by an employee who was blacklisted for refusal to participate in a price-fixing conspiracy.

Retaliatory firing has been predicated in part upon "whistle-blowing,"[40] i.e., men and women driven by courage and conscience have called attention to safety and health hazards in their workplaces. Whistle-blowing unfortunately invites retaliation, and the discharged employee then seeks justice in the form of job reinstatement or compensation for the unjust firing. One recent case, Guercio v. Brady,[41] involved the secretary of a bankruptcy court judge; she complained about corruption in the court, only to be fired by the judge. The Sixth U.S. Court of Appeals ruled that the doctrine of judicial immunity from liability did not shield the judge from suit for such a wrongful employment practice.

In Brothers v. Custis[42] the whistle-blower recouped $200,000 when fired by two officials of the Veterans Administration for reporting improprieties in an experimental drug study involving VA patients. In the State of New York, Section 740 of the New York Labor Law and Section 75b of the New York Civil Service Law safeguard private and public employees, respectively, for publicizing "a violation of law, rule, or regulation which violation creates and presents a substantial and specific danger to the public health or safety." A whistle-blower in Michigan sued his employer for discharge from his job, alleging that the firing was due to his refusal to alter sampling results on pollution reports. In Trombetta v. Detroit, T & I Railroad,[43] the Michigan court protected the plaintiff employee, like another public-interested employee in Kansas Gas & Electric Co. v. Brock,[44] where the Tenth U.S. Court of Appeals observed that the Energy Reform Act[45] protected the whistle-blower for contacts he made with governmental agencies as well as with private agencies.

Other protections for the whistle-blower are found in Section 215(a)(3) of the Fair Labor Standards Act,[46] which declares it unlawful for any person to discharge an employee for filing a complaint, for instituting a proceeding, or for testifying in connection with a violation of the act. A provision of the Asbestos School Hazard Detection and Control Act of 1980[47] prohibits state or local educational agencies receiving assistance under the act from discharging employees because the employees brought to the attention of the public the troubling problems of asbestos.

In Anderson v. Molitor Industries[48] the Colorado court observed that a company executive was fired when he reported to the chairman of the board that the company, which manufactured nuclear glove boxes used by government contractors in handling plutonium and other toxic materials, had used a common sealant that simply was not proper. The discharged employee contended that he was fired for trying to exercise a duty imposed by federal statutes to report substantial safety hazards in the manufacture of products used in nuclear facilities, and the jury awarded the discharged employee $450,000 plus interest and $100,000 punitive damages.

On the state level is the decision in Garber v. Ward,[49] where the New York court found that plaintiff police officer had been passed over for a promotion because he had a history of being a whistle-blower; on numerous occasions he had written letters reporting wrongdoing, waste, and inefficiency in the police department. Although the court recognized that public officers have broad discretion in promotion matters, the court decided that plaintiff nevertheless should be afforded the opportunity to demonstrate that the exercise of his First Amendment rights was the motivating factor in the police department's decision not to promote him:

If this contention is sustained, he is entitled to the relief requested. . . . The petitioner should be afforded the opportunity to demonstrate that his constitutionally protected conduct was the motivating factor in the respondents' decision not to promote him (see Mt. Healthy City School District v. Doyle, 429 US 274).

It is impossible to determine, based on the submissions to the court, whether in fact this is the case here. There is a triable issue of fact, as to whether petitioner was passed over for appointment because he exercised his First Amendment rights, as a "whistle blower."

Additionally, a trial is warranted with respect to the allegations of a violation of Civil Service Law section 61(2).

In summary, whistle-blowing has been characterized as a deed of "courage and anguish that attends the exercise of professional and personal responsibility.[50] It has been said that the defense of "just following orders" has long been rejected,[51] and that the whistle-blower is a modern Martin Luther whose actions should be encouraged and protected.[52] The U.S. Supreme Court more than 20 years ago in Pickering v. Board of Education[53] established legal protection for certain kinds of whistle-blowing for public employees; in a letter to the editor of a local newspaper, plaintiff high school teacher criticized the school board for its allocation of funds to athletic programs, and he was fired for this act of disloyalty or conduct "detrimental to the efficient operation and administration of the schools of the district." The highest court ruled that his "right to speak on issues of public importance may not furnish the basis for his dismissal from public employment." The right to raise such an issue publicly is protected by the First Amendment: "The question whether a school system requires additional funds is a matter of legitimate public concern on which the judgment of the school board administration, including the School Board, cannot, in a society that leaves such questions to popular vote, be taken as conclusive. On such a question free and open debate is vital to informed decision making by the electorate." The court was also aware that teachers have a special competence and interest in speaking out on issues that affect the organizations for which they work![54]

3.4 POLYGRAPH TESTING OF EMPLOYEES

Polygraph testing of employees, the subject of great controversy as to admissibility into evidence, has recently been spotlighted in cases involving negligence on the part of the testing firms.[55] In the first place, the polygraph test may not have been properly administered; second, the test results may not have been accurately maintained; and third, a third person may have been injured by the employee who tested positive for drugs, for example.

In Zampatori v. United Parcel Service,[56] an employee of defendant was given two polygraph examinations by a private detective bureau charged with investigating thefts from defendant employer. As a result of the bureau's report that plaintiff demonstrated stress and deception in the polygraph test, plaintiff was fired, and both defendant and the bureau were successfully sued by the discharged employee for negligence in the administration of the polygraph test. As emphasized in Lawson v. Howmet Aluminum Corp.,[57] a polygraph examiner owes a duty to use reasonable care in administering the test fairly and impartially; subsequent confirmatory testing should corroborate the finding.

Indeed, the polygraph measures physiological responses that are only part of the data used by a qualified polygraph examiner to draw inferences from which to render an opinion that the employee does or does not give indications of attempts at deception. By analogy, the diagnosis of a physician is based on synthesized data collected by means of instrumental or chemical testing along with the physical examination, patient history, and symptoms. The polygraph is certainly not as reliable as a fingerprint or blood type testing, but it is considered trustworthy, probative evidence.[58] A polygraph examination records the responses of the subject employee's autonomous physiological systems, such as blood pressure, pulse rate, respiration rate and depth, and perspiration or skin conductance. The responses to certain control questions are compared with the responses to the relevant questions. Greater or more persistent autonomic disturbances in answer to relevant questions are believed to indicate false-hoods.[59]

Unfortunately, polygraph examinations have become commonplace in employment situations, although the states have endeavored to regulate and in some cases to outlaw the practice.[60] In Georgia, for example, polygraph examinations are limited to a maximum of 15 questions and no fewer than 7 questions; all questions must be provided the interviewee in advance, and the employee so examined is entitled to a written copy of the polygraph results; no questions can be asked about religion, politics, race, labor organizing, or sexual activities.[61] But in Illinois the polygraph examiner may ask questions about religion, beliefs on racial matters, political opinions, labor or union organizing, sexual preferences, or sexual activities, provided that the inquiry is "directly related to employment."[62]

In Wisconsin, polygraph testing is permitted in employment situations if the employee consents in writing, if the employee is given the questions in advance, *and* if the employee is given an opportunity to retake the test. An employee cannot be fired for refusing to take the test.[63] Texas requires that polygraph testing be voluntary and that the employee be informed of the results.[64] In the State of New York no employer may require, request, suggest, or knowingly permit an applicant for employment to take a polygraph test with a psychological stress evaluator or machine that purports to detect falsehoods; neither may a New York employer use such test results, nor may a person administer such a test to an employee in New York.[65]

In Maryland both private and public employers must include the following language on all applications for employment: "An employer may not require any applicant for employment or prospective employment or any employee, to submit to or take a polygraph, lie detector, or similar test or examination as a condition of employment or continued employment."[66] The State of Michigan also bars the "lie detector" test for employees, and prohibits the discharge of an employee for failure to take such a polygraph test.[67] California[68] and Connecticut[69] prohibit the practice in private employment, but a number of states bar polygraph testing in both private and public employment.[70] However, the Eleventh U.S. Court of Appeals in Hester v. City of Milledgeville[71] approved lie detector testing for public employees, pointing out that the Fifth Amendment's bar against self-incrimination pertains only to the "criminal case."

A *New York Times* editorial reminded the public that

two million Americans each year are required to take lie-detector tests as a condition of employment. At least 50,000 are then denied jobs or promotions even though the results are unreliable. Now, after years of desultory debate, Congress appears convinced that this injustice is intolerable. . . . Organized labor has complained for years that companies use lie detectors to ferret out employees they consider to be troublesome or inclined to join a union. A more telling criticism, however, has to do with the effectiveness of polygraphs. They do not detect lies. Rather, they detect physiological changes that indicate anxiety. The human operator decides whether or not the anxiety is evidence of falsehood. . . . Almost half the States prohibit or limit the use of polygraphs in most private employment decisions.[72]

The First U.S. Court of Appeals decision in O'Brien v. Papa Gino's of America, Inc.[73] emphasized this truism, where the court affirmed a jury award of $448,000 for defamation of character and invasion of privacy when an employee was terminated after he failed a polygraph examination relating to his off-the-job use of cocaine; the reason for his job termination was later disclosed by his employer to a prospective employer. And in Perks v. Firestone Tire & Rubber Co.,[74] the Third U.S. Court of Appeals found a wrongful discharge because the discharge was based upon the polygraph examination, which in Pennsylvania was barred by statute for the employee suspected of theft.

The threshhold question of admissibility of scientific and subjective evidence such as polygraph results turns upon the evidentiary principles of relevancy and expert testimony. The principles are found in Articles 4 and 7 of the Federal Rules of Evidence and in similar state codifications as well as in the common law decisions of states that have not codified the state laws of evidence.[75]

In the New York case of Cohen v. Alexander, Inc.,[76] the plaintiff complained about his employer's polygraph test result, which prompted his discharge from employment. Plaintiff had managed the toy department for 13 years when he was subjected to a polygraph machine that revealed "deception" on his part. Plaintiff pointed out that the defendant employer

discriminated against him on the basis of his disabilities when it fired him following the polygraph test. Cohen asserts that the polygraph operators did not take Cohen's disabilities into account while administering the tests. Cohen states that he has high blood pressure, a stutter, sinus and throat problems and a nervous condition; that all of the above conditions affect the accuracy of any polygraph test given to him, and that he informed Crabb of his disabilities before the test was administered. Cohen claims that since the polygraph examiners did not take these disabilities into account before they administered the polygraph test, and subsequently fired him, he was fired on the basis of his disabilities in violation of Executive Law §296(1)(a).

The court agreed with plaintiff Cohen as a "member of a protected group (the disabled)," and therefore "he must be given an opportunity to demonstrate that the way in which the polygraph tests were administered . . . or the interpretation of those tests disparately affected plaintiff's ability to pass a test that was required for his continued employment."[77]

It is interesting to note that on October 21, 1988, the U.S. Labor Department issued regulations barring most private employers from using polygraph or other lie detector tests to screen job applicants, and also greatly restricted use of such devices to test present employees.[78] The Congressional Office of Technology Assessment had estimated that two million polygraph examinations were conducted in the year 1987, and that 90 percent were conducted by private employers. Under the new regulations, employers who insist that job applicants or current employees take the tests, or do not abide by other safeguards in the regulations, can be fined up to $10,000 for each violation. The regulations also given anyone required to take the test in violation of the new regulations the right to sue the employer in either federal or state court for such employment rights as reinstatement, promotion, or payment of lost wages and benefits. Exempted from the ban on polygraph usage are employees of federal, state, and local governments or federal contractors engaged in national security, intelligence, or top secret activities. Also exempted are prospective employees of armored car, security alarm, and security guard firms hired to protect operations affecting health and safety, national security, or money. Any employee asked to take a polygraph test must be given 48 hours' advance notice and also a statement in advance telling the employee of his or her rights, including the right to refuse the test or terminate it at any time.[79]

3.5 DAMAGES IN EMPLOYMENT CONTRACT CASES

In Pacter v. International Lithographing Corp.[80] plaintiff employee had signed a five-year employment sales contract with defendant that guaranteed him a $100,000 salary his first year and $125,000 annually for the next four years, for a total compensation of $600,000, plus $125,000 in deferred compensation at the end of the contract, and certain fringe benefits and bonus compensation if he exceeded a certain sales quota. Sixty days into the contract, he was fired because he had made no sales and had apparently overstated his previous sales experience. Plaintiff countered with the argument that defendant's prices were not competitive, making sales very difficult. The jury awarded him $675,662, later reduced to $535,662, as the measure of damages for breach of the employment contract. And in McKay and Williams v. Ashland Oil Co.[81] a federal court jury in Kentucky awarded two wrongfully discharged executives a total of $69.5 million in damages when they were discharged for opposing questionable foreign payments and cover-up attempts of the defendant employer. The award was the equivalent of more than one-half of defendant employer's profits for the fiscal year![82]

These two court decisions, following the pattern of the contract damages rule first enunciated in 1854 by the English court in Hadley v. Baxendale,[83] theoretically limited the damages for breach of the employment contract to what was reasonably contemplated or foreseen by the parties when they entered into the contract of employment.[84] Recently, however, the courts have begun to add to the already substantial contractual damages the tort action for wrongful breach of the employment contract. The tort action for wrongful discharge, with a greater measure of damages, requires employees to prove that they were terminated in violation of public policy or with malicious or retaliatory intent by the employer.[85]

Damages that are typically asserted in both the contract and the tort or wrongful discharge cases include lost wages or salaries, lost fringe benefits, reliance damages, and compensatory damages, as well as punitive damages. Lost wages or lost salaries encompass bonuses, commissions, and even lost profits; all damage awards for future benefits are discounted to present values, and the amount, when invested to yield the highest rate of return consistent with reasonable security, may be very substantial.[86] Fringe benefits too are substantial, including employer-sponsored, and even paid-for, medical, life, and disability insurance. The measure of damages would be the cost of duplicating the insurance coverages the employer had provided.[87] Pension benefits lost as a result of the breach of employment contract are fully recoverable.[88] An employee's expense account is also an item of damages.[89] Reliance damages are the expenses the employee incurred in reliance upon the employment.[90] A New Hampshire court in Cloutier v. Great Atlantic & Pacific Tea Co.[91] declined to restrict the discharged employee to tort damages even where the dismissal did not contravene public policy pronouncements in state statutes; the court decided that it was "best to allow the citizenry, through the institution of the American jury, to strike the appropriate balance."

In evaluating the measure of damages for wrongful discharge, a word should be said about "severance pay," which has recently become increasingly important in the workplace.[92] Most corporations have some provision for the payment of severance benefits to terminated employees. In Accardi v. Control Data Corporation,[93] the federal District Court for the Southern District of New York held that 16 employees were entitled to severance pay even though they never had been unemployed! They had worked for an IBM subsidiary until it was sold to defendant, but they now work for ADP. Nevertheless, the court ruled that the denial of severance pay benefits by defendant CDC was arbitrary and capricious in violation of ERISA. Note that plaintiff employees had worked in the same office for 15 years for three employers!

Damages are also an element in discerning insurance coverage of wrongful termination actions. At the outset, it should be noted that insurance companies never contemplated that the comprehensive general liability, or CGL, policy would provide coverage for employers in wrongful termination actions.[94] In essence, the insurers did not intend to cover intentional conduct such as that of the employer firing the employee. Nevertheless, insurance coverage depends upon the type of injuries or damages, the insurable event resulting in the claim, and the policy exclusions.[95] In Farm Bureau Mutual Insurance Co. v. Hoag[96] the Michigan appellate court ruled that a general liability insurer was not obligated to defend a complaint alleging "humiliation, public ridicule, loss of reputation, mental anguish, and suffering," all resulting from plaintiff's discharge from employment: "We believe that the term 'bodily injury' is not ambiguous and does not include humiliation and mental anguish and suffering as alleged in plaintiff's complaint."

The contrary view is seen in the Louisiana case of Holcomb v. Kincaid,[97] holding that humiliation and mental anguish are compensable under the standard bodily injury coverage if accompanied by "physical manifestations" such as tears or bad dreams. But contractual liability coverage does not create coverage for breach of contract claims in the wrongful discharge context.[98] Employee benefits liability coverage may create a basis for insurance coverage for lost wages, lost fringe benefits, and other intangible losses commonly alleged in wrongful discharge cases.[99] Standard "umbrella" liability policies create a potential for coverage since they broaden the bodily injury and property damage coverages under the primary general liability policies.[100]

It should be obvious that insurance coverage of wrongful discharge claims depends upon proof of "accident" and proof that the injuries were not expected or intended.[101] In Interco Inc. v. Mission Insurance Co.,[102] the federal district court held that a wrongful termination claim failed to satisfy the "accident" requirement of the occurrence policy; but the Eighth U.S. Court of Appeals reversed, concluding that, although the act of termination of employment was intentional, there was no showing that the insured expected or intended the resulting emotional distress.[103]

Workers compensation insurance policies generally encompass wrongful discrimination claims, particularly Coverage B, which insures employers against certain types of common law liability to their employees.[104] In Wojciak v. Northern Package Corp.[105] the Minnesota Supreme Court concluded that an employee's claim of retaliatory discharge for requesting workers' compensation benefits was within the exclusive purview of workers' compensation insurance and therefore insured under Coverage A, which is to indemnify for all compensation an employer must pay under the workers' compensation statute. Unfortunately, there is a lack of judicial guidance on the interplay between the general liability insurance policies and the workers' compensation and employers' liability policies in the wrongful termination or discharge situation.

NOTES

1. See Blumberg, "Loyalty, Obedience and the Role of the Employee," 24 Okla L Rev 1 (1971).

2. 346 U.S. 464 (1953).

3. See generally Manley, "Charges and Discharges," INC. Magazine 124 (March 1988).

4. See Perritt, Employee Dismissal Law and Practice (2nd ed., 1987).

5. 732 P.2d 1364 (Nev. 1987).

6. 169 Cal. App. 3d 1223 (1985).

7. See Carey, "At-Will Employees Still Vulnerable," A.B.A.J. 66 (October 1, 1987).

8. Sorosky v. Burroughs Corp., 37 F.R.D. 1510 (D.C. Cal., 1985).

9. Supra note 7 at p. 68.

10. 521 N.Y.S.2d 672 (1987); also 132 A.D.2d 162 (1987).

11. We cannot agree that the intention of the parties with respect to the termination provision was so clearly and unambiguously expressed in the agreement that it could be determined as a matter of law. The provision in paragraph seven that "Mandelblatt may be discharged as a consultant to the company without any breach of this agreement" leaves open the question: "without any breach of the agreement" by whom—Mandelblatt or the Company? Thus uncertain wording raises a question as to what the parties to the contract intended. Given the ambiguity in this language, the court below erred in determining, as a matter of law, the intention of the parties therefrom.

The construction given paragraph seven by the court, moreover, produces an unreasonable result which would, in effect, place one party to the contract at the mercy of the other. This is "against the general policy of the law" (Fair Pavilions, Inc. v. First National City Bank, 19 NY 2d 512, 518 [1967]; Spear v. Plaza South Studios, Inc., 59 AD 2d 778 [2d Dept. 1977]). Willful and gross misconduct which causes material harm to the co-contracting party, or the willful failure to perform the services called for under a personal services agreement, are acts which normally constitute breach of contract for which the defaulting party must answer in damages and, if "morally culpable," punitive damages (Hubbell v. Trans World Life Ins. Co. of N.Y., 50 NY 2d 899, 901 [1980]). The court below, however, construed paragraph seven as effecting a waiver of appellants' right to sue respondent for any damages which his conduct might cause.

12. Serra v. Popolizio, —N.Y.S.2d—(1988).

13. 150 Cal. App. 3d 1132 (1983).

14. —A.2d—(Conn. 1987).

15. —F. Supp—(Conn. 1987).

16. —N.Y.S.2d—(1988).

17. 841 F.2d 980 (9th Cir. 1988).

18. —N.W.2d—(Minn. 1988).

19. —F. Supp— (S.D. Ga. 1987).

20. 525 N.Y.S.2d 417 (1988).

21. —N.Y.S.2d—(New York County, April 25, 1988).

22. See Kaminsky v. Leary, 28 N.Y.2d 700 (1971) and Brennan v. Ward, 520 N.Y.S.2d 781 (1987).

23. —N.Y.S.2d—(App. Div. May 31, 1988).

24. 101 A.D.2d 1028 (1984).

25. 501 N.E.2d 343 (Ill. 1986).

26. See generally Closen and Wojcik, "Lawyers Out in the Cold," A.B.A.J. 94 (November 1, 1987).

27. 709 F.2d 1043 (5th Cir. 1983).

28. 29 U.S.C. 660(c)(1).

29. Note 29 U.S.C. 657(f), 657(b), and 662(d).

30. Whirlpool Corp. v. Marshall, 445 U.S. 1 (1980).

31. Note Pavolini v. Bard-Air Corp., 645 F.2d 144 (2nd. Cir. 1981).

32. 29 U.S.C. 151 to 168.

33. Section 158(a)(4).

34. See Sisco v. J. S. Alberici Construction Co., Inc., 655 F.2d 146 (8th Cir. 1981), cert. den. 455 U.S. 976 (1982).

35. 45 U.S.C. 60.

36. See Hendley v. Central of Georgia Railroad Co., 609 F.2d 1146 (5th Cir. 1980), cert. den. 449 U.S. 1093 (1981).

37. 45 U.S.C. 441(a).

38. 433 F.2d 1031 (9th Cir. 1970).

39. 670 F.2d 1378 (9th Cir. 1982).

40. See Warren Freedman, Hazardous Waste Liability §5.11 (1987).

41. 814 F.2d 1115 (6th Cir. 1987).

42. —F.Supp.—(Kan. 1987).

43. 265 N.W.2d 385 (Mich. 1978).

44. 780 F.2d 1505 (10th Cir. 1986).

45. 42 U.S.C. 5851.

46. 29 U.S.C. 215(a)(3).

47. 20 U.S.C. 3608.

48. —P.2d—(Colo. 1986).

49. —N.Y.S.2d—(New York County, January 26, 1988).

50. See Nader, Petkas, and Blackwell, Whistle Blowing: The Report of the Conference on Professional Responsibility 10 (1972).

51. *Id.*

52. Note Harv. Bus. 53 (1975).

53. 391 U.S. 563 (1968).

54. Cf. Watts. v. Seward School Board, 454 P.2d 732 (Alaska 1969), which dwelt upon the fact that the school teacher's letter became a very disruptive force in a small Alaskan community.

55. See Herman and Bernholz, "Negligence in Employee Drug Testing," Case & Comment 3 (July–August 1987).

56. 479 N.Y.S.2d 470 (1984).

57. 449 N.E.2d 1172 (Ind. App. 1983).

58. See Rakoff, "The Mythology of Polygraphy," NYLJ 1 (July 12, 1988).

59. See Gilmartin & Papastratakos, "When to Use Polygraph Evidence," The Brief 30 (Winter 1988).

60. See Warren Freedman, The Right of Privacy in the Computer Age §4.9 (1987).

61. Ga. Code Ann. § 43–36–1.

62. Ill. Stat. Ann. §2415.1

63. Wis. Stat. Ann. §111.327.

64. Tex. Rev. Civ. Stat. Article 3313(29cc).

65. See New York Labor Law § 733.

66. Md. Ann. Code § 95, Article 100. Note Moniodis v. Cook, 494 A.2d 212 (Md. App. 1985).

67. Mich. Comp. Laws Ann. § 338.1726.

68. Cal. Lab. Code § 432.2.

69. Conn. Gen. Stat. Ann. § 31–51g.

70. See R.I. Gen. Laws § 28–6.1–1 and Mass. Gen. Laws Ann. § 19B, Chapter 149, for example.

71. 777 F.2d 1492 (11th Cir. 1985), aff'g and rev'g 598 F. Supp 1456 (1984); after remand 782 F.2d 180 (11th Cir. 1986).

72. December 8, 1985.

73. 780 F.2d 1067 (1st Cir. 1986).

74. 611 F.2d 1363 (3rd Cir. 1979).

75. Supra note 5 at 10.

76. —N.Y.S.2d—(New York County, October 13, 1987).

77.

The issue of discrimination revolves around whether the polygraphers took Cohen's disabilities into account in administering the test. The effect of the administration of a polygraph test on a person with Cohen's alleged disabilities and the accuracy of this test are disputed issues. Polygraph tests have become common methods for dealing with employee theft (see Polygraphs in the Workplace—The Use of Lie Detectors in Hiring and Firing: Hearings Before Subcommittee on Employment Opportunity of House Comm. on Ed. & Labor, 99th Cong., 1st Sess., 1986). The test measures truthfulness through an examination of the subject's heartbeat and respiratory patterns. Its accuracy in the aforementioned measurement is not universally accepted (see Nagle, The Polygraph in the Workplace, 18 U. Rich. L. Rev. 43, 1983–84). Thus, given the nature of the tests administered to Cohen and the disputed issues of fact in this action, summary judgment on the first cause of action is not appropriate.

78. See Hartford Courant, October 22, 1988, at B3.

79. Id.

80. —F. Supp.—(E.D. Pa. 1987).

81. 683 F. Supp.639 (Ky. 1988); also note New York Times, June 14, 1988, at D1.

82. Id.

83. 156 Eng. Rep. 1451 (1854).

84. See Whitehill, "Damages in Employment Contract Cases," Trial Magazine 25 (July 1988).

85. See Palmateer v. International Harvester Co., 421 N.E.2d 876 (Ill. 1981).

86. Note Canavin v. Pacific Southwest Airlines, 196 Cal. Rptr. 82 (1983).

87. See Wise v. Southern Pacific Railroad Co., 83 Cal. Rptr. 202 (1970).

88. See Estate of Schley, 161 Cal. Rptr. 104 (1979).

89. See Kolb v. Goldring, Inc., 694 F.2d 869 (1st Cir. 1982).

90. See Thomas v. Olin Mathieson Chemical Corp., 63 Cal. Rptr. 454 (1967).

91. 436 A.2d 1140 (N.H. 1981).

92. See generally Jacobs, "Severance Pay and Successors—Commentary on Court Ruling," N.Y.L.J. 1 (August 27, 1987).

93. 658 F. Supp. 881 (S.D.N.Y. 1987), aff'd. 836 F.2d 126 (2nd Cir. 1988).

94. See generally Peer and Mallen, "Insurance Coverage of Employment Discrimination and Wrongful Termination Actions," Def. Couns J 464 (October 1987) and Def. Couns J 12 (January 1988).

95. Id. at 466.

96. 356 N.W.2d 630 (Mich. App. 1984).

97. 406 So.2d 646 (La. App. 1982).

98. See Jostens v. Mission Insurance Co., 387 N.W.2d 161 (Minn. 1986).

99. Supra note 94 at p. 469.

100. See Cranford Insurance Co. v. Allwest Insurance Co., 645 F. Supp. 1440 (N.D. Cal. 1986).

101. Supra note 94 at pp. 472–473.

102. 626 F. Supp. 888 (E.D. Mo. 1986).

103. 808 F.2d 682 (8th Cir. 1987).

104. Supra note 94 at p. 12.

105. 310 N.W.2d 675 (Minn. 1981).

4

Discrimination and the Employment Contract

4.1 INTRODUCTION TO THE DISCRIMINATION ISSUE

In 1977 the *Harvard Business Review* mailed lengthy questionnaires to a random sample of its 7,000 or more subscribers, and the return of usable responses came from 28 percent or nearly 2,000 people or entities. What is alarming about the findings is the total indifference to discrimination, despite the finding of a steady broadening of support for methods of assuring "due process" to employees who feel they have been wronged by management.[1] Another finding favoring advances in the right of privacy for employees similarly made no reference to the issue of discrimination. Still another finding was "the belief that grievance procedures, privacy, equal employment opportunity, and other gains in constitutionalism are increasing the price tags of products and services."[2] In keeping with this disinterest toward discrimination is the final finding that "in the next ten years" of least concern to business people are "obstacles to individualism, including difficulties in the path of people"; of prime concern, however, "in the next ten years" were "social instability, including confusion about sexual standards, treatment of criminals, attitudes toward drugs and alcohol, respect for family and authority, breakdown of law and order, and disintegration of the work ethic."

Just 12 years later in 1989, much to the chagrin of 1977 subscribers of the *Harvard Business Review*, discrimination in employment is probably the most litigated issue in employment contracts and employment relationships. Even a bank that was found to have discriminated against female and minority employees since 1974 was held liable in 1988 for back pay to the tune of millions of dollars.[3] More than 27,000 workers each year file "age discrimination" lawsuits against their employers.[4] Racial discrimination charges against employers are even more common; in Ortiz v. Bank of America National Trust & Savings Association[5] the Ninth U.S. Court of Appeals upheld the right of the female plaintiff (who had been terminated as a clerk after 17 years of service and after settling her three workers' compensation claims for $12,500) to file racial discrimination charges against the bank based on her Puerto Rican origin. While the jury nevertheless awarded her $250,000 for the employer's breach of the covenant of good faith and fair dealing! Plaintiff employee's discharge by the bank violated her right not to be deprived unfairly of the benefits of employment.

Discrimination in employment has, for the most part, been the subject of both federal and state legislation. Employees are protected against adverse employment action and wrongful discharge or dismissal by statutes against racial, religious, sexual, and age discrimination, inter alia,[6] as well as against particular conduct on the part of the employer.[7]

4.2 SOME CONSTITUTIONAL MATTERS

The U.S. Constitution also supports employees claiming employment discrimination from violations of protected rights. The constitutional claims most frequently asserted arise under the equal protection and due process clauses of the Fourteenth Amendment.[8] In particular, the Fourteenth Amendment provides that "no State shall make or enforce any law which shall abridge the privileges or immunities of citizens of the United States; nor shall any State deprive any person of life, liberty, or property, without due process of law; nor deny to any person within its jurisdiction the equal protection of the laws." Thus, the Fourteenth Amendment restrains the several states from permitting or sanctioning discrimination in employment.

In New York State Club Association, Inc. v. City of New York,[9] the U.S. Supreme Court, upholding the constitutionality of a City of New York law barring private clubs from discriminating against women and minorities, stated: "The City's interest in protecting its citizenry from the serious social and personal harms resulting from invidious discrimination is not merely legitimate, it is compelling. . . . Discrimination based on archaic and overbroad assumptions and stereotypes about the relative needs and capacities of certain groups deprives persons of their individual dignity and denies society the benefits of wide participation in political, economic, and cultural life."

Implicit in the ban against discrimination within the Fourteenth Amendment is the requirement of "state action," which has been construed to place discrimination by purely private individuals or private entities outside the pale of the Fourteenth Amendment,[10] unless the alleged discrimination is "fairly attributable to the state" or to one of the State instrumentalities.[11] There is no hesitation about prohibiting discrimination by public employers: classifications on the basis of race, religion, national origin, sex, age, and so forth are constitutionally suspect.[12] Courts look to see whether a sufficient nexus exists between the private sector and the state to invoke the ban against discrimination on the basis of the Fourteenth Amendment.[13]

The due process clause of the Fourteenth Amendment places both substantive and procedural restrictions on the power of the state.[14] Substantive due process prohibits the state from infringing upon certain fundamental rights, including the right of privacy.[15] Procedural due process mandates that the state provide such procedural safeguards as notice, hearing, and opportunity to be heard when state action deprives individuals of "life, liberty, or property." A public employee, for example, has a protected property interest in continued employment where a reasonable expectation of continued employment is created by state statute, ordinances or regulations, contractual obligations, or even local rules.[16] The U.S. Supreme Court in Wygant v. Jackson Board of Examiners[17] focused upon the discrimination issue:

Public employers operate under two interrelated constitutional duties. They are under a clear command from this Court . . . to eliminate every vestige of racial segregation and discrimination in the schools. Pursuant to that goal, race-conscious remedial action may be necessary. On the other hand, public employers . . . also must act in accordance with a "core purpose of the Fourteenth Amendment" which is to "do away with all governmentally imposed distinctions based on race." The related constitutional duties are not always harmonious; reconciling them requires public employees to act with extraordinary care.

The compelling interest here was the employer's interest in remedying its own prior discriminatory practices. And the means or preference to achieve that desired interest must be "narrowly tailored" to avoid unnecessarily trampling on the legitimate interests of nonminorities.[18] Unfortunately, in United States v. Paradise[19] the highest court held that "quotas" were warranted to remedy persistent past racial discrimination so long as the "quotas" are reasonably related or "tailored" to the objective. Promotion "quotas" for minority fire fighters were approved in 1987 by the Sixth U.S. Court of Appeals in Youngblood v. Dalzell, where the court justified its ruling by observing that the "quotas" were sufficiently "tailored" to the finding of discrimination and not unduly disadvantageous to the white or nonblack candidates for fire fighter positions.

The constitutional guarantees against discrimination in employment, as set forth in the Fourteenth Amendment, are supplemented by the numerous federal and state statutes.

4.3 CIVIL RIGHTS ACT OF 1964

Title VII of the Civil Rights Act of 1964 is the most important nondiscrimination statutory scheme, providing a comprehensive mechanism for the investigation of charges of discrimination by an independent agency, the Equal Employment Opportunity Commission (EEOC).[20] In brief, Title VII makes it unlawful for an employer to refuse to hire or to discharge any individual, or otherwise to discriminate against any individual with respect to compensation or terms and conditions of employment, because of such individual's race, color, religion, sex, or national origin.[21] But Title VII permits discrimination on the basis of religion, sex, or national origin where the characteristic is a bona fide occupational qualification reasonably necessary to the operation of the business.[22] Title VII spells out the short list of prohibitions for an employer:

fail or refuse to hire or to discharge any individual, or otherwise to discriminate against any individual with respect to his compensation, terms, conditions, or privileges of employment because of such individual's race, color, religion, sex or national origin.[23]
limit, segregate, or classify his employees or applicants for employment in any way which would deprive or tend to deprive any individual of employment opportunities or otherwise adversely affect his status as an employee, because of such individual's race, color, religion, sex or national origin.[24]
discriminate against any individual because of his race, color, religion, sex or national origin in admission to, or employment in any program established to provide apprenticeship or other training.[25]
discriminate against any of his employees or applicants for employment, . . . because he has opposed any practice made an unlawful employment practice by this subchapter, or because he has made a charge, testified, assisted, or participated in any manner in an investigation, proceeding, or hearing under this subchapter.[26]
print or publish or cause to be printed or published any notice or advertisement by such an employer . . . indicating any preference, limitation, specification, or discrimination, based on race, color, religion, sex, or national origin.[27]

The scope of this short list of discriminations means that Title VII should be and is liberally construed; for example, such matters as statutes of limitations, burdens of proof, class certifications,[28] and the like have been accorded flexible interpretations in the context of employment discrimination law.[29]

It is said that most discrimination cases may be categorized as "disparate impact" or "disparate treatment," the former describing the disproportionate impact on a protected group that is not necessarily job related or justified by business necessity, and the latter describing the different treatment accorded similarly situated employees due to race, color, religion, sex, or national origin. The U.S. Supreme Court pronouncement in Griggs v. Duke Power Co.[30] authorized challenges to employment practices that, although neutral on their face, nevertheless had a disproportionate impact on the protected group. Disparate impact here means placing various forms of statistical analysis of disparate impact in the very front of discrimination litigation. Therefore a wide range of employment practices may be illegal even though such practices would not appear discriminatory to a casual and uninitiated observer. Disparate impact does not require proof of intent to discriminate.[31] Title VII, it should be noted, does exempt the United States and government corporations and agencies, as well as "bona fide private membership clubs," from its coverage.[32]

Disparate treatment cases arise generally in situations where a person or persons believe that race, sex, or any other proscribed classification is the cause of his, her, or their employment problem.[33] The prohibition against religious discrimination, for example, has been held to protect "all forms and aspects of religion, however eccentric";[34] but Title VII does not protect every personal belief merely because a person or persons claim that the belief is religious.[35] Disparate treatment is argued whenever there is a majority movement that does not include the minority, as illustrated in Board of Trustees v. Sweeney,[36] where it was contended that sex bias existed in the promotion decisions of the employer because only four women had ever attained the rank of full professor, there never had been more than two women professors in any academic year, and, despite the fact that women were 20 percent of the faculty, males held more than 90 percent of the ranks of full professors. In International Brotherhood of Teamsters v. United States[37] the U.S. Supreme Court voiced the necessity of proving intent to discriminate as the essential ingredient in a claim of disparate treatment. In this case, it was found that only eight employees were black and only five employees were Spanish-surnamed out of 1,828 employees in the better-paying jobs. Proof of intent may be direct or indirect, i.e., intent may even be inferred from circumstantial evidence showing that the plaintiff was treated worse than similarly situated persons with other racial, religious, or gender characteristics.

It should be observed that Title VII covers all employees of interstate businesses with 15 or more employees, whether the employee is a part-time typist or the chief executive. Title VII also established the Equal Employment Opportunity Commission (EEOC), with whom all discrimination charges are filed; charges may also be filed with a state referral agency whose decision is, however, not binding on the EEOC in the event of an appeal.[38] The filing of the complaint charging discrimination must occur within 300 days of the employer's adoption of new work rules even if the employer's new work rules do not immediately affect the complaining employees, according to the Seventh U.S. Court of Appeals.[39] Here the court dismissed the suit by three women who said that a restructured seniority system had discriminated against them on the basis of their sex. The EEOC, a five-person, presidentially appointed group, has the initial task of interpreting Title VII, investigating complaints, settling the complaints if possible through conference or conciliation, and finally enforcing decisions in the federal courts. Once a complaint has been filed, the EEOC has 180 days of exclusive jurisdiction, after which the affected employee or employees may request from the EEOC letters of "right to sue" prefatory to a private legal action in the federal courts. Note that Title VII protects all employers including state and local governments, labor organizations, and labor unions, as well as employment agencies.[40]

Historically, Title VII had its roots in the 1875 Civil Rights Act, which forbade racial discrimination in private sector facilities such as restaurants, theaters, business establishments, and railroads. But the U.S. Supreme Court in The Civil Rights Cases[41] declared Sections 1 and 2 to be unconstitutional because Congress was empowered by the Fourteenth Amendment to enact legislation appropriate to enforce its prohibitory language only, which meant unwarranted "state action" only. Thus private citizens, unlike the state itself, were free to discriminate on the basis of race if private citizens chose to do so. The highest court then observed that the Thirteenth Amendment "simply abolished slavery," while the Fourteenth Amendment

prohibited the States from abridging the privileges or immunities of citizens of the United States from depriving them of life, liberty, or property without due process of law, and from denying to any person the equal protection of the laws. . . . It has power to counteract and render nugatory all State laws and proceedings which have the effect to abridge any of the privileges or immunities of citizens of the United States or to deprive them of life, liberty, or property without due process of law, or to deny to any of them the equal protection of the laws.[42]

Thus, the court in 1883 endorsed state policies disenfranchising and segregating black citizens through literacy tests, poll taxes, and the like. In Plessy v. Ferguson[43] the highest court later endorsed Louisiana's "separate but equal" facilities in public transportation. The dissent of Mr. Justice Harlan is particularly stinging:

[I]n view of the constitution, in the eye of the law, there is in this country no superior, dominant, ruling class of citizens. There is no caste here. Our constitution is color-blind, and neither knows nor tolerates classes among citizens. In respect of civil rights, all citizens are equal before the law. The humblest is the peer of the most powerful. The law regards man as man, and takes no account of his surroundings or of his color when his civil rights as guaranteed by the supreme law of the land are involved. It is therefore to be regretted that this high tribunal, the final expositor of the fundamental law of the land, has reached the conclusion that it is competent for a state to regulate the enjoyment by citizens of their civil rights solely upon the basis of race. [163 U.S. at 553]

It took many years before the highest court reversed that trend in Brown v. Board of Education,[44] outlawing segregation in the nation's public schools. The Civil Rights Act of 1964 had presaged the turn of events and given meaning to antidiscrimination provisions. However, the road has been bumpy, as seen in Kremer v. Chemical Construction Corp.,[45] where the highest court held that a state court's affirmance of an adverse state agency determination would bar the plaintiff from bringing a Title VII claim. The theory was simply that 28 USC 1738 required federal courts to give the same respect to any state judicial proceeding that the courts of that state would give. The same preclusive effect is seen in Buckhalter v. Pepsi Cola General Bottlers, Inc.,[46] where the federal district court concluded that the procedural adequacy of the Illinois agency determination, binding the Illinois courts, would also bind the federal district court.[47] In 1974 the U.S. Supreme Court in Alexander v. Gardner-Dever Co.[48] had held that an arbitration proceeding would not bar the Title VII claim because Congress intended for employees to be able to bring their discrimination claims to the federal district courts despite prior attempts at resolution of the dispute, and because an arbitration proceeding is procedurally inadequate in that generally the arbiter only interprets and applies the terms of the agreement and lacks the authority to go beyond the scope of the agreement and uphold a federal statute. Later, in Chandler v. Roudebush,[49] the highest court held that a federal employee may bring an action in federal court after an adverse decision by the Civil Service Commission, thus indirectly indicating that private employees were entitled to trial de novo after an adverse state agency determination.

In addition to the comprehensive scheme established by Title VII, there is Title VI,[50] which precludes discrimination against particular protected groups in the program or activity receiving federal financial assistance: "Nothing contained in this chapter shall be construed to authorize action . . . by any department or agency with respect to any employment practice of any employer, employment agency, or labor organization except where a primary objective of the Federal financial assistance is to provide employment."[51] Title VI applies only to public employees where the employer is the recipient of federal funding, the purpose of which is to provide employment. The U.S. Supreme Court in Guardians Association v. Civil Service Commission of the City of New York[52] ruled that Title VI does not permit individuals to bring a private cause of action, unless the evidence shows intentional discrimination practices; only in suits by the government itself can unintentional and "disparate impact" discrimination be arrested.

In Leake v. Long Island Jewish Medical Center[53] the federal District Court for the Eastern District of New York was called upon to decide whether the Civil Rights Restoration Act of 1987 should be applied retroactively.[54] In 1984 in the Grove City case[55] the highest court had held that federal civil rights statutes prohibiting discrimination by federally assisted programs or activities applied only to the particular program or activity actually receiving the federal funds. In the instant case plaintiff was a one-armed worker in the defendant hospital's housekeeping department; he refused to work in the laboratory because "he would be required to wear gloves and was unable to do so because of his handicap." He was then discharged for his refusal to work in the hospital laboratory. The hospital had received federal monies for specific research and treatment programs, but no federal monies for the housekeeping department. The New York Division of Human Rights found no probable cause to support his charge of unlawful discrimination. The federal district court decided to apply the 1987 act retroactively to cover plaintiff in view of congressional intent to prohibit discrimination in *any* program or *any* activity conducted by a federal grant recipient.

4.4   THE CIVIL RIGHTS ACT OF THE RECONSTRUCTION ERA

Probably the most important civil rights legislation on discrimination in employment is found in 42 USC 1981, 1983, and 1985, the Civil Rights Act of the Reconstruction Era. Section 1981 provides that "all persons within the jurisdiction of the United States shall have the same right in every State and Territory to make and enforce contracts, to sue, be parties, give evidence, and to the full and equal benefit of all laws and proceedings for the security of persons and property as is enjoyed by white citizens and shall be subject to like punishment, pains, penalties, taxes, licenses, and exactions of every kind, and to no other."

The vast majority of Section 1981 claims have relied, either explicitly or implicitly, on the contract clause, i.e., to make and enforce contracts. The section was originally enacted as part of the Civil Rights Act of 1866, but had laid dormant until the year 1968 when the U.S. Supreme Court in Jones v. Alfred H. Mayer Co. had applied its companion Section 1982 to private racial discrimination; and in 1975 in Johnson v. Railway Express Agency[56] the highest court held that racial discrimination in private employment also applied under Section 1981. But, most important of all, the court pointed out that Section 1981 provided remedies completely independent of Title VII of the Civil Rights Act of 1964. Section 1981 contains no requirement that the employer have a certain number of employees, and Section 1981 covers the independent contractor relationship as well as the employment relationship. Section 1981 clearly applies to private employment discrimination, particularly on the basis of race, including reverse discrimination challenges to affirmative action programs;[57] but Section 1981 apparently does not apply to discrimination on the basis of sex or religion.[58]

In Chaiffetz v. Robertson Research Holding, Ltd.[59] the Fifth U.S. Court of Appeals had occasion to review *both* Title VII and Section 1981 in the same suit brought by a U.S. citizen against a Texas corporation employer and against the British corporate parent, alleging that he had been discriminatorily discharged because he was an American, while foreign employees were retained. In reversing, the federal appellate court held, inter alia, that employment discrimination based only on one's country of birth, whether in the United States or elsewhere, contradicts the purposes and intent of Title VII. The defendants were not entitled to dismissal of the Title VII claim on the basis that they had retained their foreign employees because they had made a greater investment in those employees, where the alleged investments in the foreign employees consisted of legal assistance in obtaining work visas for them, payment for accounting assistance in preparing their U.S. federal income tax returns, and the expense-paid annual home trips. However, the court did hold that, to the extent that plaintiff's suit was based on Section 1981, it was subject to dismissal because Section 1981 does not encompass discrimination based solely on national origin.[60]

Also note that Section 1981 does not preempt state remedies; the coexistence of Section 1981 with state laws is illustrated by Neulist v. County of Nassau:[61]

One of the purposes underlying [Section 1981] was "to provide a remedy in the federal courts supplementary to any remedy any state might have." [citing McNeese v. Board of Education, 373 U.S. 668, 672 (1963)] We believe that a common law action for malicious prosecution brought in this state may co-exist with a pending Federal Civil Rights Action based upon the same facts.

The landmark 1976 decision of the U.S. Supreme Court in Runyon v. McCrary,[62] furthering the national consensus against racial discrimination, became a cause célèbre in 1988 in Patterson v. McLean Credit Union,[63] when 110 national organizations representing millions of Americans filed amicus curiae briefs asking the highest court not to disturb its 1976 holding. The prime argument was that "stare decisis" applies with compelling force to sustain the Runyon case holding,[64] and that none of the reasons that may justify a departure from precedent was present in the Patterson case.[65] Note that the Patterson case originally concerned the issue of cognizability of racial harassment claims under Section 1981. The plaintiff, a black woman employed as a teller and file coordinator for ten years, was laid off in 1982 when she refused to do menial jobs such as sweeping up the office that, allegedly, her white coworkers were not forced to do.[66] The defendant employer's argument to overrule the Runyon case was that

members of racial or other minorities may coerce private individuals into contract relations they do not wish to enter. The principle that contracts are private and presuppose two willing parties is not entirely sacrosanct. But, surely it must receive some principled consideration, before being cast aside and replaced by the ad-hoc judicial determination in *Runyon* that a public policy of non-discrimination requires new and even more intrusive restraints on private conduct.[67]

The decision of the highest court is expected in late June 1989.

The American Bar Association, inter alia, filed an amicus curiae brief in Patterson urging that the U.S. Supreme Court affirm its 1976 ruling that Section 1981 "reaches private conduct" and "embodies a policy of the highest order of importance . . . the policy of extirpating racial discrimination. . . . Section 1981 has become a vital, everyday part of civil rights jurisprudence and practice" and "no legal or social development of the past several years could conceivably justify a retreat from *Runyon*." The ABA brief concluded that the ABA's interest "flows from its opposition to racial discrimination and its concern that the abandonment of such an important and well considered Supreme Court precedent as *Runyon* would be harmful to the legal system."[68]

In the Runyon case the U.S. Supreme Court in 1976 had described the private school's policy of excluding black students as "a classic violation of Section 1981" because it denied the black student the opportunity to make a "contractual relationship'' with the school. The court predicated its holding on the Thirteenth Amendment giving Congress the power to reach private actors. The dissent argued that Section 1981 was an exercise of congressional Fourteenth, not Thirteenth, Amendment powers because the Fourteenth Amendment operates only against state governments!

The measure of damages for violation of Section 1983 was delineated by the U.S. Supreme Court in Memphis Community School District v. Stachura,[69] which held that compensatory damages based on the abstract value of constitutional rights may not be awarded by a jury. Since the primary purpose of Section 1983 was compensation of individuals for particular injuries, it was inappropriate for a jury to award damages based on its ''subjective perception of the importance of constitutional rights as an abstract matter.'' According to the Court, Congress intended to deter future violations solely through the compensation for *actual* injuries suffered. The Court was well aware of the delicate nature of the task of adapting common law rules to compensate for constitutional injuries. However, the Court found that it did not need to undertake that task because of the award of actual and punitive damages. It is sufficient to state that such ''injuries'' simply do not fit easily into traditional tort remedy categories such as mental or emotional suffering![70]

4.5 AGE DISCRIMINATION

The Age Discrimination in Employment Act of 1967 (ADEA)[71] prior to 1986 prohibited employers from discriminating because of age against persons in the age group 40 to 70. This protection worked both ways: it is equally a violation of ADEA to favor a 65-year-old over a 45-year-old as it is to favor a 45-year-old over a 65-year-old. But in 1986 Congress amended ADEA to remove the age ''cap'' of the protected class, and effective January 1, 1987, the maximum age limitation was removed for all protected employees except those employees covered by a collective bargaining agreement that was in effect on June 30, 1986, and terminated after January 1, 1987.[72] ADEA applies to all employers with 20 or more employees in an industry affecting interstate commerce and to all state and local government employers.[73]

ADEA is a composite statute that incorporates substantive elements of Title VII of the Civil Rights Act of 1964 as well as enforcement provisions of the Fair Labor Standards Act.[74] Section 2 of ADEA states its purpose ''to promote employment of older persons based on their ability rather than age; to prohibit arbitrary age discrimination in employment; to help employers and workers find ways of meeting problems arising from the impact of age on employment.'' ADEA applies equally to private employers and to public employers, whether they are employment agencies or labor unions. As expressed in Purtil v. Harris,[75] ADEA provides the exclusive remedy for age discrimination in federal employment.

For ADEA to be successfully invoked, age must be *the* factor in the layoff decision, as illustrated in Ackerman v. Diamond Shamrock Corp.,[76] where the Sixth U.S. Court of Appeals entered summary judgment in favor of the employer because ADEA "was not intended as a vehicle for judicial review of business decisions." It appeared here that the only reason plaintiff had been selected for retirement was "a legitimate business decision to eliminate plaintiff's job and divide his duties between two other employees. . . . The only motivation for that decision, from the evidence in the record, was the desire to increase corporate efficiency . . . [and the employer] may make a subjective judgment to discharge an employee for any reason that is not discriminatory."[77]

ADEA specifically permits employers to discriminate on the basis of age where age is a bona fide occupational qualification, or BFOQ; also ADEA expressly protects employers' rights to discharge or otherwise discipline employees for cause and to differentiate among employees based on reasonable factors other than age. Age is apparently recognized, however, as accompanied by impairments in sensory and functional capacities that affect a person's ability to perform certain jobs safely. The BFOQ defense has been applied in situations where the public safety would be endangered if job functions were performed by persons having disabilities associated with aging that cannot be feasibly detected by individual screening.[78]

Note that ADEA does not preempt state common law causes of action;[79] in addition, as pronounced by the U.S. Supreme Court in Oscar Mayer, Inc. v. Evans,[80] ADEA "permits concurrent rather than sequential State and federal administrative jurisdiction in order to expedite the processing of age discrimination claims. . . . The purpose of expeditious disposition would not be frustrated were ADEA claimants required to pursue State and federal administrative remedies simultaneously."[81] A review of recent age discrimination cases in the state courts illustrates the many facets of the problem:

1. New York: In Wiener v. Kreuzer[82] the defendant synagogue sought a stay of all state proceedings while litigating the plaintiff rabbi's age discrimination suit in the federal court. But the court denied the motion, finding that, since the state action involved contract and employment issues distinct from the federal civil rights issue of age discrimination, the disposition of the federal action would not resolve the state issues and thus the court should not halt the state proceedings.

In Mueller v. Young & Rubicam, Inc.[83] the female plaintiff sued for constructive discharge based upon age discrimination; she alleged that defendant failed to define her duties and eventually hired a younger person in her place. The court found that plaintiff had pleaded all the necessary elements of the cause of action for age discrimination.[84]

In Grant v. New York State Division of Human Rights[85] the defendant state agency found that there was no probable cause to believe that the employer had engaged in age discrimination, since petitioner's position was eliminated in a staff cutback; statistical evidence did not reveal a pattern of discrimination against older workers. The court agreed that the initial complaint lodged with the federal EEOC and then forwarded to defendant state agency simply did not state a cause of action for age discrimination.[86]

In Murphy v. American Home Products Corp.[87] the New York Appellate Division, First Department, ruled that the fired employee suing on an age discrimination claim was entitled to a jury trial when he sought money damages only and not reinstatement to the job or other equitable relief.[88]

And in Tolley v. Brown & Wood[89] it was held that partners are not protected against age discrimination; plaintiff was a partner in the defendant law firm from 1971 to 1985 when he resigned. Unable to find legal employment, he was driving a taxicab when he commenced suit for age discrimination, alleging that he had been ousted to "make room for younger employees and/or partners." The court found no cause of action, based in part on the U.S. Supreme Court's holding in Hishon v. King & Spaulding,[90] to the effect that ADEA "does not reach partners in a law firm. . . . the court's opinion should not be read as extending Title VII to the management of a law firm by its partners. The reasoning of the court's opinion does not require that the relationship among partners be characterized as an employment relationship to which Title VII would apply." Plaintiff's argument, however, is that he was only a nominal partner and more realistically should be categorized as an employee. Specifically, he states that he had no power to determine clients, the fees to be charged to those clients or any other clients for that matter, or the persons who would be admitted as partners. Plaintiff's argument, taken to its logical conclusion, would force the Court into an absurd analysis of the relative powers of each and every member of a small or large law firm. An attorney who chooses to be a partner may obtain greater income than he could achieve on his own, but must sacrifice some measure of personal freedom to do so. Plaintiff had the right to vote at partnership meetings and quite clearly would have been held liable on the firm's lease had it come to that. It appears from the present state of the law that regardless of his status as a partner he had clearly forfeited any "employee" protections which might have been available to him had he chosen to remain an associate.

2. *Florida*: In Gross v. Culbro Corp.[91] the plaintiff, a cigar salesman, was 63 years of age when defendant employer reduced his hours as part of an employee cutback. He brought suit under ADEA, and his part-time employment was terminated. The court found for the employer, pointing out that the employee failed to make out a prima facie case of age discrimination because he could not show intent to discriminate; he had been terminated for legitimate business reasons.

3. *Illinois*: In Brown v. Mars[92] the employee had worked for defendant for 22 years and at the age of 47 he was discharged, then earning $71,000 annually. The suit for willful and reckless age discrimination brought a jury verdict for the discharged employee of $1.1 million; the employer had offered $40,000 in settlement![93]

4. Massachusetts: In Shapiro v. Halmar Distributors, Inc.[94] plaintiff was demoted as marketing manager after 32 years' service, just one month short of his 55th birthday. No explanation for the demotion was given, and shortly thereafter he filed an age discrimination charge against his employer with the Massachusetts employment practices agency. He then took a medical leave of absence due to harassment on the job, and his salary and benefits were immediately terminated by the defendant employer. He then brought suit under ADEA, alleging that he had been wrongfully terminated because of his age; the employer countered with the contention that plaintiff was demoted and terminated for poor performance. The Massachusetts jury awarded him $294,494 for back pay, benefits, and emotional distress damages for willfulness under ADEA and for loss of consortium. Plaintiff was reinstated in his job, and also was awarded interest plus attorney's fees.

5. Ohio: In Strong v. Xenia City School[95] the plaintiff, a 49-year-old white teacher, was denied promotions from school teacher to administrator 19 times; he then filed under ADEA, contending that blacks, women, and teachers 10 to 15 years younger consistently received promotions. The federal district court jury in Ohio found that he had been denied promotions 13 times for discriminatory reasons—2 for sexual discrimination; 4 for racial discrimination; 6 for age discrimination; and 1 for retaliation. The jury awarded him $260,356, of which $110,000 was for compensation, $100,000 was for emotional distress and loss of reputation, and $50,000 was for punitive damages.

It should be noted that class actions under Rule 23 of the Federal Rules of Civil Procedure are not available under ADEA,[96] although a limited form of class action for age discrimination is permitted under the provisions of the Fair Labor Standards Act.[97] Actions for violation of ADEA can be brought by private claimants or by the government,[98] although the government must first attempt conciliation before filing suit.[99] No "right to sue" letter is required before an employee can bring suit, as required under Title VII, and ADEA expressly mandates jury trials.[100] As Laugesen v. Anaconda Co.[101] points out, once the plaintiff alleges a prima facie case under ADEA, the burden of proof does not shift to the defendant employer to prove a nondiscriminatory reason for the discharge, and the plaintiff employee can recover only if the jury finds that one factor in the discharge was age, and that age in fact made the difference in the employer's decision to terminate the employee.[102]

In October 1988 the Sixth U.S. Court of Appeals was called upon in Public Employees Retirement System of Ohio v. Betts[103] to decide whether age-based distinctions in employee benefit plans have to be justified by a substantial business purpose as specified in ADEA. The court responded in the affirmative, overturning a provision in Ohio's pension system that gave larger disability benefits to employees forced to quit work before the age of 60 than those workers who were disabled after reaching 60. The provision was illegal because Ohio officials had failed to prove that it was justified by a substantial business purpose, such as major extra costs.

4.6 EQUAL PAY ACT OF 1963

The Equal Pay Act of 1963[104] antedates Title VII of the Civil Rights Act of 1964 and is limited in scope to but one aspect of employment discrimination: wage discrimination based upon sex. The Equal Pay Act was inserted into the middle of the Fair Labor Standards Act.[105] The thrust of the act is to ensure that "employees doing equal work should be paid equal wages, regardless of sex,"[106] and therefore the act does not apply to conditions of employment,[107] job opportunities,[108] or offers of employment.[109] The act is concerned exclusively with wage and fringe benefit differentials based on sex.[110]

The wording of the act is subject to the definitions of the Fair Labor Standards Act[111] and, in general, covers employees who are "engaged in commerce or in the production of goods for commerce" or who are employed in "an enterprise engaged in commerce or in the production of goods for commerce."[112] Even if a business has fewer than two employees, the act is applicable if annual sales or business reaches $362,500.[113] Labor unions are not covered, but "no labor organization representing employees of an employer who has covered employees shall cause or attempt to cause such employer to discriminate against an employee in violation of the Act." Exempt from the provisions of the act are certain employees in certain very small retail and service establishments, amusement and recreation establishments, fisheries and fish processing plants, some agricultural businesses, and some small newspapers and telephone companies, as well as the crews on foreign vessels and occasional employees in some forms of domestic service.[114] And as Ritter v. Mount St. Mary's College[115] indicates, religious institutions and schools are exempt due to possible violation of their First Amendment rights of freedom of religion. Coverage of the act extends to most employees of the federal government[116] and all state and local government employees who are not specifically exempted under Section 3(e)(2)(C) of the Fair Labor Standards Act.[117]

The provisions of the act prohibit sex-based pay differentials "within any establishment," defined as a distinct physical place of business rather than the entire business or industry. However, in AFSCME v. County of Nassau[118] the federal District Court for the Eastern District of New York held that for public employees "physically separate workplaces can constitute a single establishment under the Equal Pay Act if there is a significant functional interrelationship between the work of the employees in the various locations." Hence, school districts, counties, and even the entire federal civil service system may constitute a single establishment subject to the act.[119] And in Hodgson v. Hasam Realty Corp.[120] the Fifth U.S. Court of Appeals affirmed the lower court finding that a hotel, two motels, and two country clubs in two counties of Florida, all operated by one employer as one unit, constituted one establishment for purposes of the act.

Equality of work is a troublesome concept in the enforcement of the act; it is evident that, in order for a plaintiff to prove a violation of the act, he or she must show not only that his or her job involves levels of skill, effort, and responsibility equal to those of the higher paid job but also, at the beginning, that the compared jobs are substantially the same in content, although the jobs need not be identical in all respects. But "equal work" does not mean "comparable work," i.e., only jobs that are substantially the same can be compared.[121] In Wirtz v. Muskogee Jones Store Co.[122] the court ruled that the defendant did not violate the act by paying male department heads in the men's clothing department less than female department heads in the women's clothing department because their skills were different, although the jobs were "substantially identical." Job titles or job classifications are not controlling on the issue of job equality.[123] An employer who is found to be in violation of the act cannot eliminate the pay differential by reducing the pay of the favored sex to a lower level; the lower pay level must be increased.[124]

Thus, it is evident that for a substantial violation of the Equal Pay Act the plaintiff must prove (a) the discrimination is based on sex; (b) the employees work under similar working conditions; (c) the differential in pay is not permitted by any enumerated defense; (d) the employees are performing equal work, similar in content and equal in skill, effort, and responsibility; and (e) the employees are in the same establishment.

It should be observed that the Equal Pay Act, recognizing salary differences based on seniority, a merit system, and an incentive pay system, was amended in 1966 and in 1972 to include nearly all employees. Today perhaps 45 states, the District of Columbia, and Puerto Rico have equal pay laws that include employees not covered under the Equal Pay Act, as amended.

In summary, note that Corning Glass Works v. Brennan[125] was the only Equal Pay Act case to reach the U.S. Supreme Court; in 1974 the highest court established a limited definition of "similar working conditions." Where all men worked on the night shift and all women worked on the day shift, the court ruled that working conditions under the act did not refer to time of day when work was performed. Accordingly, different shifts do not justify a pay differential. The Tenth U.S. Court of Appeals in Marshal v. Security Bank & Trust Co.[126] later defined the requirements that must be met to justify pay differentials through a bona fide training program—the program must be open to both sexes, all employees must be notified of training opportunities, the program must have a definite beginning and a definite ending, and the program must have a definite course of study and advancement opportunities upon completion of the course. The landmark case of EEOC v. Aetna Insurance Co.[127] set forth the specific guidelines for a bona fide merit pay plan: the employee must believe that good performance will result in additional compensation, there must be a direct correlation between amount of pay and the exceptional performance, the employee must understand the merit pay plan to eliminate surprise at a later evaluation of the merit pay plan, the performance must be measured accurately by objective performance appraisals or standards, the base pay must not be reduced because the employee is on a merit pay plan, the merit pay plan must be updated periodically, managers must believe in the merit pay plan and be trained to administer it properly, and the plan must be free of bias or leniency.

4.7 RELIGIOUS, SEXUAL, AND RACIAL DISCRIMINATION IN EMPLOYMENT

A. *Religious discrimination* in employment is barred under Title VII of the Civil Rights Act of 1964 but not under 42 USC 1981, which bars only racial discrimination. Courts have frequently been called upon to draw the line between claims of racial discrimination within the meaning of Section 1981 and claims of religious discrimination. A federal court in Michigan in Marlowe v. General Motors Corp.[128] concluded that the claims of discrimination against Jews were not claims of religious discrimination but were claims of racial discrimination falling within Section 1981. Eight years later in Wald v. Teamsters[129] a federal court in California, on the other hand, determined that Jews did not constitute a race for purposes of Section 1981, and that therefore Jews should pursue claims of religious discrimination under Title VII.[130]

The U.S. Supreme Court in 1987 decided Francis College v. Al-Khazraji[131] and Shaare-Tefila Congregation v. Cobb,[132] holding unanimously that whites and blacks who have been victims of discrimination may sue under Section 1981 to prevent and redress unconstitutional bias against their respective religions. The court spoke of discrimination based upon "their ancestry or ethnic characteristics" instead of their religious differences. In the Francis College case the U.S. citizen, born in Iraq, claimed to have been denied tenure due to his Arab origin, while in the Shaare-Tefila case suit was brought against eight men accused of spray painting the synagogue with large Nazi and other anti-Semitic symbols and slogans; and religious discrimination was indeed the target, which the Court chose to overlook. The highest court overruled the lower court judgment that Arabs and Jews were not members of distinct nonwhite races and hence not protected under Section 1981. The Court, in order to provide protection against employment discrimination, said that "most biologists and anthropologists criticize racial classifications as arbitrary and of little use in understanding the variability of human beings. . . . The particular biological traits which have generally been chosen to characterize races have been criticized as having little biological significance." Accordingly, the meaning of Section 1981 should be determined on the basis of the intentions of those who passed the law, since even those who might be deemed white today were not thought to be white when the statute was enacted.[133]

Note that the Fifth U.S. Court of Appeals in Boureslan v. Aramco, Inc.[134] ruled that the U.S. corporate defendant operating abroad need not comply with Title VII because Congress had not intended to extend civil rights nondiscrimination protection to U.S. citizens employed abroad. According to the court, "the religious and social customs practiced in many countries are wholly at odds with those of this country. . . . . Requiring American employers to comply with Title VII in such a country could well leave American corporations the difficult choice of either refusing to employ U.S. citizens in the country or discontinuing business." The bitter dissenting opinion observed that "today's decision means that one U.S. citizen assigned to the Saudi office of a U.S. corporation, and another citizen working for the same company in Texas could experience identical acts of discrimination but only the latter will have a remedy. . . . This situation creates a dilemma for minorities and women: foreign assignments will be less attractive while refusal of such an assignment could limit an individual's opportunity for advancement."[135]

In Corporation of the Presiding Bishops of the Church of Jesus Christ of Latter-Day Saints v. Amos[136] the issue was whether a religious entity, the Mormon Church, acting as an employer, may discriminate on the basis of religion in jobs that are arguably secular in nature. The federal district court in Utah said "no" and observed that Section 702 of Title VII provided that Title VII "shall not apply to . . . a religious corporation, association, educational institution, or society with respect to employment of individuals of a particular religion to perform work connected with the carrying on by such corporation, association, educational institution, or society, of its activities." Of the six plaintiffs employed by defendant, two held positions in the personnel department of Beehive Mills, which manufactures garments and Temple clothing, two were in seamstress jobs, one was in maintenance at Deseret Gymnasium, and one was a truck driver at Deseret Industries, which operates under the church's welfare programs. The court ruled that, as applied to secular nonreligious activities, Section 702 violated the First Amendment's establishment clause; the government must remain neutral and not interfere with employment decisions of religious institutions. It was unconstitutional to grant religious organizations "an exclusive authorization to engage in conduct which can directly and immediately advance religious tenets and practices." The court found that the maintenance worker was engaged in secular activity but the truck driver was engaged in religious activity, and therefore only the maintenance worker was entitled to reinstatement and back pay for unlawful discrimination.

It appears obvious that Section 702 advances religion impermissibly by granting the religious employers a privilege denied to all others. The exemption extends benefits to church-owned businesses at the expense of its employees and competing nonreligious employers. The exemption grants religious organizations a powerful means of coercing religious obedience from employees; the exemption creates a symbolic link between government and religion forbidden by the First Amendment. And the statutory provision is not necessary to insulate government from religious activities, since the application of Title VII prohibitions to religious employers in the context of gender and racial discrimination is well accepted.

In New York and Massachusetts Service, Inc. v. Commission[137] the highest Massachusetts court found that the procedure for adjudication under the Massachusetts statute prohibiting discrimination against an employee on the basis of religion did not violate the employer's right to equal protection of the laws. The commonwealth statute in question allowed the employee to transfer the case to the superior court but the defendant employer was not accorded that right.

"Reasonably accommodate" is the mandate for employers with respect to an employee's religious beliefs. Title VII defines the term "religion" as including "all aspects of religious observance and practice, as well as belief, unless an employer demonstrates that he is unable to reasonably accommodate to an employee's or prospective employee's religious observance or practice without undue hardship on the conduct of the employer's business." The U.S. Supreme Court in Ansonia Board of Education v. Philbrook[138] had occasion to make a pronouncement on a collective bargaining agreement that allowed three days of paid leave for religious holidays. The employee, a high school teacher, requested three additional days to celebrate six religious holidays observed by the Worldwide Church of God. The highest court ruled 8–1 that the school district was not required to accept the employee's demand under these circumstances when the school was open for classes.

It should be noted that a state may not deny unemployment benefits to individuals whose refusal to accept employment is based on sincerely held religious beliefs.[139]

B. *Sexual discrimination* is illustrated by Graham v. Texasgulf, Inc.,[140] where plaintiff alleged tht she was terminated after a series of reductions in the work force solely due to her sex. The federal district court in Connecticut made clear that sex discrimination is not easy to prove: "A plaintiff must prove (a) she belonged to a class of persons protected by Title VII; (b) she suffered an unfavorable employment action at the hands of her employer; (c) she was qualified to assume another position at the time of her discharge; and (d) the employer did not treat gender neutrally, but discriminated based upon it." The court here found that plaintiff did not meet either the third or fourth prong of its test, even though a male coworker was retained, because the male coworker was not less qualified than plaintiff, and the decision was based on subjective criteria.[141] In Hopkins v. Price Waterhouse[142] the U.S. Court of Appeals for the District of Columbia found that "sex stereotyping played a significant role in blocking" plaintiff from a partnership in defendant company, despite the evidence that plaintiff was denied promotion due to her inability to work with other people. The defense burden was upon the defendant employer to show by clear and convincing evidence that the decision would have been the same, absent discrimination.

In Matter of State Division of Human Rights on the Complaint of Cottongin v. County of Onondaga[143] the New York Court of Appeals had occasion to find an "inference of discrimination." Here the complainant, a white female employee-at-will as a deputy sheriff, was fired by defendant employer after five years of employment, allegedly because of her association with a black deputy sheriff. A state human rights commissioner found in her favor that she was fired on the basis of sex discrimination and ordered her reinstatement. In affirming, New York's highest court stated,

The record amply supports the Commissioner's conclusion that complainant was discriminated against on the basis of her sex and race. First, the record sufficiently supports the conclusion that complainant made out a prima facie case of discrimination by showing that she, as a white woman, was disciplined differently from her black male co-employee, Deputy Stevens. The Sheriff's Department argues, however, that the difference in treatment raises no inference of discrimination in this case because complainant was an "at will" employee, while Deputy Stevens was protected by the Civil Service Law. Notwithstanding this difference in employment status, however, the Commissioner could rationally find that the differential treatment of complainant and Deputy Stevens raised an inference of discrimination.

In Sobel v. Yeshiva University[144] the Second U.S. Court of Appeals ruled that the federal district court had improperly dismissed plaintiff's sex discrimination claim in light of the 1986 decision of the U.S. Supreme Court in Bazemore v. Friday.[145] The highest court had held there that the discriminatory treatment of blacks constituted a Title VII violation after Title VII became applicable to their employers, even though the Title VII violation had occurred before that date. Accordingly, the Second U.S. Court of Appeals explained that the Bazemore case applied to sex discrimination claims as well, and that the trial court's exclusion of evidence of discrimination occurring prior to 1972 when Title VII was made applicable to universities[146] was inconsistent with the 1986 holding of the U.S. Supreme Court. It should be noted that the plaintiffs in the Sobel case had switched midway through the trial from a "disparate treatment" case to a claim of "disparate impact." The federal district court rejected plaintiff's "disparate impact" claim because it was brought too late in the proceedings to be considered and because the allegedly discriminatory acts occurred prior to the date that Title VII became applicable to universities.[147] On remand, the federal District Court for the Southern District of New York[148] had sought to distinguish the Bazemore and Sobel cases on their facts—the former case involved presumably illegal racial discrimination affecting all blacks, whereas the latter case did not involve sex discrimination but only a pay differential attributable to "several gender-neutral factors." The federal district court in 1987 had reaffirmed its dismissal of plaintiffs' "disparate impact" claim on procedural grounds as well. The federal appellate court, somewhat annoyed by the need to review the case for a second time, stated that it was "disturbed by the manner in which the district court treated this case on initial remand" and ruled that plaintiffs were not procedurally barred from raising the "disparate impact" claim, and that the court should have noted the university's "failure to equalize salaries, separate and apart from the operation of the guideline system."

Disparate treatment on the basis of sex was evident in City of Los Angeles Dept. of Water and Power v. Manhart,[149] where the employer required a higher monthly contribution to a retirement plan from females than from males; the alleged longer life expectancy of women simply did not justify the sexual discrimination under Title VII. By the same token, retirement plans requiring fewer years of employment for females and giving women "added benefits" violated Title VII.[150] One such "added benefit" for women might be pregnancy benefits, but the U.S. Supreme Court in General Electric Co. v. Gilbert[151] ruled that an employer benefit plan that excluded pregnancy-related disability from temporary disability coverage did not constitute sexual discrimination. But Congress reacted to this decision of the highest court by enacting the Pregnancy Discrimination Act of 1978,[152] which provides that sexual discrimination encompasses discrimination "because of, on the basis of pregnancy, childbirth or related medical conditions. . . . Women affected by pregnancy, childbirth or related medical conditions shall be treated the same for all employment-related purposes, including receipt of benefits under fringe benefit programs, as other persons not so affected but similar in their ability or inability to work."

The "no spouse" rule in employment situations simply means that the employer does not permit spouses to work together; in many instances the spouse must transfer or resign or not seek employment from the same employer. Obviously, this form of sexual discrimination has been attacked with the result that courts have placed the burden of justification of the "no spouse" rule upon the employer.[153] In Whirlpool Corp. v. Civil Rights Commission[154] a woman applied for a job at the place where her husband was working but was not hired due to the no spouse rule. The Michigan Supreme Court observed that less than 13 percent of the employer's workforce was female, and therefore there was a reasonable basis for its holding of sex discrimination. Unfortunately, the court found that the no spouse rule was not inherently unfair and could be reasonably justified by the employer.

In Harper v. Trans World Airlines, Inc.[155] plaintiff and her husband were employed as telephone agents along with 373 other employees on a 24-hour daily basis. Plaintiff contended that the no spouse rule, though neutral on its face, was nevertheless discriminatory in fact because it will cause more women than men to terminate their employment. But plaintiff's argument under the Civil Rights Act of 1964 was devoid of proof!

In Meier v. Evansville-Vanderburgh School Corp.[156] the federal court in Indiana ruled that plaintiff lost the right to recover for sexual discrimination because the employee and spouse had a choice as to who would transfer or resign but left the decision to the employer!

But in Yuhas v. Libbey-Owens-Ford Co.[157] the no spouse rule did not extend to management or to coworkers who married after being hired, and the trial court found the rule to be sexually neutral. The Seventh U.S. Court of Appeals agreed that the rule was not gender based and did not intentionally discriminate against women. However, both courts observed that 71 of the 74 applicants who were disqualified by the rule were women; nevertheless, according to the federal appellate court, there was no showing that there is no equally effective nondiscriminatory alternative that would have avoided the problems.[158] Furthermore, the sexual discrimination here was unintentional since more men than women opted to work in this plant, while a majority of workers in the other plants of the same employer were female. The employer's argument pointed out that, when spouses worked together, intense emotions interfered with job performance, loyalty to the employer, and supervisory matters, particularly when one spouse supervised the other spouse; furthermore, the employer contended that double absenteeism frequently resulted when one spouse was ill and that scheduling work assignments and vacations of spouses was very complicated. But the employer had no empirical proof of these assertions. Yet the court upheld the no spouse rule as reasonably related to the efficiency of the work force and therefore valid and not sexually discriminatory.

The Eighth U.S. Court of Appeals in EEOC v. Rath Packing Co.,[159] however, found that the employer had intentionally discriminated against women, as attested to by statistics and the lack of objective hiring practices. The employer was therefore unable to justify the rule in terms of business necessity or "compelling need" to perpetuate the rule.

C. *Racial discrimination* is covered by Section 1981 exclusively; allegations of discrimination against Slavic[160] and Ukrainian citizens,[161] for example, have been held not to state a claim under Section 1981.[162] However, in Budinsky v. Corning Glass Works[163] the court relied upon a pragmatic definition of "race" and concluded that Hispanics (often perceived as nonwhite) constitute a racial classification for the purposes of Section 1981. According to the federal District Court for the Western District of Pennsylvania,

The terms "race" and "racial discrimination" may be of such doubtful sociological validity as to be scientifically meaningless, but these terms nonetheless are subject to a commonly-accepted, albeit sometimes vague, understanding. Those courts which have extended the coverage of §1981 have done so on a realistic basis, within the framework of this common meaning and understanding. On this admittedly unscientific basis, whites are plainly a "race" susceptible to "racial discrimination." Hispanic persons and Indians, like blacks, have been traditional victims of group discrimination, and, however inaccurately or stupidly, are frequently and even commonly subject to a "racial" identification as "nonwhites." There is accordingly both a practical need and a logical reason to extend section 1981's proscription against exclusively "racial" employment discrimination to these groups of potential discriminatees.

Two years later the Tenth U.S. Court of Appeals in Manzanares v. Safeway Stores, Inc.[164] focused not on whether particular groups are racial classifications but rather on whether the group to which the plaintiffs belong is an identifiable group whose rights can be measured against those rights accorded the majority group. And in Lopez v. S. B. Thomas Inc.[165] the Second U.S. Court of Appeals had no difficulty in concluding that the record (showing constructive discharge of a person of Puerto Rican descent), "reveals circumstances surrounding plaintiff's termination of employment with Thomas from which a trier of fact could infer racial discrimination." After working satisfactorily for seven years the employee had directed at him by his employer "degrading obscenities . . . [and was] told that he would be discharged."[166] Since the discharged employee had demonstrated the fact of discrimination, "the burden of production shifts to the employer to articulate a legitimate, non-discriminatory reason for the discharge. . . . If the employer satisfies his burden, the plaintiff (employee) has an opportunity to show that employer's stated reason is pretextual."

The Minnesota Supreme Court in Department v. Commission[167] ruled that, in employment discrimination cases involving disparate treatment claims, the triers of fact must articulate the threefold test of prima facie case, answer, and rebuttal, as set forth by the U.S. Supreme Court in McDonnell Douglas Corp. v. Greene;[168] accordingly, the finding of racial discrimination in the Minneapolis Police Department was reversed. On the other hand, the New York court in Prophet v. Long Island Lighting Co.[169] found that "plaintiff had alleged and presented evidence of a prima facie case of discrimination. . . . In response, defendant had produced evidence that plaintiff was denied appointment . . . for legitimate nondiscriminatory reasons. . . . Whether the reasons offered for its action were legitimate or merely a pretext for discrimination present triable issues of fact precluding summary determination."

Reverse racial discrimination should not be overlooked, as the U.S. Supreme Court stated in 1976 in McDonald v. Santa Fe Trail Transportation Co.[170] The highest court made it clear that whites enjoy Title VII protection against racial discrimination as well as minorities. However, this does not mean that "affirmative action" programs are prohibited under Title VII, as shown in the following seven decisions of the U.S. Supreme Court between 1979 and 1987:

1. *United Steelworkers of America v. Weber*:[171] The employer voluntarily established a 50 percent minority quota in a skilled crafts training program, although the plant's craft workers were exclusively white and there had been no evidence of discriminatory hiring procedures; the Court held that Title VII permits private employers to voluntarily institute race-conscious measures in order to "eliminate conspicuous racial imbalance in traditionally segregated job categories."

2. *Memphis Firefighters v. Stotts*:[172] The lower court's remedial powers under Title VII were held not to include the abrogation of seniority rights to benefit individuals who had not been proven victims of past discrimination.

3. *Wygant v. Jackson Board of Education*:[173] A school board was found to have violated the Fourteenth Amendment when it laid off teachers on the basis of race in order to maintain a set percentage of minority faculty pursuant to a collective bargaining agreement.

4. Local 93 of the International Association of Firefighters v. City of Cleveland:[174] The promotion quota was found to have been voluntarily implemented and therefore was not subject to the limitations of judicial authority under Title VII's remedial provisions.

5. Local 28 of the Sheet Metal Workers International Association v. EEOC:[175] The union was found guilty of "persistent and egregious discrimination" in refusing to admit minorities, and the Court therefore endorsed affirmative action measures including a 29 percent minority membership goal to redress past racial discrimination.

6. United States v. Paradise:[176] The Court upheld a lower court–ordered promotion quota based on race imposed on the Alabama Department of Public Safety, after finding blatant and persistent discrimination.

7. Johnson v. Transportation Agency:[177] The Court ruled that race (or gender) could be used as one factor in promotions in order to remedy a manifest statistical imbalance in the work force.

NOTES

1. See Ewing, "What Business Thinks About Employee Rights," 5 Harv. Bus. Rev. 55 (1977).

2. Id.

3. See United States v. Harris Trust & Savings Bank of Chicago, as reported in the New York Times, March 10, 1988, at A22.

4. See U.S. News & World Report 71 (March 7, 1988).

5. 824 F.2d 692 (9th Cir. 1987).

6. See generally Perritt, Employer Dismissal Law and Practice (1984). Note in particular, Title VII of the Civil Rights Act of 1964, 42 U.S.C. § 2000e (1981); Age Discrimination in Employment Act, 29 U.S.C. §§ 621–634 (1975 & Supp. 1982); Rehabilitation Act of 1973, Pub. L. No. 93–112, 87 Stat. 355 (codified as amended in scattered sections of 29 U.S.C.); Reconstruction Civil Rights Acts, 42 U.S.C. §§ 1981, 1985(3) (1981); Exec. Order No. 11,246, 30 Fed. Reg. 12,319 (1965), *as amended by* Exec. Order No. 11,375, 32 Fed. Reg. 14,303 (1967); Exec. Order No. 11,478, 34 Fed. Reg. 12,985 (1969); Exec. Order No. 12,086, 43 Fed. Reg. 46,501 (1978), *reprinted in* 42 U.S.C. § 2000e app. at pp. 28–30 (1981).

7. See National Labor Relations Act, 29 U.S.C. §§ 151–169 (1973 & Supp. 1981); § 704(a) of the Civil Rights Act of 1964, 42 U.S.C. § 2000e–3(a)(1981); Federal Employers' Liability Act, 45 U.S.C. §§ 55, 60 (1972); Federal Railroad Safety Act, 45 U.S.C.A. § 441 (West Supp. 1982); Occupational Safety & Health Act of 1970, 29 U.S.C. § 660(c) (1975); Clean Air Act, 42 U.S.C. § 7622(a)(1982); Fair Labor Standards Act, 29 U.S.C.A. § 215(a)(3) (West 1976 & Supp. 1982); Consumer Credit Protection Act, 15 U.S.C.A. § 1674 (West 1982).

8. See generally Brandin & Copus, In Defense of Public Employers (1988).

9. 108 S.Ct. 62 (1985); for lower court opinion, see 505 N.E.2d 915 (N.Y. 1983).

10. See Jackson v. Metropolitan Edison Co., 419 U.S. 345 (1974) and Shelly v. Kramer, 334 U.S. 1 (1948).

11. Note Rendell-Baker v. Kohn, 457 U.S. 830 (1982).

12. See Benson v. Arizona State Board of Dental Examiners, 673 F.2d 272 (9th Cir. 1982).

13. Cf. Gilinsky v. Columbia University, 488 F. Supp. 1309 (S.D.N.Y. 1980), holding that the university's failure to appoint a woman as a professor was not "state action."

14. Supra note at p. 37.

15. Note Roe v. Wade, 410 U.S. 113 (1973).

16. See Goetz v. Windsor Central School District, 698 F.2d 606 (2nd Cir. 1983).

17. 106 S. Ct. 1842 (1982).

18. Note United Steel Workers of America v. Weber, 443 U.S. 193 (1979).

19. 41 Fair Empl. Prac. Cas. (BNA) 1 (1987).

20. 42 U.S.C. 2000e et seq.

21. See 42 U.S.C. 2000–2(a)e.

22. See 42 U.S.C. 2000–2(e)(1). Also see generally Brandin & Copus, In Defense of Public Employers (1988).

23. 42 U.S.C. 2000c–2(a)(1).

24. 42 U.S.C. 2000c–2(a)(2).

25. 42 U.S.C. 2000e–2(d).

26. 42 U.S.C. 2000e–3(a).

27. Note Pub. L. 88–352, 78 Stat. 253, as amended, and Pub. L. 92-261, 86 Stat. 109.

28. See East Texas Motor Freight System, Inc. v. Rodriguez, 431 U.S. 405 (1977).

29. Supra note at xxiv.

30. 401 U.S. 424 (1971). See New York Times, Jan. 18, 1988, at A10.

31. See generally Perritt, Employer Dismissal Law and Practice (1984); also see Cline v. Roadway Express, Inc., 689 F.2d 481 (4th Cir. 1982) and McDonnell Douglas v. Green, 411 U.S. 792 (1973).

32. Note 42 U.S.C. 2000e(b).

33. See Brown v. A. J. Gerrard Manufacturing Co., 643 F.2d 273 (5th Cir. 1981).

34. See McDonald v. Santa Fe Trail Transportation Co., 427 U.S. 273 (1976).

35. See Brown v. Pena, 441 F. Supp. 1382 (S.D. Fla. 1977), aff 589 F.2d 1113 (5th Cir. 1979), where the petitioner claimed a religious belief in eating cat food on the job!

36. 439 U.S. 24 (1978).

37. 431 U.S. 324 (1977).

38. Note discussion hereinafter on state court affirmances.

39. See Lorance v. A T & Technologies, Inc., —F.2d—(7th Cir. October 5, 1988).

40. 42 U.S.C. 2000e(b), (c), and (e).

41. 109 U.S.3 (1883).

42. See Shaw and Wolfe, The Structure of the Legal Environment: Law, Ethics and Business (1987).

43. 163 U.S. 537 (1895).

44. 347 U.S. 160 (1954).

45. 456 U.S. 461 (1981).

46. 590 F. Supp. 1146 (N.D. Ill. 1984).

47. Cf. Jones v. Progress Lighting Corp., 595 F. Supp. 1031 (Pa. 1984).

48. 415 U.S. 36 (1974).

49. 425 U.S. 840 (1976).
50. 42 U.S.C. 2000d et seq.

No person in the United States shall, on the ground of race, color, or national origin, be excluded from participation in, be denied the benefits of, or be subjected to discrimination under any program or activity receiving Federal financial assistance.

51. 42 U.S.C. 2000d–3.
52. 463 U.S. 582 (1983).
53. —F. Supp.—(E.D.N.Y. 1988).
54. Note that the act expressly overruled Grove City College v. Bell, 465 U.S. 555 (1984).
55. Id.
56. 392 U.S. 409 (1968).
57. See, for example, McDonald v. Santa Fe Trail Transportation Co., 427 U.S. 273 (1976).
58. See Runyon v. McCrary, 427 U.S. 160, 167 (1976).
59. 798 F.2d 731 (5th Cir. 1988).
60. See generally 84 A.L.R. Fed. 114.
61. 375 N.Y.S.2d 402 (1975).
62. Supra note 58.
63. 108 S.Ct. 1419 (1988).
64. According to the brief for amici,

Stare decisis always carries special weight in matters of statutory construction, for Congress is free to change the Court's interpretations of a statute. Its failure to do so imports approval of the judicial construction. That is particularly true in the civil rights field, because civil rights decisions are uniquely visible, given the definitional role they play in society. The Court's interpretations of civil rights statutes have been revisited frequently by Congress, and frequently reversed when found to have placed too narrow a construction on those statutes.

Congress has not overturned *Runyon*, but instead has knowingly accepted and ratified it, incorporating it into subsequent legislation. Thus, the evidence of Congressional ratification is substantial. Even before *Runyon* had been decided, but in the aftermath of *Jones*, the Congress refused to make Title VII of the 1964 Civil Rights Act the exclusive remedy for employment discrimination. The proponents of doing so were seeking to repudiate lower court decisions which, in light of *Jones*, had read § 1981 as creating a parallel, but independent, remedy. Their successful opponents determined that Congress ought not to abolish a 100-year-old remedy for racial discrimination, and that it was in any event appropriate to allow victims of racial discrimination a choice of remedies.

Several years later, Congress again treated *Runyon* as part of the body of civil rights law when it incorporated it into legislation enacted in response to *Alyeska Pipeline Service Co. v. Wilderness Society*, 421 U.S. 240 (1975), allowing courts to award attorneys fees in cases brought, *inter alia*, under § 1981.

Congress is not alone in treating *Runyon's* interpretation of § 1981 as a settled aspect of the law of civil rights. This Court has done so as well. The *Runyon* holding was foreshadowed in *Jones v. Alfred H. Mayer Co.*, 392 U.S. 409 (1968) and made explicit in *Tillman v. Wheaton-Haven Recreation Association*, 410 U.S. 431 (1973), and *Johnson v. Railway Express Agency*, 421 U.S. 454 (1975). Since *Runyon*, the Court has repeatedly applied § 1981 to private conduct. But the Court has not limited its use of *Runyon* to direct applications to discriminatory conduct. It was cited in *Bob Jones University v. U.S.*, 461 U.S. 574, 593 (1983), as evidence of a "fundamental national policy against racial discrimination in private education."

Yet another indication that *Runyon* is inextricably interwoven into the fabric of the law is the extent to which it is cited by the lower courts. The clear development of the law has led parties, in reliance on *Runyon*, to forego Title VII remedies in favor of § 1981. Overruling now would dash their legitimate expectations in a way that "would be intolerable," as Judge Cardozo put it.

Stare decisis reflects a judgment that the very fact of change in a rule of law has a social impact that must be justified by the incremental benefits of the new rule over the old. Where, as in this case, it is the existing rule that serves the higher social objectives, there is no reason to discard the old rule.

65. According to the brief for amici,

Judge Cardozo described circumstances that warrant departures from *stare decisis*:

If judges have wo[e]fully misinterpreted the *mores* of their day, or if the *mores* of their day are no longer those of ours, they ought not to tie, in helpless submission, the hands of their successors. *The Nature of the Judicial Process, supra*, at 151–52. Stare decisis does not require the Court blindly to "perpetuate the injustice," *Jones v. U.S.*, 366 U.S. 213, 221 (1967) of an earlier decision. Stability and predictability are valuable principles, but they are not the only, nor necessarily the most important, values for the legal system.

There is nothing of that sort to weigh in this case against *stare decisis*. Respect for "the *mores* of [our] day" counsels an entirely opposite judgment.

The national needs that underlay *Runyon* are as pressing today for its reaffirmation. Although racial discrimination is now generally regarded as unacceptable, the unfortunate fact remains that, like the grand jury discrimination considered in *Vasquez v. Hillery, supra*, it has not become unacceptable in practice. Statutory protections for racial minorities are not mere surplusage, relics of a battle long ago won, which unnecessarily clutter the United States Code. The construction of §1981 to cover private conduct is as essential now as it was in 1976 when *Runyon* was decided. . . .

There is no comparable change of circumstances to support overruling in this case. Contracts are still an indispensable part of doing business, and doing business is still a crucial aspect of life in the United States. Private racial discrimination is as offensive as it ever was.

B. The *Runyon* Decision Places No Unusual Burdens on the Judicial System

Amici have discovered no case overturning prior statutory decisions because of changed economic or social conditions alone. There have, of course, been some cases involving departure from *stare decisis* because of changed legal circumstances. In these cases departing from precedent, not adhering to it, brings unity and cohesiveness to the law, the very goals *stare decisis* is intended to further. No such special circumstances are present here.

In *Puerto Rico v. Branstad*, 107 S.Ct. 2802 (1987), this Court overruled the holding of *Kentucky v. Dennison*, 24 How. 66 (1861), that the federal courts could not order state officials to comply with the mandatory provisions of the Extradition Clause, Art. IV, §2 *Dennison* reasoned that a federal order to a state official would violate the sovereignty of the states. That conception of the relation of the states to the federal government no longer prevailed, at least after *Ex parte Young*, 209 U.S. 123 (1908). . . .

The combined impact of these social, factual and legal changes left *Swain* an obstacle to "the court's unceasing efforts to eradicate racial discrimination in the procedures used to select the venire from which individual jurors are drawn." Hence it was overruled. *Runyon*, by contrast, is part of "the court's unceasing efforts to eradicate racial discrimination;" it is essential as ever to those efforts.

C. The *Runyon* Rule Has Not Proven Unworkable

A rule of law which in the abstract is thought to be sound may prove unworkable in practice. *Stare decisis* is no barrier to the discarding of such a rule. Such was the case of *Gulfstream Aerospace Corp. v. Mayacamas Corp., supra*, overruling *Enelow v. N.Y. Life Ins. Co.*, 293 U.S. 379 (1935), and *Ettelson v. Metropolitan Life Ins. Co.*, 317 U.S. 188 (1942).

Enelow and *Ettelson* held that whether stays of certain actions were immediately appealable depended on whether the underlying action was one at law or in equity. Given the merger of the law and equity sides of the District Court, and the difficulty of determining retrospectively and hypothetically whether modern causes of action would have been considered equitable or legal at the time that those terms had substantial significance, the *Enelow-Ettelson* doctrine "lost all moorings to the actual practice of the federal courts," was "deficient in utility and sense," "unsound in theory, unworkable and arbitrary in practice," and "unnecessary to achieve any legitimate goals." *Gulfstream Aerospace Corp. v. Mayacamas Corp.*, 108 S. Ct. at 1140. Understandably, with so little to recommend it, the *Enelow-Ettelson* doctrine was abandoned.

As is the case with every prohibitory statute, there is always the question of how far a statute should sweep. The *Jones-Runyon* reading of §§ 1981 and 1982 raises fewer problems in this regard than do decisions under Title VII, the Sherman Anti-Trust Act, the Clean Air Act, or hundreds of other statutes.

The familiar problem of setting limits, to be dealt with case by case, is no ground for overruling a precedent that gives rise to the problem. There are, in a word, no reasons of substance for discarding the settled interpretations of §§ 1981 and 1982 so long accepted by the Congress and the affected citizenry.

66. See New York Times, October 13, 1988, at A1 and A23.

67. See A.B.A.J. 38 (September 1, 1988):

In Title VII of the Civil Rights Act and other anti-discrimination laws (e.g., the Age Discrimination in Employment Act), Congress struck a reasonable and widely accepted balance between contractual freedom and anti-discrimination policy. For example, Congress excluded enterprises with fewer than 15 employees from Title VII, while making it easier to prove discrimination under Title VII than under Section 1981.

Runyon is not so much a natural expansion of this system as it is a judicially created end run around it. Scores of plaintiffs have made Section 1981 claims to redress acts of discrimination covered by Title VII, or appended 1981 claims to Title VII complaints. The reason, simply put, is that the available remedies can make it worth their while.

The punitive damages awarded in these cases can amount to three or four times the compensatory damages. Some plaintiffs have recovered damages for mental distress; others have collected back pay above the limits set by Title VII. In short, 1981 cases have less to do with achieving racial justice in employment, a purpose that is substantially accomplished by Title VII, than with collecting monetary awards.

So far, the monetary impact of Section 1981 appears to have been modest. Intentional discrimination is still fairly hard to prove, and damage awards are negligible compared to, say, product liability awards.

This may change, though. A few more generous findings of intent to discriminate, a few more compassionate juries and deep pockets—and Section 1981 may become an integral part of the tort litigation explosion. This would not make it an instrument of a coherent anti-discrimination policy but an entry ticket to a lottery with windfall settlements or judgments. The costs could be considerable both to businesses and to minorities who remain unhired because prospective employers fear that they might be buying themselves an expensive Section 1981 lawsuit.

68. See A.B.A.J. 80 (November 1, 1988).

69. 106 S.Ct.2537 (1986). See generally Note, 100 Harv. L. Rev. (1986) at 268 et seq.

70. Id. at 273.

71. 29 U.S.C. 621–634.

72. Pub. L. 99–592, codified at 29 USC 631(a).

73. Note E.E.O.C. v. State of Wyoming, 103 S.Ct. 1054 (1983).

74. 29 U.S.C. 201–219; also see Section 4.10 of this volume.

75. 658 F.2d 134 (3rd Cir. 1981), cert. den. 462 U.S. 1131 (1983).

76. 670 F.2d 66 (6th Cir. 1982).

77. See generally A.B.A.J. 70 (October 1, 1987); also see Parcinski v. Outlet Company, 673 F.2d 34 (2nd Cir. 1982).

78. See Usery v. Tamiami Trail Tours, Inc., 531 F.2d 224 (5th Cir. 1976).

79. See 29 U.S.C. 623(a) and note Cancellier v. Federated Department Stores, 672 F.2d 1312 (9th Cir. 1982).

80. 441 U.S. 750, 757 (1979).

81. See U.S. News & World Report 71 (March 7, 1988), delineating Paolillo v. Dresser Industries, Inc., 813 F.2d 583 (2nd Cir. 1987) and other recent suits.

82. —N.Y.S.2d—(New York County, June 22, 1988).

83. —N.Y.S.2d—(New York County, August 1988).

84. According to the New York court,

The branch of defendants' motion which seeks to dismiss the cause of action for age discrimination is denied.

As recently stated by the Second Department in Mayer v. Manton Cork Corp., 126 A.D.2d 526 (1987):

"In order to make out a prima facie case of age discrimination, the plaintiff must (1) demonstrate that he was a member of the protected class; (2) prove that he was discharged; (3) prove that he was qualified for the position he held; and (4) either (a) show that he was replaced by a person younger than himself; (b) produce direct evidence of discriminatory intent; or (c) produce statistical evidence of discriminatory conduct. Such a showing raises an inference of discrimination which serves to shift the burden to the defendant to produce evidence that the plaintiff's discharge was founded on valid business reasons which were independent of age considerations."

Note that Section 296(3a) of the New York Executive Law stated: "It shall be an unlawful discriminatory practice: (a) For an employer . . . because an individual is between the ages of eighteen and sixty-five . . . to terminate from employment such individual, or to discriminate against such individual in promotion, compensation or in terms, conditions or privileges of employment."

The court thereupon pointed out—"Since plaintiff alleges that she was fifty-three years of age when she signed her complaint, and was "replace" by a person approximately thirty years old, the first and fourth elements of a prima facie case of age discrimination have been sufficiently pleaded. . . . "

And the court concluded: "Here, plaintiff states in her affidavit (p. 5) that she was singled out as the only Chapman employee not eligible to receive a bonus in 1987, that she was wrongfully admonished for taking an extra day which other managers at the agency also took (p. 6), and that she received no responses from the agency president to her request for definition of her responsibilities (p. 7). Thus, even if the acts alleged were to fall short of constructive discharge, which they in fact do not, the disparate treatment allegedly accorded plaintiff states a claim for discrimination."

85. —N.Y.S.2d—(New York County, February 1, 1988).

86. According to the court,

More specifically, the Respondent, State Division found that (1) there were insufficient facts to support the allegations of age discrimination; (2) that petitioner's position was eliminated in a staff cutback in which several positions in his department [approximately one hundred and fifty positions overall] were eliminated; (3) the statistical evidence did not reveal a pattern of discrimination against older workers at ITT's Security Department; and (4) that the record taken as a whole did not support the petitioner's contention that age was a consideration in ITT's decision to eliminate his position and to terminate his services. The petitioner had the opportunity to and indeed did furnish the State Division with written position statements and documentation upon no fewer than three different occasions. . . .

87. 451 N.Y.S.2d 770 (App Div., 1st Dept., April 11, 1988); also note 461 N.Y.S.2d 232 (1988) and 512 N.Y.S.2d 752 (1988).

88. According to the court,

The cause of action here in issue is a new one created by Executive Law §297 (9). That section confers upon any person claiming to be aggrieved by an unlawful discriminatory practice (including discrimination in employment because of age) a cause of action in any court of appropriate jurisdiction for damages and for such other remedies as may be appropriate. It is significant that the only specific remedy mentioned is that of "damages" without qualification. . . . Contrary to defendant's argument, plaintiff's ritualistic use in the prayer for relief of the language "and such other and further relief as to this court seems just and proper," does not change the legal character of the relief demanded. While the use of that language may evidence the reluctance of lawyers to depart from legalistic formalism and embellishment . . . such language in no way changes the exclusively monetary nature of the relief actually sought, nor does it alter the fact that such money damages alone will afford a full and complete remedy based upon the facts set forth by the plaintiff.

89. —N.Y.S.2d—(New York County, May 2, 1988).
90. 467 U.S. 69 (1984).
91. —F.Supp.—(N.D. Fla. 1987).
92. —N.E.2d—(Ill. 1987).
93. See generally Freund & Prager, "Is an Early Retirement Incentive a Benefit— or a 'Gilded Shove,' " NLJ 28 (September 14, 1987). See also McGinley v. Burroughs Corp., 407 F. Supp. 903 (E.D. Pa. 1975).
94. —N.E.2d—(Mass. 1988).
95. —F.Supp.—(S.D. Ohio, April 20, 1988).
96. 29 U.S.C. 216(b).
97. 29 U.S.C. 626(c).
98. See Marshall v. Sun Oil Co., 605 F.2d 1331 (5th Cir. 1979), cert. den. 444 U.S. 826 (1974).
99. Cf. 42 U.S.C. 2000e-5(f) with 29 U.S.C. 626(c).
100. 29 U.S.C. 626(c)(2).
101. 510 F.2d 307 (6th Cir. 1975).
102. Note Douglas v. Anderson, 656 F.2d 528 (9th Cir. 1981).
103. —F.2d— (6th Cir. October 30, 1988).
104. 29 U.S.C. 206(d)(1).
105. 29 U.S.C. 201 et seq.
106. See H. R. Rep No. 309, 88th Cong. 1st Sess.
107. Note Lancaster v. Holt, Rinehart & Winston, Inc., —F.Supp.— (N.D. Fla. 1982).
108. Id.
109. See Torres v. Action for Boston Community Development, Inc.,—F.Supp.— (Mass. 1981).
110. See EEOC v. Fremont Christian School, 609 F.Supp. 344 (N.D. Cal. 1984), aff'd 781 F.2d 1362 (9th Cir. 1986).
111. Supra note 105.
112. See generally Diedrich & Gaus, Defense of Equal Employment Claims (1982).

113. See generally Shaw & Wolfe, The Structure of the Legal Environment: Law, Ethics and Business (1987).

114. 29 U.S.C. 213(a)(2)–(15).

115. 495 F.Supp. 724 (Md. 1980).

116. 29 U.S.C. 203(e)(2)(A),(B).

117. 29 U.S.C. 203(e)(2)(C).

118. 609 F.Supp. 695, 706 (E.D.N.Y. 1985).

119. See Grumbine v. U.S., 586 F.Supp. 1144 (D.D.C. 1984).

120. 442 F.2d 1336 (5th Cir. 1971), aff'g Shultz v. Hasam Realty Corp., 316 F.Supp. 1136 (S.D. Fla. 1970).

121. See, for example, Chapman v. Pacific Telephone & Telegraph Co., 456 F.Supp. 65 (N.D. Cal. 1978).

122. 293 F.Supp. 1034 (E.D. Okla. 1968).

123. See Epstein v. Secretary of the Treasury, 739 F.2d 274 (7th Cir. 1984).

124. Supra note 113.

125. 417 U.S. 188 (1974).

126. 572 F.2d 276 (10th Cir. 1978).

127. 616 F.2d 719 (4th Cir. 1980).

128. —F.Supp.—(E.D. Mich. 1972).

129. —F.Supp.—(C.D. Cal. 1980).

130. See 42 U.S.C. 2000e et seq.

131. 107 S.Ct. 2022 (1987).

132. 107 S.Ct. 2019 (1987).

133. See Bernstein, "Discrimination," Trial Magazine 17 (August 1987).

134. —F.2d—(5th Cir. October 17, 1988).

135. See New York Times, October 18, 1988, at A23.

136. —F.Supp.—(Utah 1984).

137. —N.E.2d—(Mass. 1988).

138. —U.S.—(1988).

139. See Hobbie v. Unemployment Appeals Commission of Florida, 107 S.Ct. 1046 (1987); Thomas v. Review Board of the Indiana Employment Security Division, 450 U.S. 707 (1981); Sherbert v. Verner, 374 U.S. 398 (1963).

140. 662 F.Supp. 1451 (Conn. 1987).

141. See Maskin v. Chromally American Corp., —F.Supp.—(E.D. Pa. 1986).

142. —F.R.D.—(D.C. Cir. 1988).

143. —N.E.2d—513 N.Y.S.2d 68, 127 A.D.2d 986 (1988) (New York, April 26, 1988).

144. 839 F.2d 18 (2nd Cir., February 4, 1988).

145. 106 S.Ct. 3000 (1986).

146. See 42 U.S.C. 2000e–2(a)(1).

147. Note 566 F.Supp. 1166 (S.D.N.Y. 1983).

148. 656 F.Supp. 587 (S.D.N.Y. 1987).

149. 435 U.S. 702 (1978).

150. Note Rosen v. Public Service Electric & Gas Co., 477 F.2d 90 (3rd Cir. 1973).

151. 429 U.S. 125 (1976).

152. 42 U.S.C. 2000e(k).

153. See generally Kent and Feinschreiber, "Are 'No Spouse' Rules Valid?" Case & Comment 9 (July–August 1987).

154. 390 N.W.2d 625 (Mich. 1986).
155. 525 F.2d 409 (8th Cir. 1975).
156. 416 F.Supp. 748 (S.D. Ind. 1975), aff'd 539 F.2d 713 (7th Cir. 1976).
157. 411 F.Supp. 77 (N.D. Ill. 1976), rev'd 562 F.2d 496 (7th Cir. 1977).
158. Supra note 26 at p. 13.
159. 787 F.2d 318 (8th Cir. 1986), cert. den. 107 S.Ct. 307 (1986).
160. See Sokolski v. Corning Glass Works, —F.Supp.—(W.D. Pa. 1977).
161. See Hiduchenko v. Minnesota Medical Center, 467 F.Supp. 103 (Minn. 1979).
162. See Jones v. United Gas Improvement Corp., 68 F.R.D. 1 (E.D. Pa., 1975).
163. 427 F.Supp. 786 (W.D. Pa. 1977).
164. 593 F.2d 968 (10th Cir. 1979).
165. 831 F.2d 1184 (2nd Cir. 1987).
166. According to the court,

This case presents for our consideration whether unchecked ethnic epithets directed towards an employee may contribute to the employee's constructive discharge from his employment, and whether this type of harassment may also serve as the basis for a hostile work environment claim entitling plaintiff to relief in his civil rights suit against his employer. Although we recognize that an employer is unable to guarantee a working environment uncontaminated by foul invective, the law nonetheless provides that when an employer knows or reasonably should know that co-workers are harassing an employee because of that individual's race, color, religion, sex, or national origin, the employer may not stand idly by. In our view, the allegations in the instant case are sufficient to avoid dismissal of the employee's constructive discharge claim.

167. —N.W.2d—(Minn. June 17, 1988).
168. 411 U.S. 792 (1973).
169. —N.Y.S.2d—(Nassau County, June 28, 1988).
170. 427 U.S. 273 (1976).
171. 443 U.S. 193 (1979).
172. 467 U.S. 561 (1984).
173. 106 S.Ct. 1842 (1986).
174. 106 S.Ct. 3063 (1986).
175. 106 S.Ct. 3019 (1986).
176. 55 U.S.L.W. 4211 (1987).
177. 55 U.S.L.W. 4379 (1987).

5

Discriminatory Problems of the Handicapped

5.1 INTRODUCTION TO THE FEDERAL STATUTES ON THE DISCRIMINATION OF THE HANDICAPPED

It has been estimated that 18 percent of the noninstitutionalized civilians in the United States are physically handicapped.[1] There are millions of employables who are blind or have visual impairment; millions who are deaf or have hearing impairment; millions who have orthopedic handicaps that affect arms, hands, legs, or feet; and still other millions with diverse physical or mental handicaps. But, unlike employment discrimination on the basis of sex, age, national origin, religion, or race, employment discrimination on the basis of handicap is not generally prohibited by federal law, with the sole exception of the Vocational Rehabilitation Act of 1973, as amended.[2] This act imposes employment obligations toward the handicapped on nearly all federal contractors and on nearly all recipients of federal financial assistance.

Under Section 503 of the act most federal contracts and subcontracts must contain a provision that "in employing persons to carry out such contract . . . [the contractor] shall take affirmative action to employ and advance in employment qualified handicapped individuals." Section 503 also mandates an administrative complaint procedure for handicapped individuals and for waiver of affirmative action requirements when "special circumstances in the national interest so require." Authority to implement Section 503 is delegated to the Office of Federal Contract Compliance Programs of the U.S. Department of Labor. Excluded from Section 503 provisions are employer-contractors in contracts involving less than $2,500.[3] Section 503 applies to an employer only if its prime federal contract or subcontract is for the "procurement . . . for the United States" of personal or real property or of nonpersonal services including construction and furnishing of supplies. Section 503 does not cover work performed outside the United States.

"Handicap" is broadly defined to include mental as well as physical impairment.[4] As set forth in Prewitt v. U.S. Postal Service,[5] discrimination in employment on the basis of handicap is banned so long as the individual "meets all employment criteria except for the challenged discrimination criterion and can perform the essential functions of the position in question without endangering the health and safety of the individual or others." Both drug addiction and alcohol addiction, for example, are handicap criteria, if the impairment substantially limits or restricts the performance of the employment; but the act does not protect "any individual who is an alcoholic or drug abuser whose current use of alcohol or drugs prevents such individual from performing the duties of the job in question or whose employment, by reason of such current alcohol or drug abuse, would constitute a direct threat to property or safety of others."[6] Under Section 504 of the act, both drug and alcohol addiction are considered "physical and mental impairments." While the employer can take action against a current drug or alcohol user whose job performance is adversely affected by the drug or alcohol abuse, the employer may have a duty to provide reasonable accommodation to persons known to be so handicapped.[7] Note that in Walker v. Weinberger[8] the termination of a recovered alcoholic violated the act because the termination was based on both pretreatment and posttreatment absences of the employee.

5.2 STATE STATUTES ON HANDICAP DISCRIMINATION

It appears that most states prohibit handicap discrimination, particularly discrimination against drug addicts or alcohol addicts.[9] Some states have statutory prohibitions or restrictions on medical examinations for applicants and for employees, particularly examinations involving drug and alcohol testing. As illustrated in Turner v. Fraternal Order of Police,[10] some states recognize an employee's common law right of action for the invasion of privacy such as drug testing; but in Brotherhood of Maintenance Way Employees v. Burlington Northern Railroad Co.,[11] the Eighth U.S. Court of Appeals vacated an injunction halting a drug testing program for employees because the court found that the new drug testing program represented only a minor change in working conditions, i.e., the addition of the urine test to confirm or refute a work supervisor's observation that an employee is impaired.[12]

In the New York case of Dooley v. International Paper Co.[13] the discharged employee sought damages for discrimination based upon his disability as an epileptic. Under Section 296(1)(a) of the New York Executive Law a disability is defined as "a physical, mental or medical impairment resulting from anatomical, physiological, or neurological conditions which prevents the exercise of a normal bodily function or is demonstrable by medically accepted clinical or laboratory diagnostic techniques." The New York statute was amended in 1983 to "expand its protection to those individuals who are merely perceived as being disabled." The court ruled that plaintiff "has come forward with sufficient evidence to raise a factual issue as to whether he had an actual disability at the time he was terminated. The statute in effect at the time did not require that the disability be conclusively diagnosed."

It is evident that 45 states and the District of Columbia have laws prohibiting discrimination based upon handicap.[14] In California in February 1987 the question was raised as to whether AIDS can be considered a handicap under the California physical handicap antidiscrimination statute.[15] A quality control employee was not allowed to return to work after doctors diagnosed his condition as AIDS. The administrative law judge ruled that AIDS was not a handicap because it did not impair sight, hearing, or speech, as defined under the California statute, and therefore there was no discrimination. But the commission itself reversed and ruled that to deny reinstatement to the employee violated the California statute prohibiting discrimination against the handicapped. The commission defined a physical handicap as any physical condition of the body that has a disabling effect, or may handicap in the future without any present disabling effect. And in Massachusetts in Cronan v. New England Telephone Co.[16] it was held that an employee discharged due to AIDS could bring a claim against the employer under the Massachusetts Fair Employment and Practices Act. The court specifically ruled that AIDS qualified as a handicap under the act.

5.3   AIDS AS A HANDICAP DISCRIMINATION

The disease of acquired immune deficiency syndrome, or AIDS, has been held under state law in California and Massachusetts, inter alia, to be a handicap that can constitute the subject of employment discrimination.[17] In June 1986 the Office of Legal Counsel of the U.S. Department of Justice issued an opinion that Section 504 of the Vocational Rehabilitation Act of 1963, prohibiting discrimination against qualified handicapped persons in federally conducted or federally assisted programs, bars discrimination against persons who suffer from the disabling effects of AIDS, but does not bar discrimination against seropositive individuals who are carriers of the disease.[18] But the U.S. Supreme Court in School Board of Nassau County, Florida v. Arline[19] the very next year rejected that opinion that Section 504 of the act does not apply to communicable disease, i.e., where the employee is the carrier of the communicable disease. Here the highest court found that tuberculosis, also a contagious disease, is a handicap, even though the disease went into remission for 20 years. According to the Court, the discharged employee had a record of

physical or mental impairment that substantially limited one or more of her person's major life activities. . . . Arline's contagiousness and her physical impairment each resulted from the same underlying condition, tuberculosis. . . . [But] this case does not present, and we therefore do not reach, the questions of whether the carrier of a contagious disease such as AIDS should be considered to have a physical impairment or whether such a person could be considered, solely on the basis of contagiousness, a handicapped person as defined by the Act.

Criminal liability for willfully or knowingly exposing another person to the AIDS virus is found in state statutes in Florida and Idaho, for example.[20] The federal government in October 1988 issued a legal opinion supporting federal policies that bar discrimination against AIDS victims who work for the federal government or for employers who receive federal funds.[21] In effect, the federal antidiscrimination statute extends to employees infected with the AIDS virus treatment equal to all others in the federal workplace, unless they pose substantial health or safety risks. The AIDS virus is alleged to have infected 1.5 million persons, and more than 37,000 persons have died from the virus.[22]

Can AIDS be a disability incurred in the course of employment? What about the case of a worker who, while at a remote residence, engages in sexual activity and contracts AIDS?[23] On the basis of the only reported case,[24] where the employee contended that his employer condoned his practice of consorting with prostitutes, which was apparently the mores of the community, the hearing resulted in victory for the employee because the employer was found to have sanctioned the mores of the community, and the resulting AIDS could reasonably have been expected.[25]

In passing, we note that there is probably no right of private action under the Vocational Rehabilitation Act of 1963, at least judging by the decision in Trageser v. Libbie Rehabilitation Center,[26] where the Fourth U.S. Court of Appeals held that no private judicial remedy exists for employment discrimination by employers receiving federal funds, unless the employment is a primary objective of the federal aid received by the defendant employer or unless the discrimination in employment necessarily causes discrimination against primary beneficiaries of the federal aid. But a contrary view is seen in LeStrange v. Consolidated Rail Corp.,[27] where the Third U.S. Court of Appeals in 1982 ruled that the prohibition against discrimination can be enforced by means of a private civil action.

5.4 HOMOSEXUALITY AS A HANDICAP DISCRIMINATION

Homosexuality is recognized as a handicap for purposes of discrimination, as perhaps best illustrated in Watkins v. U.S. Army,[28] where the Ninth U.S. Court of Appeals in 1988 held that Army regulations that barred homosexuals from military service constituted discrimination in violation of the Fourteenth Amendment's equal protection clause. Plaintiff had enlisted in the Army in 1967 at the age of 19; at that time he filled out a standardized questionnaire marking "yes" in response to a question asking whether he then or in the past had homosexual tendencies. An Army psychiatrist nevertheless found him qualified for military service; note that there was no outright prohibition in 1967 against homosexuals in the Army. He received an honorable discharge in 1970, reenlisted, and in 1976 was accepted for a six-year term of duty. But in 1975 a board of officers was convened to determine whether he should be discharged for his homosexual tendencies. His commanding officer and coworkers testified to his outstanding work and stated that his homosexuality caused no problems. Plaintiff was retained in the military service; in 1979 he reenlisted for another three years despite the fact that his security clearance had been revoked, based upon his admission that he was a homosexual.

In 1981 Army regulations eliminated the discretion of commanding officers as to homosexuality, with the result that new regulations focused heavily on a soldier's intent or mental state with respect to homosexual acts.[29] Pursuant to these new regulations the Army rejected Watkins's application to reenlist, and the federal district court agreed with the Army determination. On appeal to the Ninth U.S. Court of Appeals, he argued that the new Army regulations violate the First Amendment by penalizing him for his statements regarding his homosexuality and also violate the Fifth Amendment and the Fourteenth Amendment equal protection guarantees by discriminating against him because of his homosexual orientation.

The Ninth U.S. Court of Appeals ruled that, even if his statements declaring his homosexual orientation are protected under the First Amendment, the Army regulations provide alternative grounds for disqualification. But the court found that the regulations did discriminate against persons of homosexual orientation, noting that the regulations provided that if a person is found to have engaged in homosexual acts, he or she may still qualify for the Army by proving his or her orientation is heterosexual rather than homosexual; and furthermore that the regulations explicitly state that the Army's policy is to allow "retention only of nonhomosexual soldiers" who, even if they have engaged in homosexual acts, can demonstrate that there were "extenuating circumstances" as specifically set out in the regulations.[30] The court observed that homosexuals have been the victims of pernicious discrimination as well as sustained hostility and violence;[31] and that

sexual orientation (like race) plainly has no relevance to a person's ability to perform or to contribute to society. . . . Racial discrimination . . . would not suddenly become constitutional if medical science developed an easy, cheap, and painless method of changing one's skin pigment. . . . It may be that some heterosexuals and homosexuals can change their sexual orientation through extensive therapy, neurosurgery or shock treatment. But the possibility of such a difficult and traumatic change does not make sexual orientation "mutable" for equal protection purposes.[32]

It should be noted that this decision may conflict with the U.S. Supreme Court's decision in Hardwick v. Bowers,[33] rejecting a homosexual's constitu-

tional challenge to Georgia's sodomy law and holding that there is no constitutional right of privacy that protects acts of homosexual sodomy. The highest
court in 1986 disclosed "willingness to condone anti-homosexual animus in the
actions of the government."

There are innumerable acts of state and local legislative bodies on homosexual discrimination, one of the most "liberal" being the Act of the City Council
of the City of New York, amending the Administrative Code by adding a new
Section B1-7.2, prohibiting discrimination on the basis of sexual orientation.[34]

5.5   VETERANS AND DISCRIMINATION

Federal law imposes on private employers many nondiscriminatory obligations
toward veterans. For example, private employers may not deny an employee
job retention, advancement, or any other benefit because of the employee's
obligations as a member of a reserve component of the military forces.[35] Employers must grant leaves of absence to their employees for active military
duty,[36] and reinstate their former employees upon request after periods of military duty.[37] And federal contractors must engage in affirmative action programs toward certain veterans as applicants for employment and as employees.[38] All of these obligations benefiting veterans are in effect prohibitions against
discrimination; but in Monroe v. Standard Oil Co.[39] the highest court pointed
out that employers need not make accommodations to provide reservists or
veterans with special benefits due to their lost work time; the only accommodations required are leaves of absence and nondiscrimination due to such absences.

Enlistees in the military services must satisfy several conditions in order to
have reemployment rights upon timely application for employment, such as
release from the armed forces under honorable conditions, application for employment filed after not more than four years' total military service up to 1961,
and up to five years' total military service after 1961.[40]

NOTES

1. See U.S. Dept. of HEW, Digest of Data on Persons with Disability 3, table 1
(May 1979).
2. 29 U.S.C. 701–796.
3. See 41 C.F.R. 60–741.3(a)(1).
4. 29 U.S.C. 707(a) defines "handicapped person" as "any person who (i) has a
physical or mental impairment which substantially limits one or more major life activities, (ii) has a record of such an impairment, or (iii) is regarded as having such an
impairment." 45 C.F.R. § 84.3(j)(2) (1982) defines *physical or mental impairment* to
include: (A) any physiological disorder or condition, cosmetic disfigurement, or anatomical loss affecting one or more of the following body systems: neurological; musculo-
skeletal; special sense organs; respiratory including speech organs; cardiovascular; re-
productive, digestive, genito-urinary; hemic and lymphatic; skin; and endocrine; or (B)

any mental or psychological disorder, such as mental retardation, organic brain syndrome, emotional or mental illness, and specific learning disabilities.
See E. E. Black, Ltd., v. Marshall, 497 F.Supp. 1088 (Hawaii, 1980).

5. 662 F.2d 292 (5th Cir. 1981).

6. See Davis v. Bucher, 451 F.Supp. 791 (E.D. Pa. 1978). Also note Trial Magazine 29 (July 1987).

7. Note Whitlock v. Donovan, 598 F.Supp. 126 (D.D.C. 1984).

8. 600 F.Supp. 757 (D.D.C. 1985).

9. See Schlei & Grossman, Employment Discrimination Law (2d ed., 1979).

10. 500 A.2d 1005 (D.D.C. 1985).

11. 802 F.2d 1016 (8th Cir. 1986).

12. See Trial Magazine 31 (July 1987).

13. —N.Y.S.2d—(New York County, July 18, 1988).

14. See 7 Legal Notes and Viewpoints Q 45 (1986).

15. Dept. of Fair Employment and Housing v. Raytheon Co., —Cal. Rptr.— (1987).

16. —N.E.2d— (Mass. 1986).

17. Supra notes 14, 15, and 16.

18. 55 U.S.L.W. 2009 (July 1, 1986).

19. 107 S.Ct. 1123 (1987).

20. See New York Times, August 27, 1987, at 14.

21. See New York Times, October 7, 1988, at A17.

22. Id.

23. See generally Danzig, "Compensability for A.I.D.S. Under Workers' Compensation Laws," N.Y.L.J. (October 21, 1988).

24. Paul Trejo, Claimant Case No. 85 BGN 100-539, Workers' Compensation Appeals Board, May 1987.

25. See also A.B.A.J. 24 (October 1, 1988), posing the dilemma for all employers, i.e., avoiding discrimination while addressing coworkers' fears.

26. 590 F.2d 87 (4th Cir. 1978).

27. 687 F.2d 767 (3rd Cir. 1982).

28. 837 F.2d 1428 (9th Cir. 1988).

29. A.R. 635-200, 635–280, as follows:

A.R. 635-200
15-2 Definitions

a. Homosexual means a person, regardless of sex, who engages in, desires to engage in, or intends to engage in homosexual acts.

b. Bisexual means a person who engages in, desires to engage in, or intends to engage in homosexual and heterosexual acts.

c. A homosexual act means bodily contact, actively undertaken or passively permitted, between soldiers of the same sex for sexual satisfaction.

15-3 Criteria

The basis for separation may include preservice, prior service, or current service conduct or statements. A soldier will be separated per this chapter if one or more of the following approved findings is made:

a. The soldier has engaged in, attempted to engage in, or solicited another to engage in a homosexual act unless there are further approved findings that—

(1) Such conduct is a departure from the soldier's usual and customary behavior, and

(2) Such conduct is unlikely to recur because it is shown, for example, that the act occurred because of immaturity, intoxication, coercion, or a desire to avoid military service, and

(3) Such conduct was not accomplished by use of force, coercion, or intimidation by the soldier during a period of military service, and

(4) Under the particular circumstances of the case, the soldier's continued presence in the Army is consistent with the interest of the Army in proper discipline, good order, and morale, and

(5) The soldier does not desire to engage in or intend to engage in homosexual acts.

Note: To warrant retention of a soldier after finding that he or she engaged in, attempted to engage in, or solicited another to engage in a homosexual act, the board's findings must specifically include all *five* findings listed in (1) through (5) above. In making these additional findings, boards should reasonably consider the evidence presented. For example, engagement in homosexual acts over a long period of time could hardly be considered "a departure from the soldier's usual and customary behavior." The intent of this policy is to permit retention *only* of *nonhomosexual* soldiers who, because of extenuating circumstances (as demonstrated by findings required by para 15-3a (1) through (5)) engaged in, attempted to engage in, or solicited a homosexual act.

b. The soldier has stated that he or she is a homosexual or bisexual unless there is a further finding that the soldier is not a homosexual or bisexual.

c. The soldier has married or attempted to marry, a person known to be of the same biological sex (as evidenced by the external anatomy of the person involved) unless there are further findings that the soldier is not a homosexual or bisexual (such as, where the purpose of the marriage or attempt to marry was the avoidance or termination of military service.)

A.R. 635-280

Applicants to whom the disqualifications below apply are ineligible for RA (Regular Army) reenlistment at any time and requests for waiver or exception to policy will not be submitted. . . .

c. Persons of questionable moral character and a history of antisocial behavior, sexual perversion or homosexuality. A person who has committed homosexual acts or is an admitted homosexual but as to whom there is no evidence that they have engaged in homosexual acts either before or during military service is included. (See note 1) . . .

k. Persons being discharged under AR 635-200 for homosexuality . . .

Note: Homosexual acts consist of bodily contact between persons of the same sex, actively undertaken or passively permitted, with the intent of obtaining or giving sexual satisfaction, or any proposal, solicitation, or attempt to perform such an act. Persons who have been involved in homosexual acts in an apparently isolated episode, stemming solely from immaturity, curiousity [sic], or intoxication, and in the absence of other evidence that the person is a homosexual, normally will not be excluded from reenlistment. A homosexual is a person, regardless of sex, who desires bodily contact between persons of the same sex, actively undertaken or passively permitted, with the intent to obtain or give sexual gratification. Any official, private, or public profession of homosexuality, may be considered in determining whether a person is an admitted homosexual.

30. Id.

31. See High Tech Gays v. Defense Industrial Security Clearance Office, —F. Supp.— (N.D. Cal. 1987).

32. Supra note 28 at p. 1446.
33. 106 S. Ct. 2841 (1986).
34.

To amend the administrative code of the City of New York, in relation to unlawful discriminatory practices.

Be it enacted by the Council as follows:

§1. Legislative declaration. The Council reaffirms its finding and declaration articulated in the law establishing the city commission on human rights that in the city of New York, with its great cosmopolitan population consisting of large numbers of people of diverse backgrounds, beliefs, and ways of life, there is no greater danger to the well-being of the city and its inhabitants than the existence of groups prejudiced against one another and antagonistic to each other. It further reiterates that prejudice, intolerance, bigotry, and discrimination occasioned thereby threaten the rights and proper privileges of the city's inhabitants and menace the institutions and foundation of a free democratic state.

The Council notes that, throughout the history of the city, many New Yorkers have encountered prejudice on account of their sexual orientation. In some instances the prejudice has impaired access to employment, housing, and other basic necessities of life leading to deprivation and suffering. In addition, it has fostered a general climate of hostility and distrust, even to the point of physical violence against those perceived to be homosexual.

The Council hereby finds and declares that discrimination on the basis of sexual orientation exists, that it unjustly threatens the well-being of thousands of New Yorkers, and that it should be prohibited in regard to employment, housing, land, commercial space and public accommodations.

In doing so, the Council wishes to make clear that it is not the function of this civil rights statute to promote a particular group or community; its purpose is rather to ensure that individuals who live in our society will have the opportunity to pursue their own beliefs and conduct their lives as they see fit within the limits of the law.

§2. Title B of chapter one of the administrative code of the City of New York is amended by adding a new section B1-7.2 to read as follows: B1-7.2 Unlawful discriminatory practices—sexual orientation.

1. The provisions heretofore set forth in section B1-7.0 as unlawful discriminatory practices shall be construed to include discrimination against individuals because of their actual or perceived sexual orientation.

2. Nothing in this section shall be construed to: a. Restrict an employer's right to insist that an employee meet bona fide job-related qualifications of employment; b. Authorize or require employers to establish affirmative action quotas based on sexual orientation or to make inquiries regarding the sexual orientation of current or prospective employees; c. Limit or override the present exemptions to the human rights law, including those relating to employment concerns having fewer than four employees, as provided in subdivision five of section B1-2.0; owner-occupied dwellings, as provided in paragraph (a) of subdivision five of section B1-7.0; or any religious or denominational institution or organization, or any organization operated for charitable or educational purposes, which is operated, supervised or controlled by or in connection with a religious organization, as provided in subdivision nine of section B1-7.0; d. Make lawful any act that violates the penal law of the state of New York; or e. Endorse any particular behavior or way of life.

3. As used in this section, the term "sexual orientation" shall mean heterosexuality, homosexuality, or bisexuality.

§3. This local law shall take effect immediately.

35. See 38 U.S.C. 2021(b)(3), which provides that "any person who holds a position . . . [other than a temporary job] shall not be denied retention in employment or any promotion or other incident or advantage of employment because of any obligation as a member of a Reserve component of the Armed Forces."

36. See 38 U.S.C. 2024(d),(e), and (f).
37. See 38 U.S.C. 2021(a) and 2024.
38. See 38 U.S.C. 2021(a).
39. 101 S. Ct. 2510 (1981).
40. See 38 U.S.C. 2024(a) and (g).

6

Sexual Harassment in the Workplace

6.1 INTRODUCTION

In recent years sexual harassment has become a cause célèbre as a cause of action directed against employers, who perhaps in prior years had not recognized the widespread practice.[1] It was in 1976 that a federal court first recognized sexual harassment as a cause of action under Title VII of the Civil Rights Act of 1964. This decision of Williams v. Saxbe[2] was followed by such cases as Barnes v. Costle,[3] holding that the sexually harassed plaintiff must show that her supervisor conditioned the granting or denying of economic benefits upon the receipt of sexual favors, and Bundy v. Jackson,[4] holding that the sexually harassed plaintiff need not demonstrate such economic reprisal if she can show that she was forced to suffer "sexually stereotyped insults and demeaning propositions" in an environment pervaded by hostile sexual innuendo and behavior.

And in Meritor Savings Bank, FSB v. Vinson[5] the U.S. Supreme Court unanimously upheld the extension of Title VII to embrace claims for sexual harassment, although in 1986 the highest court did not hold employers in the hostile environment situation "strictly liable" for the harassment perpetrated by supervisors. The Court was concerned that evidence of a plaintiff's speech and dress should be "relevant" to a determination of whether the alleged sexual advances were unwelcome to the plaintiff! The court opined that "sexual misconduct constitutes prohibited 'sexual harassment' whether or not it is directly linked to the grant or denial of an economic quid pro quo." In point of fact, sexual harassment, according to the Court, meant unwelcome sexual advances where "such conduct has the purpose or effect of unreasonably interfering with an individual's work performance or creating an intimidating, hos-

tile, or offensive working environment." Yet the court was unwilling to set a
guideline calling for strict liability on the part of employers in cases of quid
pro quo sexual harassment, preferring to state simply that the "absence of
notice to an employer does not necessarily insulate that employer from liability."

Among federal government employees it was estimated in 1981 that 42 percent of the 694,000 women and 15 percent of the 1,168,000 men had experi-
enced some form of sexual harassment in the federal workplace.[6]

6.2 STATES AND SEXUAL HARASSMENT

The states have also enacted legislation on the issue of sexual harassment in
the workplace, and today the vast number of actions in the state courts attest
to the popularity of state remedies, as illustrated by the recent New York case
of Perez v. Merrill Lynch Pierce Fenner & Smith.[7] Here the plaintiff employee
brought a personal injury suit against her employer, alleging that she had been
sexually assaulted by a coworker in an elevator at the place of business. The
court pointed out that "workers' compensation is the exclusive remedy for
injuries sustained by an employee in the course of employment. . . . Nor can
the court sanction circumvention of the statutory remedy by permitting an employer to be sued in his capacity as property owner or lessee and thus be treated
as a dual legal personality." However, the New York court held that she could
amend her pleading to maintain a civil rights action against her employer under
Section 40-c of the New York Civil Rights Law for allegedly allowing sexual
harassment in the workplace.

In California in Vinson v. Superior Court[8] it was held that a woman who
alleged sexual harassment cannot be "grilled" about her own private sex life.
The California Supreme Court observed that the plaintiff widow had suffered
severe emotional distress during a school employment interview when the in-
terviewer made salacious remarks and told her that she would not be hired
unless she had sexual relations with him. However, the plaintiff must submit
to a limited psychiatric examination with respect to her claim of emotional
distress. Thus, the prospective employee's right of privacy was upheld.

And in the District of Columbia in Broderick v. SEC[9] the court held that the
female lawyer with the SEC was the victim of sexual harassment because she
worked in a hostile environment where those who submitted to sexual advances
received preferential treatment. The pervasive sexual atmosphere was found to
have undermined the motivation and work performance of the female plaintiff.
The court approved a settlement involving promotion retroactive eight years
and back pay.[10]

Individuals who have suffered sexual harassment are not limited to Title VII
claims but may also seek redress for their injuries in state courts for a variety
of claims. In the New Hampshire case of Monge v. Beebe Rubber Co.[11] the
termination of an employee who refused to date her supervisor was held to

violate an implied-in-fact covenant of good faith and fair dealing between employer and employee. Traditional tort theories have also been successfully advanced in sexual harassment cases.[12]

6.3   TITLE VII AND SEXUAL HARASSMENT

A review of court decisions on Title VII of the Civil Rights Act of 1964 spells out the many interesting details of the basic issue that sexual harassment is a blatant form of discrimination. But in Corne v. Bausch and Lomb, Inc.[13] the federal district court in Arizona ruled that the verbal and physical sexual advances of a supervisor against two female employees was a "personal proclivity, peculiarity or mannerism" and in no way related to the nature of the employment. Accordingly, that behavior did not subject the employer to any liability under Title VII for discrimination. However, in Barnes v. Costle,[14] two years earlier, the District of Columbia Court of Appeals had ruled that "an employer is chargeable with Title VII violations occasioned by the discriminatory practices of supervisory personnel," although once the employer discovers the practices, the employer "may be relieved from responsibility under Title VII" if the employer immediately rectifies the situation. But liability may be imposed against an employer for acts of sexual harassment by coworkers where the employer knew of, but failed to redress, the sexual harassment.[15] In Tomkins v. Public Service Electric & Gas Co.[16] the Third U.S. Court of Appeals found that before an employer can be liable for sexual harassment by one of its supervisory personnel, the employer must have participated "directly or vicariously" in the sexual harassment, and thus have "actual or constructive knowledge" of the sexual harassment. In Henson v. City of Dundee[17] the Eleventh U.S. Court of Appeals weakened the standard of employer liability by asserting that, unlike the supervisor who, in the case of quid pro quo harassment, "relies upon his apparent or actual authority to extort sexual consideration," a supervisor creating a hostile environment "does so for his own reasons . . . [and] thus acts outside the actual or apparent scope of the authority he possesses as a supervisor."

It should be observed that Title VII allows courts to award a victorious plaintiff reinstatement in the position, back pay, or "any other equitable relief as the court deems appropriate."[18] Thus, Title VII can effectively stifle sexual harassment and operate to redress discrimination against protected groups rather than individuals only. Some of the equitable remedies include injunctions forbidding sexual harassment or mandating the establishment of grievance procedures, as well as back pay awards, reinstatement, promotion, attorneys' fees, and court costs.[19] In Guyette v. Stauffer Chemical Co.[20] the federal district court in New Jersey not only found sexual harassment under Title VII but also allowed state law tort claims of assault and battery, intentional and negligent infliction of emotional distress, and interference with contractual relations, inter alia. The court found that "the State and federal claims arose out of the same nucleus of operative fact."

NOTES

1. See generally 10 Harv. L. Rev. 276 et seq. (1986).

2. 413 F. Supp. 654 (D.D.C. 1976), rev'd on other grounds sub nom Williams v. Bell, 587 F.2d 1240 (D.C. Cir. 1978).

3. 561 F.2d 983 (D.C. Cir. 1977).

4. 641 F.2d 934 (D.C. Cir. 1981).

5. 106 S.Ct. 2399 (1986).

6. See Dolkart and Malchow, "Sexual Harassment in the Workplace: Expanding Remedies," 33 Torts & Ins. L. J. 181 (Fall 1987).

7. —N.Y.S.2d— (New York County, July 14, 1988).

8. —Cal. Rptr.— (September 14, 1987).

9. —F.R.D.— (D.D.C. 1988).

10. See A.B.A.J. 21 (August 1, 1988).

11. 316 A.2d 549 (N.H. 1974).

12. See Montgomery, "Sexual Harassment in the Workplace: A Practitioner's Guide to Tort Actions", 10 Golden Gate U. L. Rev. 879 (1980).

13. 309 F. Supp. 161 (Ariz. 1979).

14. 561 F.2d 983 (D.D.C. 1977).

15. See Kyriazi v. Western Electric Co., 461 F. Supp. 894 (N.J. 1978). Also supra note 6.

16. 568 F.2d 1044 (3rd Cir. 1977).

17. 682 F.2d 897 (11th Cir. 1982).

18. 42 U.S.C. 2000-e-5 (g).

19. See Bundy v. Jackson, 641 F.2d 934 (D.C. Cir. 1981).

20. 518 F.Supp. 521 (N.J. 1981).

7

Other Federal Statutes on Employment

7.1 PREEMPTION GENERALLY

The existence of the many federal statutory remedies for employment situations may preclude resort to common law or state or local judicial remedies. "Preemption," or statutory preclusion,[1] arises when a federal statutory remedy and a state common law, for example, exist for the same conduct. The consequence is that the supremacy clause of the U.S. Constitution applies,[2] or that the "primary jurisdiction" doctrine authorizes the particular federal agency to address the same factual circumstances first.[3] However, most federal laws covering employee relations either present no federal-state jurisdictional conflict or set conditions for preemption if conflicts arise. In broad terms "preemption" means the overriding authority of Congress and the federal government to decide whether a given federal statute applicable to the facts of the situation shall set the minimum standards and allow states and localities to set higher standards, or whether the given federal statute shall accomplish the opposite or reverse. The Fair Labor Standards Act,[4] for example, sets minimum wages, maximum hours for child labor, and maximum hours that may be worked without the employer paying overtime wages; state laws may supersede the FLSA by imposing higher minimum wages, lower maximum hours for child labor, and lower maximum hours that may be worked without overtime payment.

Preemption problems are likely to arise in employment discrimination instances where res judicata and collateral estoppel are important issues.[5] When the scheme of federal regulation is determined to be so pervasive as to make reasonable the inference that Congress left no room for the state to supplement it, or when the state policy is found likely to produce a result inconsistent with the objective of the federal statute, the doctrine of preemption is invoked.[6]

Preemption arises when an employee seeks to assert a state claim that is also the subject of an unfair labor practice under federal law.[7] Preemption is also an issue when an employee covered by a collective bargaining agreement brings an action for wrongful discharge.[8] A state court may still retain jurisdiction even if it must apply federal laws.[9]

7.2 TITLE IX OF THE EDUCATION AMENDMENTS OF 1982

The operative language of Title IX of the Education Amendments of 1982 states that "(a) no person in the United States shall, on the basis of sex, be excluded from participation in, be denied the benefits, or be subjected to discrimination under any program or activity receiving Federal financial assistance. . . . " In North Haven Board of Education v. Bell[10] the U.S. Supreme Court held that Title IX covers employment discrimination, irrespective of whether the purpose of the funding is to provide employment. The issue of "federal funding" was addressed in Grove City College v. Bell,[11] where the highest court found that the college was subject to Title IX because some of its students received scholarship funds under the Federal Basic Education Opportunity Grant Program and the federal funds reached the college in the form of tuition payments. In short, if federal funds "support a program which is infected by a discriminatory environment, then termination of such funds is proper."[12]

A private right of action is available to enforce the prohibition on sex discrimination, as in Cannon v. University of Chicago.[13] Here the Court held that female medical school applicants who were discriminatorily denied admission could sue in federal court for violation of their rights protected under Title IX because Title IX "has no time limits for action and no conciliation provisions."[14]

7.3 FAIR LABOR STANDARDS ACT OF 1938

The Fair Labor Standards Act of 1938[15] is probably the most important federal statute for protecting the unrepresented, nonunion worker; FLSA led to a standard 40-hour work week, payment of time and a half for overtime, and a minimum wage for all but a few categories of workers. FLSA covers all employees engaged in interstate or foreign commerce if the business has two or more employees who produce goods exceeding $275,000 per year. Exempt under Section 203 are such enterprises as "mom and pop" businesses where only the family is employed, and owners of non-profit organizations not having a business purpose. Also exempt are professional, executive, and administrative workers, as delineated at length in Brock v. Superior Care, Inc.[16] Here the Secretary of Labor brought an action under FLSA alleging that defendant had failed to pay nurses on a time and a half basis for overtime work; defendant countered with the argument that nurses were exempted from the act. The defendant was engaged in the business of referring nurses for temporary duty in hospitals, nursing homes, and patient residences; and defendant paid the nurses on an hourly basis. The Second U.S. Court of Appeals responded to defendant's argument that "even if the nurses are 'employees' under FLSA, they are bona fide professional employees exempt from the overtime pay requirements of FLSA pursuant to Section 13(a)(1) of the Act." The court observed that this section did provide an exemption for

any employee employed in a bona fide professional capacity (as such terms are defined and delimited by regulations of the Secretary of Labor). . . . One of the criteria in the regulations for bona fide professional employees is compensation for services "on a salary or fee basis at a rate of not less than $170 per week". . . . Compensation on a salaried basis occurs when an employee regularly receives, each pay period, a predetermined amount, not subject to reduction because of variations in the quality or quantity of work performed. An employee is paid on a fee basis when he received a fixed sum for a single job regardless of the time required for its completion.

The court concluded that "the nurses do not come within the definition of bona fide professional employees . . . because they are paid on an hourly basis and not by fee or salary."[17]

Preemption[18] of FLSA by state statute adds to and does not weaken the requirements of wage and hour practices.[19] Such issues as compensable work time, meal periods,[20] off-duty and on-call time,[21] compensable waiting time, and compensatory travel time are all frequently litigated.

7.4   ERISA, OR EMPLOYEE RETIREMENT INCOME SECURITY ACT

The Employee Retirement Income Security Act, or ERISA, is one of the more complicated pieces of federal regulation that greatly affect the employment contract.[22] It has been held that ERISA preempts state law claims over medical insurance programs that qualify as ERISA "employee benefit plans."[23] In that case a husband and wife had each filed suit in an Alabama state court charging bad faith and fraud in the failure of the employer to provide their children with surgical benefits. The Second U.S. Court of Appeals in Dister v. The Continental Group, Inc.[24] outlined the standard of proof required to establish that an employer had wrongfully discharged an employee in order to avoid paying pension benefits to the employee. The court found discrimination, since the plaintiff was discharged just four months short of the date he would be entitled to enhanced pension benefits.[25] The three-step process, first set forth by the U.S. Supreme Court in its 1973 decision in McDonnell Douglas Corp. v. Green,[26] required that the employee show a prima facie case of discrimination; then, the burden shifts to the employer to offer some "legitimate, nondiscriminatory reason" for the employer's conduct; and finally, the employee must prove by a "preponderance of the evidence" that the employer's reasons for termination were not legitimate but a pretext for discrimination.[27]

The U.S. Supreme Court in Pilot Life Insurance Co. v. Dedeaux[28] in 1987 held that state common law causes of action relating to improper processing of claims under employee welfare benefit plans regulated by ERISA are preempted by ERISA's broad exemption provision, Section 514(a). Here the employee in 1975 injured his back in an accident related to his employment; his employer sponsored a long-term disability plan that qualified as an employee benefit plan under ERISA for employees who became permanently disabled. The insurance company actually administered the plan and provided the injured employee with benefits for the first two years, but thereafter repeatedly reinstated and terminated benefits until 1980 when his benefits were terminated permanently. He sued both the employer and the insurer, alleging state common law claims for tortious breach of contract and for breach of fiduciary duty and fraud. The insurer successfully moved for summary judgment on the ground that ERISA preempted his state law claims and that ERISA provided the exclusive remedy for the alleged mishandling of his benefits. The Fifth U.S. Court of Appeals reversed[29] on the ground that his state common law claims were "saved" under the ERISA saving clause because they constituted state laws that "regulate insurance." But the U.S. Supreme Court then reversed, holding in favor of preemption: "The express preemption provisions of ERISA are deliberately expansive and designed to establish pension plan regulation as exclusively a federal concern."

In Teper v. Park West Galleries, Inc.[30] the Michigan Supreme Court ruled that the award of future pension benefits in a wrongful discharge law suit against an employer under Michigan law is not precluded by the preemption provision of ERISA. The court observed that the action was not against the employee benefit plan or an administrator or the fiduciary of the plan. Thus, the court reinstated the trial court's award of future pension benefits.

In summary, it should be noted that ERISA, in protecting the pension interests of employees, requires that administrators of a pension fund must handle it so as to protect the employees' interest. The fact that the employer contributed all or part of the money to the pension fund does not entitle the employer to use the fund as though the money still belonged to the employer! Administrators of pension funds must make detailed reports to the U.S. Secretary of Labor. ERISA requires "pension portability," i.e., when an employee moves or transfers to another job or another employer, the employee may transfer the interest to an IRA, or Individual Retirement Account, which may be retained as an individual account or added to the pension plan of the new employer with the latter's consent. ERISA also establishes an insurance plan to protect employees when the employer goes out of business: a Pension Benefit Guaranty Corporation guarantees that the employee will receive benefits in much the same pattern as the FDIC protects bank depositors. This corporation is financed by payments made by employers for every employee covered by the pension plan. And ERISA makes it a crime to fire, discriminate against, or threaten any employee who exercises any right conferred by ERISA.

7.5 UNEMPLOYMENT COMPENSATION

A dismissed employee under appropriate state employment compensation law usually can obtain unemployment compensation benefits if the dismissal was for any reason other than misconduct connected with work.[31] Interestingly, eligibility for unemployment compensation benefits is defined by state and federal law under the cooperative state-federal system.[32] Claimants, on denial of benefits, must have an opportunity for a fair hearing to dispute the denial as well as an opportunity for appeal or review of the determination.

In the Unemployment Relief Act of 1933[33] federal prohibitions against discrimination were first launched, followed by Executive Order 8587 seven years later, prohibiting race and religious discrimination in the federal civil service.[34] But today unemployment compensation insurance laws are state-administered; the first compulsory, public unemployment compensation plan was introduced in 1916 by the Massachusetts legislature. However, the Social Security Act of 1934 contains a mandatory unemployment compensation provision that allows the states to decide which type of plan best fits their needs. This Social Security provision was enforced by the mandatory federal collection of tax on employers and redistribution to the states with conforming unemployment programs.

The state plans are designed in favor of the employee, with the burden of proof on the employer to establish why a benefit should not be paid. State statutes delineate benefit amounts, eligibility requirements, and reasons why an unemployed person should be denied benefits or be disqualified from receiving further unemployment insurance benefits.

7.6 EXECUTIVE ORDER 11246

Executive Order 11246, as amended,[35] requires that all federal government contractors refrain from employment discrimination and furthermore develop affirmative action plans for all their employees.[36] Executive Order 11246 requires an immense amount of paperwork, provides for substantial penalties for noncompliance, and ensures remedial action that can be imposed as a condition of doing business with the federal government. Exemptions are common, ranging from contracts with financial institutions and depositories holding federal funds to contracts not exceeding $10,000 other than government bills of lading. Regulations permit case-by-case exemptions for specific contracts, facilities, and the like.[37] Underpinning Executive Order 11246 are such legislative enactments as the Federal Property and Administrative Services Act of 1964, as amended;[38] Titles VI and VII of the Civil Rights Act of 1964;[39] and the Equal Employment Opportunity Act of 1972.[40]

Under Executive Order 11246 all nonexempt contracts and subcontracts must include an equal opportunity clause that sets forth the federal contractor's obligation during the performance of the contract. These obligations extend to the relationship with present and prospective employees, the government itself, and third parties to the contract.[41]

It appears that there is no private right of action for violation of Executive Order 11246,[42] but a private person may bring an action in the nature of mandamus to compel administrative action to enforce the executive order.[43]

7.7   CIVIL RIGHTS ATTORNEY'S FEES AWARDS ACT

To facilitate private enforcement of civil rights laws by enabling winning plaintiffs to recover attorneys' fees was the avowed purpose of the Civil Rights Attorney's Fees Awards Act.[44] But the efficacy of the act has been diminished by the simultaneous negotiation of damages, injunctive relief, *and* attorneys' fees, perhaps conditioning favorable offers regarding the merits of the case on the immediate acceptance of full or partial waivers of attorneys' fees by the lawyer for the plaintiff seeking redress for a civil rights violation.[45]

In Sears v. Atchison, Topeka & Santa Fe Railroad Co.[46] the Tenth U.S. Court of Appeals refused to apply retroactively a limitation on contingency fees in civil rights actions. In 1972 the attorney agreed to represent 22 black railroad employees alleging racial discrimination in pay and in promotion. Plaintiffs agreed that the attorney would receive a contingency fee of 40 percent of the total recovery if an appeal was taken and the plaintiffs prevailed. The case subsequently became a part of a class action with 73 plaintiffs, and the attorney served as lead counsel for the class action. He secured a final judgment of $8.2 million for his 22 clients. The federal district court awarded him $400,000 under the act, and the attorney appealed, seeking a fee of $1.5 million. The federal appellate court reversed, refusing to accept Cooper v. Singer,[47] which held that attorneys' fees are limited to the statutory fee determined by the federal district court as reasonable under the act: "Mr. Paup pursued this complex, difficult litigation as lead counsel over a period of some thirteen years. He performed diligently and skillfully. He represented clients with limited finances. He assumed the risk of nonrecovery in prolonged and combative litigation. Under all the circumstances, the contingent fee contracts were reasonable."

And in Hamner v. Rios[48] the Ninth U.S. Court of Appeals held that statutory attorneys' fees cannot be denied in a federal civil rights action merely because the winning plaintiff agreed to pay his lawyer a contingency fee. The U.S. Supreme Court in Evans v. Jeff D.[49] in 1986 ruled that it was within each trial court's discretion to approve or not to approve simultaneous negotiations and fee waivers, thus perhaps crippling civil rights litigation to a great extent.[50]

NOTES

1. See Warren Freedman, Res Judicata and Collateral Estoppel (1988).
2. See Article VI thereof.
3. See U.S. v. Western Pacific Railroad Co., 352 U.S. 59 (1956).
4. See infra Section 7.3.
5. Supra note 1.
6. Note Napier v. Atlantic Coast Line Railroad Co., 272 U.S. 605 (1926) and Cloverleaf Butter Co. v. Patterson, 315 U.S. 148 (1942).
7. See Belknap, Inc. v. Hale, 103 S.Ct. 3172 (1983).
8. See chapter 3.
9. See Clafin v. Houseman, 93 U.S. 130 (1876).
10. 456 U.S. 512 (1982).
11. 465 U.S. 555 (1984).
12. See Iron Arrow Society v. Heckler, 702 F.2d 549 (5th Cir. 1983).
13. 441 U.S. 677 (1979).
14. Note Strong v. Demopolis City Board of Education, 515 F.Supp. 730 (S.D. Ala. 1981) involving a suit by a school teacher employee.
15. 29 U.S.C. 207 et seq.
16. 840 F.2d 1054 (2nd Cir. 1988).
17. The Second U.S. Court of Appeals also expounded on the issue of "whether the workers are employees or independent contractors:"

The FLSA defines "employee" as "any individual employed by an employer," and to "employ" as including "to suffer or permit to work." 29 USC §§203(e)(1), 203(g) (1982 & Supp. Ill 1985). The definition is necessarily a broad one in accordance with the remedial purpose of the Act. See *United States v. Rosenwasser*, 323 U.S. 360, 363 (1945); *Real v. Driscoll Strawberry Associates, Inc.*, 603 F.2d 748, 754 (9th Cir. 1979).

Several factors are relevant in determining whether individuals are "employees" or independent contractors for purposes of the FLSA. These factors, derived from *United States v. Silk*, 331 U.S. 704 (1947) (Social Security Act), and known as the "economic reality test," include: (1) the degree of control exercised by the employer over the workers, (2) the workers' opportunity for profit or loss and their investment in the business, (3) the degree of skill and independent initiative required to perform the work, (4) the permanence or duration of the working relationship, and (5) the extent to which the work is an integral part of the employer's business. See *id.* at 716; *Rutherford Food Corp. v. McComb*, 331 U.S. 722, 730 (1947); *Donovan v. DialAmerica Marketing, Inc.* 757 F.2d 1376, 1382–83 (3d Cir.) cert. denied, 474 U.S. 919 (1985); *Real v. Driscoll Strawberry Associates, Inc.* supra, 603 F.2d at 754; *Usery v. Pilgrim Equipment Co., Inc.*, 527 F.2d 8, 12 (2d Cir. 1984) (considering somewhat different factors in "economic reality" test where question was whether an employment relationship existed between a prison inmate and an outside employer). No one of these factors is dispositive; rather, the test is based on a totality of the circumstances. See *Rutherford Food Corp. v. McComb*, supra, 331 U.S. at 730; *Usery v.Pilgrim Equipment Co., Inc.*, supra, 527 F.2d at 1311. The ultimate concern is whether, as a matter of economic reality, the workers depend upon someone else's business for the opportunity to render service or are in business for themselves. See *Bartels v. Birmingham*, 332 U.S. 126, 130 (1947) (Social Security act); *Donovan v. Tehco, Inc.*, 642 F.2d 141, 143 (5th Cir. 1981) (FLSA).

The existence and degree of each factor is a question of fact while the legal conclusion to be drawn from those facts—whether workers are employees or independent contractors—is a question of law. Thus, a district court's findings as to the underlying factors must be accepted unless clearly erroneous, while review of the ultimate question of employment status is *de novo*. See *Brock v. Mr. Fireworks, Inc.*, 814 F.2d 1042, 1043–45 (5th Cir.), *cert. denied*, 108 S.Ct. 286, (1987);

Bonnette v. California Health and Welfare Agency, 704 F.2d 1465, 1469 (9th Cir. 1983). In the present case, the District Judge properly looked to the economic reality test and the *Silk* factors in deciding that the nurses were employees. Superior Care contends that some of his findings of fact were clearly erroneous and that he relied on irrelevant evidence. We disagree.

18. See Supra Section 7.1.

19. See Mumblower v. Callicott, 526 F.2d 1183 (8th Cir. 1985).

20. See Ballard v. Consolidated Steel Corp., 61 F.Supp. 996 (S.D. Cal. 1945).

21. See Skidmore v. Swift & Co., 323 U.S. 134 (1944).

22. See 29 U.S.C. 1001 to 1461.

23. Belasco v. WKP Wilson & Sons, —F.2d— (11th Cir. 1987).

24. —F.2d— (2nd Cir. October 3, 1988).

25. Note that Section 510 of ERISA makes it illegal for employers to discharge any employee for the purpose of cutting off employee benefits.

26. 411 U.S. 792 (1973).

27. See Hartford Courant, October 4, 1988, at 1 et seq.

28. 107 S.Ct. 1548 (1987).

29. 770 F.2d 1311 (5th Cir. 1985).

30. —N.W. 2d— (Mich. August 24, 1988).

31. See generally 76 Am. Jur. 2d §§52–58 (1975).

32. Note Federal Unemployment Tax Act, 26 U.S.C. 3304 (a)(10).

33. 48 Stat. 22, Act of March 31, 1933.

34. 5 Fed. Reg. 4445 (1940).

35. Exec. Order No. 11,246, §202(1), 30 Fed. Reg. 12,319 (Sept. 28, 1965), *reprinted in* 42 U.S.C. §2000e, at 19 (West 1981), *as amended by* Exec. Order No. 11,375, 32 Fed. Reg. 14,303 (Oct. 17, 1967). Executive Order 11,246 was signed September 24, 1965, and became effective October 24, 1965. It superseded Executive Orders 10,925 and 11,114, which contained similar provisions but provided for administration by the President's Committee on Equal Employment Opportunities. Executive Order 11,375 was signed on October 13, 1967, effective in part on November 12, 1967, and in part on October 14, 1968, and amended Executive Order 11,246 by substituting the word *religion* for *creed* and adding the word *sex.*

36. Written affirmative action plans are required of employers with 50 or more employees and a contract or subcontract worth $50,000 or more, 41 C.F.R. §60-2.1 (1982).

37. See 41 C.F.R. §60-1.5(b), for example.

38. 40 U.S.C. 471 et seq.

39. 42 U.S.C. 2000d et seq.

40. 42 U.S.C. 2000e et seq.

41. See U.S. v. Mississippi Power & Light Co., 553 F.2d 480 (5th Cir. 1977).

42. See Weiss v. Syracuse University, 522 F.2d 397 (2nd Cir. 1975).

43. See Chamber of Commerce v. Legal Aid Society, 447 U.S. 921 (1980).

44. 42 U.S.C. 1988 (1982); see also 100 Harv. L. Rev. 258 et seq. (1986).

45. Note Lazar v. Pierce, 757 F.2d 435 (1st Cir. 1985), upholding a civil rights plaintiff's waiver of attorney's fees in the same consent decree.

46. 779 F.2d 1450 (10th Cir. 1985).

47. 719 F.2d 1496 (10th Cir. 1983).

48. 769 F.2d 1404 (9th Cir. 1985).

49. 106 S.Ct. 1531 (1986).

50. See 100 Harv. L. Rev. 259 (1986).

8

Workplace Injuries to Employees

8.1 INTRODUCTION

Lawsuits by employees for workplace injuries are common, not only because of the expansion of tort and contract law theories favorable to injured employees, but also because of the sophistication of lawyers representing injured employees. The insurance industry[1] is particularly alert to this growing trend of compensating injured employees far beyond the avowed limits of workers' compensation statutes.[2]

State and local legislative bodies have been greatly concerned about workplace injuries, as Suffolk County, New York, most recently illustrated in Local Law No. 21, "A Local Law Providing Employee Protection Against Video Display Terminals."[3] This unusual piece of local legislation was attacked in ILC Data Device Corp. v. Suffolk County[4] by a local corporation employing "approximately 2,000 people," on diverse grounds including (a) the work-related injury "may very well have been pre-empted" by ERISA[5] and by New York State's Workers' Compensation Law, "which requires employers to provide examinations and eye-glasses in connection with work related to injury or disability"; (b) Local Law No. 21 "may very well impede the free flow of interstate commerce and violate the Commerce Clause of the U.S. Constitution";[6] and (c) "plaintiffs have further demonstrated that they will suffer irreparable financial hardship, absent the granting of a preliminary injunction inasmuch as plaintiffs will be forced to incur substantial expenses which cannot be reimbursed if it is ultimately decided that Local Law No. 21 is invalid." The most salient argument advanced against the local legislation by the plaintiffs is the lack of evidence that "operators of video display terminals are at risk of any immediate injury or of any permanent injury to their vision." Accordingly, the New York court here granted the preliminary motion to stop Suffolk County from implementing the local legislation, which would have required plaintiff employers to pay 80 percent of the cost of eye examinations and glasses for employees operating video display terminals.

Workplace injuries of employees are generally covered by insurance, particularly workers' compensation.[7] In addition, employers will generally have a comprehensive general liability, or CGL, policy that covers "all sums which the insured shall become legally obligated to pay as damages because of . . . bodily injury."[8] The unfortunate aspect of such insurance coverage, in the absence of exclusivity of workers' compensation, is that employee claims are not limited to physical injury but also encompass emotional distress, mental anguish, and suffering, along with the physical symptoms of such suffering. A majority of courts have concluded that these tangential "injuries" do not constitute "bodily injury" under the standard CGL policy.[9] A minority of cases like Loewenthal v. Security Insurance Co.[10] hold that the CGL policy's definition of "bodily injury" did include "pain, suffering and mental anguish."

A novel type of injury is illustrated in Butler v. Michigan Mutual Insurance Co.,[11] where a former employee sued his employer alleging that the employer had made defamatory statements about the former employee's work performance; that the former employee had been stealing and embezzling money from the employer. Since the CGL policy excluded coverage for obligations of the employer under workers' compensation, unemployment compensation, disability benefits, and similar laws, the Alabama Supreme Court entered summary judgment for the insurer on the ground that the insured employer's defamatory statements clearly were "directly or indirectly related to the employment of such person by the named insured," which coverage is expressly excluded under the CGL policy.

8.2 WORKERS' COMPENSATION INSURANCE FOR EMPLOYEE WORKPLACE INJURIES

Workers' compensation probably evolved from English legislation under King Henry I in the year 1100, which stated that if a person were to die during the course of a mission, the creator of the mission would be held responsible. Early German law similarly held a master liable for a servant's death and required him to make a monetary payment. It was not until 1884 in Germany that the first modern workers' compensation law was enacted, requiring employers to make mandatory contributions for compulsory insurance for industrial accidents to employees. In the United States the first workers' compensation law was passed in 1911 in the State of Wisconsin, and within 30 years all states had similar statutes. The inherent philosophy behind such statutes was simply a recognition that workplace injuries to employees were social problems for the government and not exclusively individual problems. State workers' compensation laws generally pay medical expenses, some portion of wages while the injured employee is incapacitated, and benefits to dependents in case of the employee's death.

Workers' compensation laws, inter alia, were designed to overcome the many common law defenses of employers, such as the fellow servant rule,[12] assumption of risk,[13] and contributory negligence.[14] The purpose of the state legislation was to "spread the loss more evenly throughout the industry"[15] in the sense that occupational injuries are deemed an expense of production. Workers' compensation is a "social compromise"[16] that balances the interests of the employer, the employee, and the government, but the employee exchanges his or her common law right of action for the certainty of a no-fault recovery.[17] Workers' compensation benefits are financed through (a) private insurance,[18] (b) insurance purchased through governmental agencies set up for the purpose,[19] and (c) self-insurance.[20]

The heart of every workers' compensation statute is its coverage formula. The vast majority of the states as well as the federal government in the Federal Longshoreman's and Harbor Workers' Compensation Act (1927) adopted the "arising out of and in the course of employment" formula, as illustrated by the State of Maryland:

Every employer subject to the provisions of this article, shall pay or provide as required herein compensation according to the schedules of this article for the disability or death of his employee resulting from an accidental personal injury sustained by the employee arising out of and in the course of his employment without regard to fault as a cause of such injury.[21]

In contrast, a minority of states and the Federal Employees' Compensation Act (1916) use simply an "in the course of employment" formula and do not favor the "arising out of" concept:

Liability under this chapter shall exist against an employer only where the following conditions concur: (a) Where the employee sustains an injury; (b) Where, at the time of the injury, both the employer and employee are subject to the provisions of this chapter; (c) Where at the time of the injury, the employee is performing service growing out of and incidental to his employment; (d) Where the injury is not intentionally self-inflicted.[22]

Obviously, the different coverage formulas in similar situations and under similar circumstances can result in different remedies, particularly where the employee's conduct is deemed to be a "deviation" from the course of employment.[23] But the base for coverage is still the "accidental injury," i.e., the injury need not result from a violent external event but only from something unexpected.[24] Compensability can also be found where the workplace accelerates or aggravates a preexisting condition or injury or even combines with conditions unrelated to work to cause an injury.[25] Both time and space of employment have been expanded in recent years to encompass a reasonable amount of time and space incidental to the actual hours and locations of employment so as to provide coverage during "coffee breaks," workplace recreational activities, lunch hours, and the trip to and from work.[26]

Today the scope of injuries that are compensable in the workplace has also been greatly expanded. The "wage-loss principle"[27] has been replaced by the increasing recognition that certain permanent injuries, for example, are worthy of compensation even though their effect on wage-earning capacity cannot be readily observed or measured. There has been a proliferation and expansion of the "schedule principle"[28] for the loss of, or loss of use of, arms, legs, fingers, toes, and other body parts, as well as loss of vision and hearing. These permanent partial benefits undoubtedly create excessive costs in both insurance rates and litigation time.[29]

8.3   EXCLUSIVITY OF WORKERS' COMPENSATION

Most states provide that where the workers' compensation statute is applicable, workers' compensation is the *exclusive* remedy for the injury, disease, or death of the employee against the employer and its insurance company, regardless of the question of negligence and the existence of other rights and remedies.[30] This is the rule even when the injury, disease, or death is not totally compensable under workers' compensation; and the burden of proving the affirmative defense that the employee is entitled only to workers' compensation rests upon the employer.[31] In Burlew v. American Mutual Insurance Co.[32] Chief Judge Cooke of the New York Court of Appeals, in reinforcing the exclusivity doctrine against an employee who had inhaled fumes at her workplace and had been hospitalized for surgery declared that

The legislative scheme for workers' compensation benefits is far-reaching. It concerns itself not only with the simple fact of a work-related injury, but it provides a thorough system of regulation, administration, and, where the Legislature has deemed them appropriate, sanctions (see, e.g. Workers' Compensation Law, §§25, 52, 120, 220). Consequently, all employer conduct that is regulated by the Workers' Compensation Law is subject to the protection of that law's exclusivity; if the employer violates any provision of the code, an employee's remedies cannot exceed those granted in the statutes.[33]

It appears that there are at least three general types of exclusivity provisions in state statutes: (1) the narrow type in which the employee waives his or her or even the spouse's common law rights, as illustrated by the New Jersey statute;[34] (2) the middle-of-the-road type in which no liability other than employer's liability to the employee for work-related injury, disease, or death may exist, as illustrated by the California statute;[35] and (3) the broad type under which the exclusion covers all actions by any person arising out of his or her employment for any injury, disease, or death suffered, as illustrated by the

Texas statute.[36] The second and third types of exclusivity provisions are the most popular, and both of these types bar actions for loss of consortium by spouses, for example, as well as actions for loss of parental society by minor children, upon the ground that such causes of action are derivative and do not come into existence until the employee suffers injury, disease, or death, and then are barred under the exclusivity provision.[37]

But the exclusivity provisions do not bar an action against a third-party tortfeasor because the thrust of workers' compensation is to extend immunity only to employers. However, to preclude double recovery, the employee must, if he or she recovers from the third-party tortfeasor, reimburse the employer for the outlay of compensation, with the excess obviously going to the successful plaintiff employee.[38] The third-party action is primarily the employee's cause of action; and where the defendant tortfeasor sues the employer for contribution or indemnity, the majority of courts will not sanction such payment by the employer under the exclusivity provisions of the workers' compensation statute.[39] However, in Skinner v. Reed-Prentice,[40] the Illinois court observed that the employer had misused the machine that injured the employee and so the court allowed a limited contribution by the employer to the defendant and third-party tortfeasor.

The workers' compensation remedy is exclusive not only as to common law tort remedies against the employer but also as to other statutory rights and remedies. An employee cannot recover against his employer under the Federal Employers Liability Act of 1908,[41] the Federal Tort Claims Act of 1946,[42] the Occupational Safety and Health Act of 1970,[43] the Outer Continental Shelf Lands Act of 1978,[44] and other federal acts.[45]

Intentional Acts Exception to Exclusivity

Of the several theories or devices to bypass the workers' compensation system for persons injured, diseased, or killed by toxic torts or hazardous waste disposal, the intentional acts exception is seemingly the most popular. An employer's intentional act that causes injury, disease, or death of an employee gives rise to a common law action for damages, on the reasoning that an intentional act is not accidental and would therefore not fall within the scope of workers' compensation. The nonaccidental character of the injury, disease, or death, however, is not sufficient itself, for liability must be predicated upon intentionally caused conduct. The New York Court of Appeals in Burlew v. American Mutual Insurance Co.[46] ruled that plaintiff's complaint "even when supported by her affidavit, does not describe any conduct remotely approaching the standard of behavior necessary to establish such a claim" based upon "intentional infliction of mental distress.[47] The New York Supreme Court, Bronx County, in Howard v. John Mini Indoor Landscapes, Inc.[48] stated that it was not proper for a court to determine the intentional nature of the employer's conduct until the workers' compensation board had first determined that the employer's conduct was intentional and therefore outside the workers' compensation statute. The court quoted the leading New York Court of Appeals decision in O'Rourke v. Long:[49]

The initial question to be resolved whenever a defense of Work[ers'] Compensation is presented is whether the plaintiff has a right to bring a plenary action. If the right to sue the employer has been stripped away by work[ers'] compensation coverage, it is an arrogation of jurisdiction to consider a tort complaint on its merits. By considering a complaint on its merits . . . the employer would be subject to fending off liability in a forum from which the Legislature provided a shield.[50] . . . [W]here, [as here], the availability of work[ers'] compensation hinges upon the resolution of questions of fact or upon mixed questions of fact and law, the plaintiff may not choose the courts as the forum for the resolution of such questions. The Legislature has placed the responsibility for these determinations with the Work[ers'] Compensation Board and there it must remain. Thus, it would be inappropriate for us to express our own views as to whether, as a matter of law, work[ers'] compensation benefits are available to plaintiff.[51]

Courts faced with the issue of intentional conduct by the employer have generally required a deliberate attempt to harm. Misrepresenting the hazard of pesticide chemicals,[52] allowing toxic fumes to continue in the workplace,[53] and even deliberately removing or rendering inoperative certain safety guards in the workplace[54] were held not to be intentional conduct or the equivalent of a deliberate intent to injure a specific employee.[55] Similarly, the New York Appellate Division in 1981[56] held that plaintiff's allegation of fraud and intentional tort simply did not escape the exclusivity bar of the workers' compensation statute, even though she had contended that her employer, GAF,

falsely and fraudulently stated and represented to plaintiff that she was physically and medically fit for her particular work assignment involving exposure to allegedly carcinogenic chemicals and substances; that from prior medical examinations GAF has actual knowledge that plaintiff was uniquely susceptible to bladder cancer by virtue of constant exposure to carcinogenic substances, yet wantonly and maliciously continued to expose her to those substances; and that GAF fraudulently and carelessly subjected her to carcinogens in persistent and willful violation of safety rules and regulations.[57]

Interestingly, some states have by statute provided that where intentional acts are shown, the compensation award will be increased by a percentage over the award normally available, as a statutory penalty for an employer's willful, intentional, or reckless misconduct.[58] California, one of those states favoring the percentage increase in benefits for intentional acts of the employer, has held that an employer commits willful misconduct when he "turns his mind" to the fact that injury to employees will probably result from his act or omission, yet fails to take appropriate precautions for their safety.[59] California, however, does not permit a tort suit, upholding the exclusivity of workers' compensation.

The Ohio Supreme Court in Blankenship v.Cincinnati Milacron Chemicals

Corp.[60] in 1982 held that workers' compensation laws do not give employers immunity from lawsuits when an employee claims that the employer intentionally caused the injury. Plaintiffs here alleged that their employer knew that poisonous fumes in the plant were causing disease and that the employer failed to correct the hazardous conditions; furthermore, plaintiffs alleged that the employer failed to warn all employees, failed to provide medical examinations as required by law, and failed to report the hazardous conditions to various state and federal agencies as required by law. The Ohio Supreme Court two years later in Jones v. VIP Development Co.[61] ruled that specific intent was not a necessary element in proving an intentional tort: "An intentional tort is an act committed with the intent to injure another, or committed with the belief that such injury is substantially likely to occur."[62] And an employer may be judged to have committed an intentional tort if he fails to warn employees of a known hazard or hazards, or defect or defects, regardless of whether the employer believed the harm was substantially certain to occur. The Ohio Supreme Court by its decision overruled three appellate court decisions that had been consolidated,[63] one of which was Hamlin v. Snow Metal Products Co., involving serious physical injuries to an employee who was exposed to toxic chemicals. Allegedly his employer knew the chemicals were toxic but had misrepresented to the employees that the working conditions were not harmful to their health and that the hazardous conditions had been corrected. The Ohio Supreme Court held that continuing to assure employees of the safety of their workplace constituted an intentional act of wrongdoing.[64] The fact that the employee applied for and received workers' compensation benefits did not bar the employee from recovering damages for an intentional tort.[65] The employer found liable for an intentional tort is not entitled to a setoff equal to the amount of workers' compensation benefits paid out to the employee.[66]

On the other hand, the North Carolina Supreme Court decision in Freeman v. SCM Corporation[67] favored the exclusivity provisions of the workers' compensation statute because the employer's act was found not to be intentional. Here the employee reported to her supervisor that the molding machine was malfunctioning, but nevertheless she was ordered to continue operating the machine. As a result she was struck in the face by a pressure bolt that blew out of the machine. The court affirmed the dismissal of this suit, although it acknowledged that the injured employee had "in fact . . . no 'selection' as to the appropriate avenue of recovery for her injuries."[68] On similar facts the Fifth U.S. Court of Appeals in Boudeloche v. Grow Chemical Coatings Corporation[69] reversed a dismissal of the injured employee's suit by finding an intentional act: "If the actor knows that the consequences are certain, or substantially certain, to result from his act and still goes ahead, he is treated by the law as if he had in fact desired to produce the result."[70] But in a series of asbestos cases the courts failed to find an intentional act or acts on the part of employers, or any support for the allegation that the employers were forewarned with knowledge of the imminent peril of asbestos.[71] However, in Johns-

Manville Products Corp. v. Rudkin[72] the California court permitted an employee to recover in tort for an aggravation of the disease because the employer fraudulently concealed the employee's disease.

A federal court in Montana in 1984 held in Mitchell v. Shell Oil Co.[73] that "any misconduct short of a genuine intentional act, however wanton, reckless or culpable such conduct might be, will not suffice to state a claim outside the exclusivity provision."[74] Similarly, in Pyle v. Dow Chemical Co.[75] in 1984 the Eighth U.S. Court of Appeals stated that the injured employee must show that the employer acted with an actual, specific, and deliberate intent to injure the specific employee. However, in Teklinsky v. Ottawa Silica Corp.[76] the federal district court in Michigan held that the exclusivity of the Workers' Compensation Disability Act did not bar recovery for injuries caused by exposure to asbestos fibers at the workplace. Plaintiff alleged that the employer knew from X-rays ordered by its company physician that plaintiff had developed serious medical problems, including asbestosis, yet deliberately withheld this information from the employee: "Where the allegations of plaintiff include concealment from the plaintiff of a known physical condition, and where no treatment or protections are afforded while medically recommended, and where plaintiff's condition is thus aggravated by such conduct, the exclusive remedy provision of the Workers' Compensation Disability Act will not bar this separate action in tort."[77]

The State of West Virginia by statute[78] defines the "actual specific intent" of an employer (so as to take the employee's claim outside workers' compensation) by requiring a finding of five elements: (1) the unsafe working condition presented a high degree of risk and a strong probability of serious injury or death; (2) the employer had a subjective realization of that working condition; (3) the condition violated a state or federal safety statute, rule, or regulation or a well-known industrial safety standard; (4) notwithstanding, the employer intentionally exposed the employee to those conditions; and (5) the exposed employee suffered serious injury or death as a proximate cause of the working condition in the workplace.

The Connecticut Supreme Court in Mingachos v. CBS, Inc.[79] upheld the exclusivity provision of the workers' compensation statute for accidental injuries caused by "the gross, wanton, willful, deliberate, intentional, reckless, culpable, or malicious negligence, breach of statute or other misconduct of the employer *short of genuine intentional injury*"[80] (emphasis added). The court also pointed out that neither the state nor federal OSHA statute or regulations provide for a private cause of action for work-related injuries and furthermore do not supersede an employer's immunity from common law actions by employees.[81]

Dual Capacity Exception to Exclusivity

An employer normally immune from tort liability to an employee under the exclusivity bar may become liable if the employer occupies in addition to his capacity as an employer a second capacity, or dual capacity, conferring obligations toward the employee independently of those obligations imposed on defendant as an employer.[82] Under the dual capacity theory or device the employer is, in effect, a third party, a separate legal entity who can be sued in his role as a product manufacturer, for example.[83] The parent corporation or subsidiary or an affiliated corporation are subject to suit as if they were independent third parties, even though one entity is the employer.[84] In Wright v. District Court of Colorado[85] the court held that the exclusivity provisions of the Colorado workers' compensation law did not bar an employee who had been treated for a workplace injury by a company physician from bringing a malpractice action against the physician, since a company doctor may operate in the dual capacity of a coemployee and physician. The leading California case, Duprey v. Shane,[86] had agreed that the physician acted in a dual capacity as employer and as treating physician of the plaintiff nurse, although in a 1976 case the California court refused to recognize the case as authoritative.[87] In 1983 in Horney v. Guy F. Atkinson Co.[88] the California Court of Appeals held that the employee of a joint venture can sue one party to the joint venture in the latter's capacity as the manufacturer of a defective product sold to the public. The court reasoned that the employee was injured by the product outside of the course of employment.[89]

It would appear that a majority of states do not recognize the dual capacity exception, or, like Delaware,[90] simply have not decided the question. The exception has been rejected outright by Illinois,[91] Louisiana,[92] Michigan,[93] Mississippi,[94] Nevada,[95] New Jersey,[96] New York,[97] North Dakota,[98] Tennessee[99] Texas,[100] Washington,[101] and Wisconsin.[102]

Other Exceptions to Exclusivity

Under the traditional approach to exclusivity, torts such as libel, false imprisonment, malicious prosecution, invasion of privacy, alienation of affections, fraud, intentional infliction of mental distress, and other nonphysical injuries are exceptions to exclusivity because they do not constitute personal injuries, diseases, or deaths by accident arising out of or in the course of employment.[103] The leading "dual injury" case is Johns-Manville Products Corp. v. Contra Costa Superior Court,[104] where the California court ruled that the injury resulting from the aggravation of asbestosis caused by the defendant's fraudulent concealment of the employee's condition stated a cause of action. Along this same line of reasoning, if an employer negligently fails to disclose to an employee the existence of a noncompensable disease, possibly in the course of a medical examination, most courts allow a separate tort action on the theory that the injury, disease, or death is not employment related.[105]

Increasing attempts by claimants to overcome the exclusive remedy of workers' compensation have spread to situations where the suit is brought against coemployees.[106]

The Standard Workers' Compensation and Employers' Liability Insurance Policy

In 1954 the Standard *Workmens'* Compensation and Employers' Liability Policy (in contrast to the 1983 Standard *Workers* Compensation and Employers Liability Policy)[107] was adopted in all states and the District of Columbia, with the exception of a small number of local California insurance companies and the six monopolistic state fund jurisdictions. The two basic coverages, workers' compensation (Coverage A) and employers' liability (Coverage B), are relatively simplified in their approaches, the former providing automatic statewide coverage for all locations and operations under the workers' compensation law and the occupational disease law of the state.[108] Any number of states may be listed in the declarations page for Coverage A because the policy is used on an interstate basis; it is a statutory coverage and covers all operations of the employer except those specifically excluded. Coverage B also provides a broad coverage and protects the employer against legal liabilities where there is a suit against the employer on account of an employee's injury, but where the injury is not covered under Coverage A. In effect, Coverage B has a worldwide effect with few exceptions; it does not apply to any employee who works permanently at a location in another country because the coverage generally is restricted to U.S. citizens or residents who are temporarily outside the United States and working in connection with operations in the state or states designated in the declarations page. Coverage B is a legal liability insurance and the laws of negligence apply to that insurance.

The insuring agreements name only the employer, not the executives or directors of the company, or the individual partners in a partnership, because coverage is afforded only for employers. The amount of coverage in dollars under Coverage A depends upon the limitations on benefits prescribed in the state workers' compensation law. On the other hand, Coverage B is generally limited to $100,000 for bodily injury including death in one accident for one or more employees, and the total limit under Coverage B for bodily injury or death by disease is $100,000 per state. Higher limits are available under Coverage B for an extra premium charge, although such coverage is unlimited in California, Massachusetts, Missouri, New Jersey, and New York.[109]

Defense, settlement, and supplementary payments are included in the insuring agreements. A defense is available even if such "proceeding or suit is groundless, false, or fraudulent," for the pleadings control and defense coverage is unlimited in amount.[110] In essence, the insurance company is required to defend any proceeding brought by an employee against the insured employer seeking benefits or seeking compensation for injury and damages. In Thill Candy Co. v. Farm Bureau Mutual Insurance Co.[111] the federal district court in Pennsylvania awarded the insured plaintiff counsel fees that the insured had incurred in the defense of the action. And in Danek v. Hommer[112] the New Jersey court declared that the insurer's duty to defend depends upon the nature of the claim, not upon the details of the accident, and the duty to defend is broader than the duty to pay!

Insurance companies under the policy have particularly noted in recent years the number of cases where attempts are made to avoid the exclusive remedy defense so as to bring protection under Coverage B. For example, the following fall within Coverage B: the dual capacity argument,[113] where the employer is sued whenever the duty involved did not flow exclusively from his status as an employer; loss of consortium[114] and care and loss of services, because of injury to the spouse; and the "third party over" situations, as where the injured employee sues a third party who impleads the employer, the classic case being Dole v. Dow Chemical Co.[115] On the other hand, the following situations are not covered under Coverage B: intentional acts,[116] coemployees or corporate officers who are not named insureds, and dual capacity.[117]

Courts have construed policy provisions generally in favor of the insured, as illustrated by Pennsylvania National Mutual Insurance Co. v. Spence,[118] where the Fourth U.S. Court of Appeals gave retroactive effect to the claim, despite the policy language providing coverage "by accident occurring during the policy period." Here the employee was injured before the 1972 amendments to the Federal Longshoreman's and Harbor Workers' Compensation Act (1927)[119] were effective, and died in 1973 after the insurance policy had expired; but the court ruled that coverage should be retroactively applied. In Copelin v. Reed Tool Co.[120] the Texas court, after noting that the wife's suit for loss of consortium was nullified by the exclusive remedy provision, nevertheless concluded that because there was an allegation of intentional misconduct on the part of the employer, both the employee and his wife could sue for intentional misconduct under Coverage B of the insurance policy. Similarly, courts have expanded Coverage B to encompass "liability over" or "indemnity over" suits where third-party defendants implead employers; the courts simply rule that the exclusive remedy applies only between employer and employee so that the third party sued by the injured employee is allowed to bring the employer into the lawsuit.[121]

Even Section 3602 of the California Labor Code (enacted in 1982), which precluded operation of the dual capacity exception,[122] has been altered by at least four exceptions allowing an employee or dependents to bring an action at law for damages against the employer (1) where the employee's injury, disease, or death was proximately caused by a willful physical assault by the employer; (2) where the employee's injury, disease, or death was aggravated by the employer's fraudulent concealment of the existence of the harm and its connection with the employment; (3) where the harm to the employee was proximately caused by a defective product manufactured by the employer and sold, leased, or otherwise transferred to an independent third person and thereafter provided for for the injured employee's use by a third person; and (4) where the harm to the employee is proximately caused by the employer's knowing removal of, or knowing failure to install, for example, a point of operation guard on a power press.[123]

8.4   RECENT CASES ON EXCLUSIVITY OF WORKERS' COMPENSATION

In the years 1987 and 1988 there were numerous interpretations and reinterpretations of exclusivity of workers' compensation that merit attention. The following court decisions lift the bar of exclusivity:

   1. Blancato v. Feldspar Corp.:[124] The employer illegally hired a minor to work in a hazardous employment as a sand operator in a mining facility; the Connecticut Supreme Court ruled that the minor's estate could avoid the illegal contract of employment and sue the employer directly in tort for wrongful death despite Connecticut's exclusivity bar.

   2. Bryant v. Fox:[125] Two professional football players with the Chicago Bears suffered football-related injuries; but, believing that they suffered additional injuries distinct from their football injuries, they sued the team physician for his negligence. The defendant team physician successfully moved to dismiss the claims on the ground of exclusivity of Illinois workers' compensation; but the Illinois appellate court reversed, finding that an issue of law existed as to whether the team physician was an employee of the Chicago Bears or an independent contractor against whom the players had a common law cause of action. Thus, the appellate court believed that it could not, as a matter of law, rule that defendant team physician was an employee of the Chicago Bears. (Interestingly, the court stated that it was unable, as a matter of law, to rule that the sport of professional football was an ultrahazardous business with automatic coverage under the Illinois Workers' Compensation Act!)

   3. Pleasant v. Johnson:[126] The North Carolina Supreme Court ruled that the injured employee who had received benefits under the state workers' compensation law was not foreclosed from bringing an action against the coemployee for the coemployee's willful and wanton negligence causing his injury; the court noted that the negligent coemployee was required neither to participate in the defense of the workers' compensation claim nor to contribute to the award, and thus was not unduly prejudiced by permitting the injured employee to sue him; a judgment recovered by the injured employee from the coemployee would be disbursed in accordance with the statute and could reduce the burden otherwise placed on the innocent employer or the innocent insurer, according to the court.

   On the other hand, the following recent court decisions upheld the exclusivity of workers' compensation:

   1. Stewart v. CMI Corp.:[127] The Utah Supreme Court refused to recognize the dual capacity exception with the result that it would not permit a strict products liability action against the employer manufacturer of a screw-auger and platform; the deceased employee's estate had received workers' compensation benefits but sought higher benefits. The court opined that the obligation of the employer to provide safe equipment was essentially the same whether the equipment was bought or made by the employer, and therefore there was no need for two actions where the obligations were not distinct or separate.

2. *Vargas v. Hercules Chemical Co.*:[128] The New York court observed that the plaintiff worker was injured when an allegedly defective bottle of acid spilled on him in the workplace; the court ruled that the defendant employer was not liable and that only the manufacturer of the defective product could be liable.

3. *Panaro v. Electrolux Corporation*:[129] The plaintiff and his wife sought damages from both the husband's employer and the nurse employed by the employer; plaintiffs claimed that the nurse failed to exercise reasonable professional care when plaintiff husband suffered a stroke in the workplace. The Connecticut Supreme Court ruled in favor of the defendants as to the exclusivity of workers' compensation and declined to carve out an exception for injuries caused by a professional nurse employed by the employer.

4. *Mermelstein v. City of New York*:[130] The plaintiff, a psychiatric resident, was attacked by a patient, and she sued the defendant hospital for negligence; but the New York court ruled that she could prevail only if she was not an employee of the hospital at the time of the incident. The court intimated that plaintiff was probably an employee who must stay within workers' compensation benefits.

8.5   OCCUPATIONAL SAFETY AND HEALTH ADMINISTRATION, OR OSHA

The Occupational Safety and Health Administration, or OSHA, was established pursuant to the OSH Act (1970),[131] and is charged with developing and promulgating occupational safety and health standards and regulations, conducting investigations and inspections to determine the status of compliance, and issuing citations and penalties for noncompliance. OSHA operates in ten regional offices around the United States and is within the U.S. Department of Labor. OSHA's primary thrust addresses workplace exposure to hazardous substances.

OSHA was severely criticized in a 1985 study by the Congressional Office of Technology Assessment, which said the agency has had little measurable effect on protecting workers from accidents; OSHA's inspections are infrequent and its penalties are so mild that companies have limited incentives for compliance with OSHA regulations. The study reported that about 6,000 people each year, about 25 every working day, died of injuries in the workplace, the highest number in the mining industry (44 for each 100,000 full-time workers in 1982). The study also disclosed that OSHA inspected fewer than 4 percent of the nation's workplaces annually. The three-year study, *Preventing Illness and Injury in the Workplace,* is a 425-page report.[132]

In sharp contrast with the Environmental Protection Agency (EPA), which regularly performs risk estimation to establish upper limits on the degree of risk,[133] OSHA rejects risk estimation on the ground that there are far too many uncertainties involved, and uncertainty is unacceptable; and that estimating the extent of risk involves placing an implicit value on human life, which OSHA argues is inappropriate and impossible.[134] Courts have taken the position that once a suspicion of carcinogenicity, for example, is raised, the regulating agency, whether it is EPA or OSHA, should err on the side of safety.[135]

In Smith v. Western Electric Co.[136] the state appellate court ruled that plaintiff's suit was not preempted by OSHA, thus laying a foundation for the argument that OSHA was not doing its administrative job. Here the employee sued his employer, claiming that he was entitled to the absence of tobacco smoke in the workplace. The court found that the employer was breaching its common law duty to provide a reasonably safe workplace by failing to exercise its control and assume its responsibility to eliminate the hazardous condition caused by tobacco smoke.

The OSH Review Commission is an independent quasi-judicial agency established by the OSH Act (1970); it is charged with ruling on cases forwarded to it by the U.S. Department of Labor when disagreements arise over the results of safety and health inspections performed by OSHA. Employers are given the right to dispute any alleged job safety or health violation found during inspection by OSHA, the penalties proposed by OSHA, and the time given by OSHA to correct any hazardous situation. The OSH Review Commission adjudicates enforcement actions contested by employers, employees, or representatives of employees; the petitioner must act within 15 working days to obtain a hearing before an administrative law judge whose decision is, however, subject to discretionary review by the OSH Review Commission upon the direction of any one member of the commission. A judicial review of the decision takes place in the U.S. Court of Appeals for the District of Columbia.[137]

8.6 FEDERAL EMPLOYERS' LIABILITY ACT, OR FELA

The Federal Employers' Liability Act, or FELA,[138] was designed to cover workplace injuries in interstate commerce, and the recent case of Schneider v. National Railroad Passenger Corp.[139] spells out an important aspect of FELA. Here plaintiff ticket agent alleged that defendant negligently failed to provide her with a safe place to work because she was attacked, robbed, and almost raped as she entered an adjoining parking lot after leaving her work. The Second U.S. Court of Appeals, in reversing, held that there was evidence to indicate that the employee was within the scope of her employment at the time of injury and that the claim was covered by FELA. The court cited with approval the lower court statement that "it generally is accepted that an employee traversing the employer's premises to report to or to leave the job within a reasonable time of her shift is fulfilling a function necessarily incident to employment." The court pointed out that the prevailing law was derived from the U.S. Supreme Court decision in Erie Railroad Co. v. Winfield:[140] "In leaving the carrier's yard at the close of his day's work the deceased was but discharging a duty of his employment. . . . Like his trip through the yard to his engine in the morning, it was a necessary incident of his day's work and partook of the character of that work as a whole, for it was no more an incident of one part than of another." After analyzing a host of cases, the federal appellate court here concluded:

All these cases reached the logical conclusion that a railroad employee's workplace does not extend as far as the railroad tracks do. But none questioned the general rule that an employer's potential FELA liability is not cut off as soon as a shift concludes, or as soon as an employee leaves his or her desk or ticket counter. As we noted in *Powers v. New York Central Railroad*, 251 F2d at 816, "An employee does not lose his character as an employee at the very moment his working time ends. An employee still on the employer's property who is leaving work within a reasonable time after the work day is over is certainly within the protection of the Federal Employers' Liability Act." (Citations omitted.)

Here, Ms. Schneider was not commuting miles away from Union Station. According to her testimony, she had walked only 15 to 18 feet out of the station door and was still on station property when she was attacked entering her car. Surely it was a necessary incident of Schneider's day's work for her to traverse the station premises in order to leave at the end of her shift. See *Erie R.R. v. Winfield*, 244 U.S. at 173. Cf. *Caillouette v. Baltimore & O. Chi. Term. R.R.* 705 F2d at 246 (switchman reporting to work on the wrong side of train yard injured while walking to a shanty to call for an engine to come and take him to the right side of the yard). Schneider's work as a ticket agent was an important part of Amtrack's business in interstate commerce. She was required to work the night shift in a downtown urban area at a station where her evidence indicates the Amtrak police ordinarily saw ticket agents safely from the station to their cars parked in the immediate vicinity.

NOTES

1. See generally Martin, "Coverage Issues in Employment Claims," For the Defense 11 (April 1988).
2. See infra Section 8.2.
3. Section 2. Definitions

A. "Commissioner" shall mean the Commissioner of the Suffolk County Department of Health Services.

B. "Employee" shall mean any person engaged to work on a constant, regular, non-intermittent basis as an operator by an employer located and/or doing business within the Suffolk County.

C. "Employer" shall mean any person, partnership, firm association or corporation located and/or doing business within the Suffolk County which operates 20 or more terminals within the Suffolk County.

D. "Operators" shall mean any employee who normally operates a terminate, for an employer, 26 or more hours per week.

E. "Terminal" shall mean any electronic video screen data presentation machine, commonly denominated as video display terminals (VDT) or cathode-ray tubes (CRT). Nothing in this article may be construed to apply to television, cash registers, memory typewriters, self-contained personal computers, or oscilloscope screens.

Section 3. Requirements

A. Vision Examinations

1) Any individual who is to be assigned by an employer as an operator shall receive, with the written consent of such employee, an ophthalmological/optometric examination conforming to the recommended components of an eye/vision examination established by the American Optometric Association with a view to the specific requirements of visual correction that may be needed by an operator for the job, before beginning an assignment, or within thirty days thereafter, and again in each subsequent year the operator is so employed. Where employees have been assigned as operators prior to the effective date of this law, they shall receive such an examination within ninety days after the effective date of this law. This examination may be performed at the direction of an employer on a day or at a time during which employee is not required to be present at his place of employment. Any operator who declines said opthalmological/optometric examination shall do so in writing. Such declination shall remain in effect during the entire calendar year in which such declination is made.

2) Every employer shall maintain records sufficient to verify its compliance with paragraph ( ) of this section.

3) The employer shall (a) pay eighty percent of the usual and customary fees, prevailing within the pertinent community in which the services are rendered, for initial and annual opthalmological or optometric examinations for each operator required under this law through an insurance policy or by direct payment to the provider of care, provided, however, that the employer may require an operator to select a provider of such eye examination services from an employer-established panel of at least three licensed providers;

(b) pay eight percent of the usual and customary fees, prevailing within the pertinent community in which the services are rendered, of any lenses and basic frames required for use by the operator as a result of the operator's work on the terminals; and

(c) permit the operator to select the provider of the examination required by this section, except as otherwise provided under any previously or subsequently negotiated group health care agreement or policy or pertinent collective bargaining agreement, provided, however, that the employer may require an operator to select a provider of such eye examination services from an employer-established panel of at least three licensed providers.

4) No employer shall use the results of any opthalmological or optometric examination required by this section to screen prospective operators for suitability for employment.

4. —N.Y.S.2d— (Suffolk County, October 19, 1988).

5. Note Section 7.4 *supra*.

6. See 29 U.S.C. 1001(a) and Article 1, Section 8, Clause 3 of the U.S. Constitution.

7. Supra note 2.

8. See Warren Freedman, Richards on the Law of Insurance §5.10 (1989).

9. See E. Z. Loader Boat Trailers, Inc. v. Travelers Indemnity Co. 762 P.2d 439 (Wash. 1986) and Bituminous Fire & Marine Insurance Co. v. Izzy Rosen's Inc., 493 F.2d 256 (6th Cir. 1974).

10. 436 A.2d 493 (Md. 1981); also *supra* note 1 at p. 13.

11. 402 So.2d 949 (Ala. 1981).

12. See generally Larson, The Law of Workmen's Compensation 25–26 (1978).

13. Id., at 27.

14. Id., at 27.

15. See Price, Workers' Compensation: Coverage, Benefits, and Costs, (1980), 46 Soc Security Bulletin No. 5 at 14–15 (1983).

16. See, for example, Spratlin v. Evans, 260 Ark. 49, 55, 538 S.W. 2d 527, 531 (1976).

17. See generally Denenberg, Eilers, Malone and Zelton, Risk and Insurance 374–375 (1974).

18. Id.

19. See Greene, Risk and Insurance 535 (1977).

20. Id.

21. Md. Ann. Code Article 101, §15.

22. New York Workmen's Compensation Law §10.

23. Supra note 12 generally.

24. Supra note 12 at Sections 37.00 et seq. and 38.00 et seq. and 39.00 et seq.

25. Supra note 12 at Sections 7.40 and 12.20.

26. See O'Leary v. Brown-Pacific-Maxon, Inc., 340 U.S. 504 (1951).

27. See 6 Wm. Mitchell L. Rev. 501, 502 (1980).

28. Id., at pp. 507–515.

29. Id., at p. 532.

30. See DeRosa v. Albert F. Amling Co., 404 N.E.2d 564 (Ill. App. 1980).

31. See Tredway v. District of Columbia, 403 A.2d 732 (D.C. app. 1979), cert. den. 101 S.Ct. 141 (1980).

32. 63 N.Y.2d 412, 472 N.E.2d 682 (1984), aff'd 63 N.Y.2d 601, 468 N.E.2d 711 (1984).

33. Id.

34. Such agreement shall be a surrender by the parties thereto of their rights to any other method, form or amount of compensation or determination thereof than as provided in this article and an acceptance of all the provisions of this article, and shall bind the employee and for compensation for *the employee's* death shall bind *the employee's* personal representatives, *surviving spouse* and next of kin, as well as the employer, and those conducting *the employer's* business during bankruptcy or insolvency. (N.J. STAT. ANN. § 34–15–8)

35. Liability for the compensation provided by this division, in lieu of any other liability whatsoever to any person except as provided in Section 3706, shall, without regard to negligence, exist against an employer for any injury sustained by his employees arising out of and in the course of the employment and for the death of any employee if the injury proximately causes death in those cases where the following conditions of compensation concur. (CAL. LAB. CODE, § 3600)

36. Section 3. The employees of a subscriber and the parents of minor employees shall have no right of action against their employer or against any agent, servant or employee of said employer for damages for personal injuries, and the representatives and beneficiaries of deceased employees shall have no right of action against such subscribing employer or his agent, servant or employee for damages for injuries resulting in death, but such employees and their representatives and beneficiaries shall look for compensation solely to the association, as the same is hereinafter provided for. (TEXAS CODE ANN. Article 8306, §6)

37. See Williams v. Byrd, 242 Ga. 80, 247 S.E.2d 874 (1978).

38. See Granger v. URDA, 44 N.Y.2d 91, 375 N.E.2d 380 (1978).

39. See Arcell v. Ashland Chemical Co., 152 N.J. Super. 471, 378 A.2d 53 (1977).

40. 70 Ill.2d 1, 374 N.E.2d 437 (1978).

41. See 45 U.S.C. 56.

42. See 28 U.S.C. 1346(b).

43. See 29 U.S.C. 651.

44. See 43 U.S.C. 1331.

45. See, for example, Blessing v. U.S., 447 F.Supp. 1160 (E.D.Pa. 1978).

46. Supra note 32.

47. Id.

Neither the agent's statement that plaintiff could not expect to be supported by the insurer forever nor the carrier's attempt to disprove plaintiff's claim was so extreme and outrageous as to exceed all bounds of decency or to be utterly intolerable in civilized society (see *Fischer v. Maloney*, 43 NY2d 553, 557). Moreover, inasmuch as this conduct cannot even be said to amount to "bad faith," it is unnecessary to decide whether plaintiff may recover as a third-party beneficiary of the insurance contract.

48. —N.Y.S.2d— (Mar. 14, 1984).

49. 41 N.Y.2d 219 (1976).

50. Id. at 221.

51. Id. at 228.

52. See Wright v. FMC Corp., 81 Cal. App. 3d 554 (1978).

53. See Sanford v. Presto Mfg. Co., 92 N.M. 746, 594 P.2d 1202 (1979).

54. See Antonio v. Hirsch, 3 A.D. S.2d 939, 163 N.Y. S.2d 489 (1951).

55. See De Coigne v. Ludlum Steel Co., 251 A.D. 662, 297 N.Y.S. 636 (1937).

56. Mylroie v. GAF Corp., 440 N.Y.S.2d 67 (1981).

57. Id. at 68–69.

58. See, for example, N.C. Gen. Stat. § 97–12; and Cal. Lab. Code § 4553.

59. See Rogers Materials Co. v. Industrial Accident Commission, 48 Cal. Rptr. 129, 408 P.2d 737 (1965).

60. 69 Ohio St. 2d 608 (1982).

61. 15 Ohio St. 3d 90, 472 N.E.2d 1046 (1984).

62. Id. at 1051.

63. In addition to Jones v. VIP Development Co., *supra* note 61, there was Gains v. City of Painesville.

64. Supra note 61 at p. 1053.

65. Supra note 61 at p. 1054.

66. See generally FOR THE DEFENSE 9–13 (Aug. 1985).

67. 311 N.C. 294, 316 S.E.2d 81 (1984).

68. Id.

69. 728 F.2d 759 (5th Cir. 1984).

70. Id. at 761.

71. See Copeland v. Johns-Manville Products Corp., 492 F. Supp. 498 (D.N.J. 1980) and Austin v. Johns-Manville Sales Corp., 508 F. Supp. 313 (D.Me. 1981).

72. 27 Cal.3d 455, 612 P.2d 948 (1980).

73. 579 F. Supp. 1326 (D. Mont. 1984).

74. Id. at 1329.

75. 728 F.2d 1129 (8th Cir. 1984).

76. 583 F.Supp. 31 (E. D. Mich. 1984).

77. Id. at p. 35. Cf. McLaughlin v. American Oil Co., 391 N.E.2d 864 (Ind. App. 1979).

78. W. Va. Code §23-4-2 (1981).

79. 196 Conn. 91, 491 A.2d 368 (1985).

80. Id. at p. 378.

81. Supra note 79 at p. 375.

82. See Douglas v. E & J Gallo Winery, 69 Cal. App. 3d 103 (1977).

83. See Mercer v. Uniroyal, Inc., 49 Ohio App. 279, 361 N.E.2d 492 (1977).

84. See Boggs v. Blue Diamond Coal Co., 590 F.2d 655 (6th Cir. 1979), *cert. den.* 444 U.S. 836 (1979).

85. 447 P.2d 727 (Colo. 1983).

86. 39 Cal.2d 781, 249 P.2d 8 (1952).

87. See Dixon v. Ford Motor Co., 53 Cal. App. 3d 273 (1976).

88. 190 Cal. Rptr. 18 (1983).

89. Id. at pp. 20–21.

90. See Kofron v. Amoco Chemical Corp., 441 A.2d 226 (Del. 1982).

91. See McCormick v. Caterpillar Tractor Co., 85 Ill. 2d 352, 423 N.E. 2d 876 (1981).

92. See Hebert v. Gulf States Utilities Co., 369 So. 2d 1104 (La. App. 1979).

93. See Neal v. Raura-Iron Works, Inc., 66 Mich. App. 273, 238 N.W. 2d 837 (1975).

94. See Trotter v. Litton Systems, Inc., 370 So.2d 244 (Miss. 1979).

95. See Frith v. Harrah South Shore Corp., 92 Nev. 447, 552 P.2d 337 (1976).

96. See Taylor v. Pfaulder Sybron Corp., 150 N.J. Super. 148, 374 A.2d 18 (1977).

97. See Billy v. Consolidated Machine Tool Corp., 51 N.Y.2d 152, 412 N.E.2d 934 (1980).

98. See Schlenk v. Aerial Contractors, Inc. 268 N.W.2d 163 (N.D. 1978).

99. See Billings v. Dugges, 50 Tenn. App. 403, 362 S.W.2d 49 (1962).

100. See Cohn v. Spinks Industries, Inc., 602 S.W.2d 102 (Tex. Cir. Ct. 1980).

101. See Thompson v. Lewis County, 92 Wash. 2d 204, 595 P.2d 541 (1979).

102. See Gerger v. Campbell, 98 Wis. 2d 282, 297 N.W.2d 183 (1980).

103. See Wilkins v. West Point Pepperell Inc., 397 So.2d 115 (Ala. 1981).

104. 27 Cal.3d 465, 612 P.2d 948 (1980).

105. See Castner v. American Airlines, Inc., 78 A.D.2d 917, 433 N.Y.S.2d 512 (1980).

106. See Jones v. Thomas, 430 So.2d 891 (La. 1983).

107. Note that in 27 states workmens' compensation laws are called "workers' " compensation laws.

108. See Wojciak v. Northern Package Corp., 310 N.W.2d 675 (Minn. 1981) where the court construed the words "other benefits" under the policy as expanding coverage for retaliatory discharge, i.e., when the employee filed a workers' compensation claim.

109. Note that the Federal Longshoreman's & Harbor Workers' Compensation Act (1927) at 4.33 herein, as well as other federal acts including maritime tort exposure, are subject to the policy limit stated in the declarations page in New York and Massachusetts, notwithstanding the unlimited liability for state act losses.

110. See Treadwell v. U.S. Fidelity & Guaranty Co., 275 N.Y. 158, 9 N.E.2d 818 (1937).

111. 171 F. Supp. 237 (E.D. Pa. 1959).

112. 28 N.J. Super. 68, 100 A.2d 198 (1953).

113. Id.

114. See Ferriter v. O'Donnell & Sons, 381 Mass. 507, 413 N.E.2d 690 (1980).

115. 30 N.Y.2d 143, 282 N.E.2d 288 (1972).

116. Id.

117. Supra note 113.

118. 591 F.2d 985 (4th Cir. 1979).

119. Supra note 109.

120. 596 S.W.2d 302 (Tex. Cir. App. 1980).

121. Supra note 110.

122. Supra note 84.

123. See Cal. Lab. Code §§6–2602 and 12–4558.

124. 522 A.2d 1235 (Conn. 1987).

125. 515 N.E.2d 775 (Ill. App. 1987).

126. 325 S.E.2d 244 (N.C. 1987).

127. 740 P.2d 1340 (Utah 1987).

128. —N.Y.S.2d— (New York County, 1988):

Here, there is no showing of negligence on the part of Widman. Although Widman may have had a duty to plaintiff as plaintiff's employer, that duty only extends to liability under the Worker's Compensation Law unless negligence or some additional breach is shown. Plaintiff's entitlement to Worker's Compensation is granted on the basis of a finding that the accident occurred during the course of plaintiff's employment. It does not reflect a finding of negligence on the part of Widman. The evidence, such as the suggestion of "frolic" on plaintiff's part, without adequate explanation by plaintiff, and evidence of plaintiff's prior experiences with substances of the sort that allegedly caused his injury leads one to question just what the employer's breach of duty was. Even if it were proven, for example, that employer failed to inform plaintiff of the dangers of the substance, the evidence set forth fully supports a finding of plaintiff's advance awareness of these dangers. Nor has plaintiff established that he was instructed by anyone in connection with his employment, to transport the "Clobber" on the particular day of the accident. It was placed in the back seat of plaintiff's car by his own initiative. The mere assertion of a dispute in the absence of evidentiary facts is insufficient to defeat the motion for summary judgment. (Rafkin v. Continental Diamond Mines, Inc., 33 Misc. 2d 156, 228 NYS2d 317, mod. 241 NYS 2d 302).

There is no connection between the alleged accident and responsibility on the part of plaintiff's employer. Nor has it been established that employer owes a legal duty to plaintiff under the circumstances of this case.

129. 208 Conn. 589 (1988).

130. —N.Y.S.2d—(New York County, August 8, 1988).

131. 29 U.S.C. 651–678.

132. See New York Times, April 18, 1985, at A18.

133. See 44 Fed. Reg. 15,926, 15,929, and 15,938 (March 15, 1979).

134. See OSHA Cancer Policy 5245–50.

135. See Environmental Defense Fund, Inc. v. EPA, 510 F.2d 1292, 1298 (D.C. Cir. 1975) and Certified Color Mfgrs. Assn. v. Mathews, 543 F.2d 284, 297–298 (D.C. Cir. 1976).

136. 643 S.W. 2d 10 (Mo. App. 1982).

137. See The United States Government Organization Manual 1985/1986 at 595–597 (GPO).

138. 45 U.S.C. 51–60 (1982).

139. —F.2d—(2nd Cir. August 9, 1988).

140. 244 U.S.—(   ):

Winfield has been followed by various circuit courts, including our own. In Powers v. New York Central Railroad, 251 F2d 813, 816–17 (2d Cir. 1958), we said that "[a]n employee still on the employer's property who is leaving work within a reasonable time after the work day is over is certainly within the protection of the Federal Employers' Liability Act" citing Erie R.R. v. Win-

field, supra, and *Morris v. Pennsylvania R.R.,* (187 F2d at 841). In *Morris* we said, "It is now too late to argue that a worker is within his employment only when actually on the job." 187 F2d at 841 citing *Mostyn v. Delaware L. & W. R.R.,* 160 F2d 15, 17 (2d Cir.) cert. denied, 332 U.S. 770 (1947); *Young v. New York, N.H. & H.R.R.,* 74 F2d 251, 252 (2d Cir. 1934) (when employee has not yet left the premises or has entered on his way to work, he is within his employment, but employment may also begin "before he reaches the premises"). Although some disputed questions of fact remain, it is apparent to us on this record that Schneider's injuries occurred in close physical and temporal proximity to her workplace, and that if the disputed facts are resolved in her favor FELA coverage is appropriate.

9

Employers' Liability to Third Parties Injured by Conduct of Employees

9.1 INTRODUCTION

Can or should an employer be liable for the acts or conduct of an employee with respect to injuries the employee caused to third persons? The Minnesota Supreme Court found in Meany v. Newell[1] that the estate of the deceased third party did not state a cause of action in negligence against the employer. Here the employer hosted a Christmas party and served intoxicating drinks; the employee was thoroughly intoxicated and when he left the party the employer was fully aware of his dangerous intoxication. The intoxicated employee thereupon smashed into another vehicle and killed a passenger in the other car and severely injured that driver; the intoxicated employee himself was killed in the accident. The court reasoned that the state Dram Shop Act was not meant to apply to a social host, and that there was no benefit-barter situation that would require the court to hold the employer liable. In effect, no common law cause of action could be brought against the employer for negligently serving alcohol to an obviously intoxicated employee.

It should be noted that Section 317 of the *Restatement (Second) of Torts* imposes a duty of reasonable care upon a master or employer if the employee or servant is on the premises or is using personal property owned by the master or employer, or if the master or employer has knowledge or reason to know that he can control the servant or employee and knew or should have known of the necessity of exercising that control over the servant or employee. The duty of reasonable care applies and requires the employer to control the employee while acting outside the scope of employment to prevent the employee from intentionally or negligently causing harm to third parties.[2]

The better view is seen in the California case of Harris v. Trojan Fireworks

Co.,[3] where, on almost similar facts, the California Court of Appeals found that the victim made out a prima facie case of vicarious liability under the theory of respondeat superior. The court concluded that the intoxication occurred during the course of employment and was the proximate cause of the accident resulting in the death and two injuries. The respondeat superior doctrine was deemed applicable because the Christmas party was of prime benefit to the employer: "Liability attaches where a nexus exists between the employment or the activity which results in an injury that is foreseeable."[4] A similar result holding the business liable is illustrated in Director v. Mazure,[5] where plaintiff was seriously injured as a passenger in a motor vehicle that hit a guard rail, where the crash was caused by the negligence of defendant's employee. (Since the employee driver was never served with process, the New York court had dismissed the case against him.) The court held that the employer was liable under respondeat superior and also rejected the defenses that the accident was caused by "potholes" in the road and that the employee driver was speeding and had no valid driver's license.

Third-party actions against employers brought by tortfeasors who are sued by injured employees are also commonplace today. The employer is impleaded or simply brought into the lawsuit as a named third-party defendant. However, in a majority of jurisdictions, such third-party actions against employers have generally been denied under a literal interpretation of the statutory language of workers' compensation insulating the employer from liability to the employee or to any other person. The rationale is that the employer, immune from liability in tort to the employee, cannot be considered a joint tortfeasor for that injury to the employee. In Paul Krebs & Associates v. Matthews & Fritts Construction Co.[6] the Alabama Supreme Court held that the employer's statutory immunity from suit due to injuries to its employees protected the employer from a suit by a third party seeking indemnity, despite express indemnity provisions in the construction contract between the employer and the defendant construction company.

On the other hand, under common law indemnity, in Miller v. DeWitt[7] the Illinois Supreme Court allowed a passively negligent tortfeasor, from whom the injured employee recovered, to obtain indemnification from the actively negligent employer of that injured employee. It would appear that the third-party plaintiff was generally without fault and that its liability to the injured employee was only vicarious, derivative, or technical due to its relationship with the actively negligent employer. Five years later the New York Court of Appeals in Dole v. Dow Chemical Co.[8] discarded the active-passive negligence concept and allowed partial indemnification between joint tortfeasors based upon their relative degree of fault. Here the employer had used a chemical manufactured by defendant to fumigate a grain storage bin; after the employee cleaned the bin, he died from exposure to the poisonous chemical in the bin, and the employee's representative sued the defendant chemical manufacturer for failure to label the chemical properly so as to warn of its dangers. The chemical manufacturer then filed a third-party complaint against the employer, alleging negligence in failing to train the employee in the use of the chemical, in failing to follow the instructions for the use of the chemical, and in failing to test or inspect the grain bin after fumigation to ensure the safety of the bin and the area. In essence, the New York Court of Appeals indicated that the amount of the employer's liability for partial indemnity or contribution was unlimited. But in Arbaugh v. Procter & Gamble Manufacturing Co.[9] the California appellate court ruled that contribution among joint tortfeasors based upon relative fault would not be extended in California to the workers' compensation area. Obviously the existence of the exclusivity remedies of the workers' compensation laws are relevant here.[10]

9.2 EMPLOYEE DEFAMATION AND JOB REFERENCES

Employee defamation cases involving liability of the employer are increasing, particularly where employee discharges can be related back to an employer's alleged defamation of the employee.[11] According to the *Wall Street Journal*,[12] about one-third of all defamation actions are libel and slander suits filed by discharged employees against their former employers! Under traditional defamation law, employers have been protected from liability by a qualified privilege when disclosing information concerning present or former employees. Support for this view stems from society's interest in facilitating communication in such situations involving candid evaluation of an employee's performance.[13]

But that qualified privilege has been gradually eroded, as illustrated by O'Brien v. Papa Gino's of America, Inc.,[14] where the First U.S. Court of Appeals held that the employer was liable for a statement that the former employee was "fired for drug use" where the employer failed to state that the discharge was also motivated by a personal grudge. The court reasoned that the jury's finding of two causes for the employee's discharge meant that a true and accurate statement of the reason for termination would be to the effect that the employee was fired "largely due to drug use but we also had retaliatory motives arising from a personal grudge." Even a statement that the employee had been terminated "for cause" can be sufficient to state a cause of action.[15] In Lewis v. Equitable Life Assurance Society[16] the former employer was held liable for damages resulting from a discharged employee's disclosure to prospective employers of the contents of defamatory statements concerning the reason for termination of employment. The reasoning here was that the employer could foresee that the former employee would be under a strong compulsion to repeat, or publish, the reasons for termination of employment in order to respond truthfully to questions from a prospective employer as to why the prior employment had been terminated, even though there was no communication of the defamatory statement to anyone other than the discharged employee.[17]

It can safely be said that there is danger in any employer giving unfavorable job references, especially when the former employee is investigating the substance of the references, as illustrated in Marshall v. Brown,[18] where the California jury found the former employer liable for telling a woman's prospective employer that the employee was "erratic in work hours, brought her personal problems to the office, had married another employee and had caused that male employee to have a mental breakdown." Communication of defamatory material solely to intracompany personnel has been held to constitute publication to a third person for defamation purposes, and defamation actions against the employer have been successful.[19] (The contrary view holds that communications by employees without direct authorization by their employers do not subject employers to defamation liability.[20])

The use of releases or waivers by employers has provoked litigation, as in Kellums v. Freight Sales Centers, Inc.,[21] where the plaintiff signed the release authorizing disclosure of employment information and releasing the employer from any liability resulting from such disclosure. The plaintiff employee later alleged that he was slandered by the former employer, who had responded to an inquiry from a prospective employer. The Florida appellate court held that, while the exculpatory clause or release could absolve the defendant employer from liability for negligence, it was against public policy to apply the release to a defamation claim, just as it was against public policy to permit a party to absolve itself of liability for an intentional tort.

Obviously, the employer loses the qualified privilege to disclose defamatory matter if the employer abuses it by publishing the statement for some reason other than the reason for which the qualified privilege was granted in the first place, or if the employer publishes it with "malice." In Pittman v. Larson Distributing Co.[22] the Colorado court found that the plaintiff employee had been hired upon the employer's promise of a certain territory and commission, and that the employer had reduced his rate of commission and territory and had later discharged him after the employer received an attorney's letter seeking back payments and restoration of his territory. In response to inquiries from a prospective employer, the employer stated that plaintiff had been discharged because he "spent too much time in the office and on the telephone" rather than calling on customers in person. The court ruled that the evidence tended to show that the plaintiff was not discharged due to "fault" but rather in retaliation for his insistence upon being paid in accordance with the original employment agreement, and therefore the employer could be held liable for the defamatory utterances.

9.3   RIGHT-TO-KNOW LAWS FOR EMPLOYEES

Still another aspect of employer's liability to third parties for acts of the employee can be seen in the right-to-know laws enacted in recent years by states and local political subdivisions in order to meet what was perceived as a dire need for the dissemination of information about toxic and hazardous substances and about hazardous waste disposal.[23] These legislative enactments generally establish a comprehensive program for the disclosure of information either in the workplace or in the general environment, or both;[24] and require employers and manufacturers to identify and report hazardous and toxic substances and dangers in hazardous waste disposal; to maintain files of basic safety and health information; to prepare specific and detailed information such as chemical or generic or trade or common names of such substances, including the specifics of the hazard as to flammability, explosiveness, or reactivity, and emergency handling procedures; ɔ ensure that containers are properly labeled; and to provide data to public agencies as well as public postings.

The State of California under its Hazardous Substances Information Act[25] compels all employers using hazardous substances as well as all persons who sell or manufacture or produce hazardous substances to disclose complete data, and the California OSH Board is required to promulgate standards prescribing an employer's duties toward employees to ensure that employees have timely access to material safety data sheets and furthermore that they are trained in first aid measures against exposure to hazardous substances.[26]

Connecticut has right-to-know laws relating to carcinogenic materials and toxic substances.[27] Employers must post a list of all carcinogenic substances used or produced in the workplace; employers must also give education and training for employees exposed to workplace toxic substances.

New York under Section 875 et seq. of the New York Labor Law has a very detailed right-to-know law including the right of an employee to be advised by signs of information regarding toxic substances found in the workplace, and the employer must obtain such data from every possible source. Forty years of recordkeeping is mandated for employers in New York.[28]

In West Virginia the state labor commission must prepare a list of chemical substances and materials that have been determined or are suspected to be hazardous or toxic to health.[29] Employers must post this information together with data on other such substances found in the workplace. In 1983 in West Virginia Manufacturers Assn. v. West Virginia[30] the federal district court affirmed the constitutionality of the legislation and in particular the lack of preemption in federal legislation with respect to right-to-know laws.

Few states and local political subdivisions have legislatively provided for compensation for personal injuries or disabilities associated with exposure to hazardous substances, as alternatives to common law rules and court decisions. Alaska expressly recognized a right of recovery in state courts for personal injuries or disabilities suffered by private persons as the result of the release of hazardous substances by creating a strict liability system.[31] Damages recoverable are not limited to "injury to or loss of persons or property, real or personal, loss of income, loss of means of producing income, or the loss of economic benefit."[32]

An interesting variation on the right-to-know laws is the problem of workers and employees with respect to exposure to tobacco smoke in the workplace. In Smith v. Western Electric Company[33] the Missouri appellate court held that an employer owes a duty to the employee to use all reasonable care to provide a reasonably safe workplace, and that by failing to exercise its control and assume its responsibility to eliminate the hazardous condition caused by tobacco smoke, the employer breached that duty. Accordingly, injunctive relief was proper because the harm was irreparable and there was no adequate remedy at law; neither did OSHA preempt the subject matter of the case.[34]

NOTES

1. 367 N.W.2d 472 (Minn. 1985).

2. See Rodriguez-Schack, ''Meany v. Newell: Employer's Liability to Third Parties Injured by Intoxicated Employees Following an Office Party'', 33 Torts & Ins. L.J. 522 (1986).

3. 174 Cal. Rptr. 452 (1981).

4. See generally Barry, ''Employer Liability for a Drunken Employee's Actions Following an Office Party'', 19 Cal. West L. Rev. 107 (1982).

5. —NYS2d—(New York County, June 24, 1988).

6. 356 So.2d 638 (Ala. 1978).

7. 37 Ill.2d 273, 226 N.E.2d 630 (1967).

8. 30 N.Y.2d 143, 282 N.E.2d 288 (1972).

9. 80 Cal. App. 3d 500 (1978).

10. Note the compilation of state exclusivity provisions in workers' compensation laws:

ALA. CODE § 25–5–52, 25–5–53 (1975)

ALASKA STAT. § 23.30.055 (1962)

ARIZ. REV. STAT. ANN. § 23–1022 (1956)

ARK. STAT. ANN. § 81–1304 (1947)

CAL. LAB. CODE § 3601, 3864 (West 1982)

COLO. REV. STAT. § 8–43–104 (1973)

CONN. GEN. STAT. ANN. § 31–293a (1958)

DEL. CODE ANN. tit. 19, § 2304 (1974)

D.C. CODE ANN. § 36–304 (1981)

FLA. STAT. ANN. § 440.11 (West 1974)

GA. CODE ANN. § 114–103 (1973)

HAWAII REV. STAT. § 386–5 (1976)

IDAHO CODE § 2–201, 2–207 (1973)

ILL. ANN. STAT. ch. 48, § 138.5, 138.11, 172–40 (Smith-Hurd 1977)

IND. CODE ANN. § 22–3–2–6 (Burns 1982)

IOWA CODE § 85.20 (1983)

KAN. STAT. ANN. § 44–510e (1980)

KY. REV. STAT. § 342.015 (1970)

LA. REV. STAT. ANN. § 23:1032 (1965)

ME. REV. STAT. ANN. tit. 39, § 28 (1964)

MD. ANN. CODE art. 101, § 15 (1957)

MASS. GEN. LAWS ANN. ch. 152, § 24 (West 1975)

MICH. STAT. ANN. § 411.4 (Callaghan 1983)

MINN. STAT. ANN. § 176.021, 176.061, 176.031 (West 1969)

MISS. CODE ANN. § 71–3–9 (1972)

MO. REV. STAT. § 287.120 (1978)

MONT. CODE ANN. § 39–71–411 (1981)

NEB. REV. STAT. § 48–148 (1976)

NEV. REV. STAT. § 616.370 (1980)

N.H. REV. STAT. ANN. § 281:12 (1983)

N.J. STAT. ANN. § 34:15–8 (West 1959)

N.M. STAT. ANN. § 52–1–9 (1978)

N.Y. WORK. COMP. LAW § 67–10–312 (McKinney 1965)

N.C. GEN. STAT. § 97–10.1 (1981)

N.D. CENT. CODE § 65–04–28 (1960)

OHIO REV. CODE ANN. § 4123.74 (Page 1980)

OKLA. STAT. ANN. tit. 85, § 12 (West 1963)

OR. REV. STAT. § 656.018 (1981)

PA. STAT. ANN. tit. 77, § 481 (Purdon 1981)

R.I. GEN. LAWS § 28–29–20 (1978)

S.C. CODE ANN. § 42–1–540, 42–1–560, 42–1–580 (Law. Co-op. 1978)

S.D. CODIFIED LAWS ANN. § 62–3–2 (1982)

TENN. CODE ANN. § 50–6–108 (1982)

TEX. CIV. STAT. art. 8306, § 3 (Vernon 1982)

UTAH CODE ANN. § 35–1–60 (1981)

VT. STAT. ANN. tit. 21, § 622 (1981)

VA. CODE § 65.1–40 (1950)

WASH. REV. CODE ANN. § 51.04.010 (1962)

W.VA. CODE § 23–2–6 (1983)

WIS. STAT. ANN. § 102.03 (1980)

WYO. STAT. § 27–12–103 (1977)

11. See "Employers Face Upsurge in Suits Over Defamation," N.L.J. 1 (May 4, 1987).

12. October 2, 1986 at 33.

13. See 50 Am Jur2d § 195 (1970).

14. 780 F.2d 1067 (1st Cir. 1986).

15. See Carney v. Memorial Hospital & Nursing Home, 485 N.Y.S.2d 984, 475 N.E.2d 451 (1985).

16. 389 N.W.2d 876 (Minn. 1986).

17. See generally McCandless and Lofholm, "False and Defamatory: Two Words that Strike Fear into Employers," The Brief 13 (Summer 1987).

18. 190 Cal. Rptr. 392 (1983).

19. See McCone v. New England Telephone and Telegraph Co., 393 Mass. 231 (1984) and Sturdivant v. Seaboard Systems, Inc., 459 A.2d 1058 (D.C. App. 1983).

20. Note Ellis v. Jewish Hospital of St. Louis, 581 S.W.2d 850 (Mo. App. 1979) and K-Mart Corporation, Inc. v. Pendergrass, 494 So.2d 600 (Ala. 1986).

21. 467 So.2d 816 (Fla. App. 1985).

22. 724 P.2d 1379 (Colo. 1986).

23. For example, see Cal. Lab. Code § 6360 et seq. (West 1980); Conn. Gen. Stat. Ann. §31-40(c) (West 1980); Conn. Pub. Act 82-251 (Laws 1982); Mass. Ann. Laws ch. 149, §142A (Michie/Law Co-op 1981); Me. Rev. Stat. Ann. tit. 2, §1701 et seq. (1980), Mich. Comp. Laws Ann. §4808.1011 (1981); N.Y. Labor Law §875 et seq. (McKinney 1981); Va. Code §40.1-51.1 (1982); NJS 1670/AB 3318 (1983); Alaska Spec. Act ch. 93 (1983); New Hampshire ch. 466 (1982); Ill HB 741 (1983); Rhode Island 161 (Laws 1983); Minn. Spec. Act ch. 316 (1983); Wash. Rev. Code Ann. §§49.17.220, .240 (West 1982); W. VA. Code §21-3-18(a) (Michie 1982); Wis. Stat. Ann. §101.58 et seq. (West 1981).

24. See 90 Yale L.J. 1792 (1981).

25. Cal. Labor. Code §6360 et seq.

26. Id. at §6398.

27. Conn. Gen. Stat. Ann. §31–49(c) and Conn. Pub. Act. 82-251 (1982).

28. New York Labor Law, §879.

29. W. Va. Code §21–3–18(a).

30. 542 F. Supp. 1247 (S.D.W.Va. 1982).

31. See Alaska Stats §46.03.822, which reads as follows:

Sec. 46.03.822 Strict liability for the discharge of Hazardous Substances.

To the extent not otherwise preempted by federal law, a person owning or having control over a hazardous substance which enters in or upon the waters, surface or subsurface lands of the state is strictly liable, without regard to fault, for the damages to persons or property, public or private, caused by the entry. In an action to recover damages, the person is relieved from strict liability, without regard to fault, if he can prove

(1) that the hazardous substance to which the damages relate entered in or upon the waters, surface or subsurface lands of the state solely as a result of

(A) an act of war,

(B) an intentional act or a negligent act of a third party, other than a party (or its employees) in privity of contract with, or employed by, the person,

(C) negligence on the part of the United States government or the State of Alaska, or

(D) an act of God; and

(2) in relation to (1)(B), (C) or (D) of this section, that he discovered the entry of the hazardous substance in or upon the waters, surface or subsurface lands of the state and began operations to contain and clean up the hazardous substance within a reasonable period of time.

32. Id., at §46.03.824.

33. 643 S.W.2d 10 (Mo. App. 1985).

34. See generally 37 ALR4th 480.

10

Enforcement of Restrictive, Noncompetitive Covenants Against Employees

Employees, upon discharge, termination, retirement, resignation, or other separation from employment, for whatever reason, are frequently subjected to restrictive, noncompetitive covenants that adversely affect their present or future employment. These covenants, for the most part, are enforceable if they are judged to be reasonable restraints, as illustrated most recently in Ingersoll-Rand Co. v. Ciavatta.[1] Here the employer sued the employee, claiming that the employee had violated the employment agreement by failing to assign his invention to the employer after leaving the employment. Employee's defense was simply that the holdover clause in the employment agreement was unenforceable. But the New Jersey Supreme Court held that holdover clauses are enforceable when reasonable, as delineated by prior New Jersey decisions on the tests of reasonableness.[2]

However, the New York court in Lord, Geller, Federico, Einstein, Inc. v. Lord, Einstein, O'Neill & Partners[3] spelled out what is reasonable and what is not reasonable. Here plaintiff advertising company, founded in 1967, was sold in 1974 to JWT advertising agency, and the sales agreement required Lord and Einstein, as employees of the new agency, to be bound by a "non-competition" clause for one year after their employment with plaintiff agency was terminated:

7. *Non-competition.* Employee agrees that, except in the event of the breach by the Company and/or JWT of this Agreement (which shall include discharge of Employee without cause) or the breach by JWT of the Management Agreement of even date herewith between JWT and the Key Employees, for a period of one year from the termination for any reason of his employment with the Company, whether during, at the end of, or after the term of employment provided for by Section 2 hereof, he shall not,

directly or indirectly, solicit or accept any of the advertising business being handled by the Company at the time his employment with the Company terminates, or handled by the Company during the twelve months immediately preceding said time, provided, however, that Employee shall be entitled to solicit or accept the business of any former client after the first anniversary of the termination of the client's relationship with the Company. For the purposes of this provision, Employee shall be conclusively deemed to have indirectly solicited or accepted any business acquired by any advertising agency during his employment by or other affiliation of any type whatsoever with (whether as stockholder, director, officer, employee, consultant, or otherwise) such agency, or during the twelve months immediately preceding such employment or affiliation, if, in connection with the solicitation or acceptance of such business by such agency, Employee has contact with or arranges for a meeting with any representative of a client or former client of the Company or if Employee has any contact or attends any meetings with any representative of such a client after the acquisition of the account by such agency. For the purposes of this provision, discharge for cause shall mean discharge of Employee for acts or omissions by Employee which constitute gross negligence or a material act of disloyalty or breach of trust by Employee against the Company or JWT (Exhibit 'B' to Lord's affidavit).

(b) A Management Agreement whereby certain ground rules for the management of LGFE are set forth. In the preamble to said agreement, the statement is made that the individuals managing the company are to conduct the company's business "on an autonomous basis." The rights of the managers relating to composition of the Board of Directors, and certain decisions to be made, are then set forth in Sections 1 and 2 of the agreement. Interestingly enough, the term of those rights is specifically limited to five years from the effective date of the sale to JWT. Further, the managers are specifically directed to comply with the wishes of JWT as to "the acceptance or resignation of any account assignments." Section 2(b)(v).

Plaintiff advertising agency prospered under the new ownership, and in 1977 its parent company JWT was acquired by Owl company, which immediately demanded that plaintiff agency withdraw from an important account. Plaintiff rebeled against that demand, which was apparently inconsistent with its management agreement with JWT, and plaintiff contacted an investment banker about a possible "buyout." Shortly thereafter the employees of plaintiff resigned and formed the defendant advertising agency; "many of the accounts serviced by LGFE (plaintiff) were notified of the departures." Plaintiff agency sought "to enjoin the former employees from attempting to obtain the business of said accounts"; defendant employees contended that both employees and the accounts have "the right to move from and to whatever agencies they wish, and that indeed it is not unusual that they do so." The New York court granted plaintiff's motions in the following particulars: (1) the individual employees were preliminarily enjoined from soliciting other employees to leave their employment and work for defendant agency; and (2) the two principal defendants were preliminarily enjoined from soliciting or accepting, directly or indirectly, any accounts of plaintiff agency that were accounts of the plaintiff for 12 months preceding their resignation, in accordance with clause 7 of the employment agreement. The court stated that

the common law implies a duty of loyalty between employer and employee which prohibits employees from conspiring to set up a competing business while they are still
working for their employer. . . . Furthermore, this common duty of loyalty survives
the termination of employment. . . . The solicitation of employees to leave their former employer constitutes a breach of this duty. . . . The mass exodus of employees,
on no notice, within days of each other, and their concomitant employment at [defen-
dant agency] . . . points strongly towards a solicitation which must be enjoined pending
determination of this action.

However, the New York Court stated that "to the extent that employees leave
[plaintiff agency] . . . of their own accord and seek employment at [defendant
agency], [defendant agency] is free to hire those employees." On soliciting
accounts of clients belonging to plaintiff agency, the court enjoined this noncompetitive practice with respect to accounts as of March 1988 because "the
preservance of goodwill of an employer's business [is] a reason to enforce an
anti-competitive provision." These employees "may not violate the terms of
their express agreement not to accept or solicit [plaintiff's] clients for one year."
The court thereupon enunciated the basic reasons why courts grant enforcement
of noncompetitive agreements: (a) the anticompetitive provision is clearly limited both as to time and as to what is prohibited; and (b) the activities prohibited only related directly to the accounts of the plaintiff agency for a further
limited time. Hence, the New York court found the restraints to be "reasonable" under the circumstances of the case.

In Hart, Nininger and Campbell Associates, Inc. v. Rogers[4] the Connecticut
appellate court observed that the plaintiff employer sought damages from three
former employees for breach of a restrictive covenant not to compete. According to the court, the nature of plaintiff employer's business was such that "the
confidential information disclosed to the defendants was regarded as such a
valuable business asset that the plaintiff required some protection from postem-
ployment competition. . . . Accordingly, as a condition of employment, each
defendant entered into a written restrictive non-competitive agreement with
[plaintiff employer] protecting [plaintiff employer] from his or her postemploy-
ment competition." The court also noted the evidence of "taped messages
[that] tracked the progress of defendant's efforts to solicit [plaintiff employer's]
clients and to form their own new business."

The trial court had found that defendants had breached their individual agreements with plaintiff employer, and the trial court rendered judgment against
each of the three defendants individually and jointly for $60,000 for each loss
of commissions caused by defendants' breach of the restrictive noncompetitive
covenants, and the court also granted injunctive relief to plaintiff employer.

The appellate court held that the trial court did not err in concluding that these restrictive covenants were reasonable and enforceable:

Employee further agrees that during his employment with the Company and for a period of two years after the termination thereof, he will not directly or indirectly for his own account or as an employee, stockholder, director, officer or consultant of another anywhere engage in any enterprise or business in the Company's Territory competitive with any business now or hereafter carried on by the Company during the term of his employment and that he will not solicit or attempt to represent or do business with any of the principals represented by the Company or customers to whom the Company sells with respect to competing or complementary product lines.

The Connecticut court found that

noncompetitive or restrictive covenants between an employer and employee usually occur when an employer is trying to protect his trade secrets, customer lists or territory. . . . It is a well settled rule that an anticompetitive covenant ancillary to a lawful contract is enforceable if the restraint upon trade is reasonable. . . . Our Supreme Court has set out a five-part test for determining the reasonability of a restrictive covenant: (1) the length of time the restriction is to be in effect; (2) the geographical area covered by the restriction; (3) the degree of protection afforded to the interest of the party in whose favor the covenant is made; (4) the restrictions imposed on the employee's ability to pursue his occupation; and (5) the potential for undue interference with the interests of the public. *Scott v. General Iron & Welding Co.,* 171 Conn. 132, 137, 368 A.2d 111 (1976) . . . .

The court thereupon concluded, as did the trial court, that the noncompetitive agreement was "reasonable and reasonably necessary . . . to protect the interest" of the employer, and that there was a "reasonable relationship between the type of business interests to be protected and the scope of the geographical restrictions." Interestingly, one defendant had argued that the restrictive covenant should not be enforceable as against her because she was forced to sign the employment agreement without the benefit of counsel, to which the court replied: "The argument is wholly without merit or support in the record and requires no further discussion."

The contrary position that restrictive, noncompetitive covenants against employees are not enforceable is illustrated by the Texas Supreme Court holding in Bergman v. Norris of Houston, Inc.,[5] which reversed the trial court that had enjoined four hairdressers, formerly employed by defendant, from competing for three years within a 15-mile radius. The highest Texas court ruled that barbering and hairstyling are a common calling, and as such, covenants not to compete in those areas are unenforceable, as there is no sale of a business or imparting of specialized knowledge or information involved.

The holding of the New York Court of Appeals in Leo Silfen, Inc. v. Cream[6] was similar, but with an unexpected result. Here defendant was an officer and employee of plaintiff employer, and after he was discharged, he went into business under the name Real Estate Maintenance Chemical Specialty Corporation. The former employee thereupon solicited former customers of his exemployer, who then sought, along with an associate corporation, to enjoin the exemployee and to recover damages. The trial court entered judgment in favor of the plaintiff employer. The highest New York court observed that

plaintiff corporations are engaged in selling building maintenance supplies to industrial and commercial users. Plaintiffs purchase their inventory from independent supply houses and then, at a substantial markup, resell to customers under their own label. Plaintiff Silfen sells soaps, polishes, waxes, finishers, and disinfectants, while plaintiff Formula 33 Corporation specializes in ice and snow melting compounds.

In 1949 defendant Cream joined Silfen, then engaged only in the paper and twine business. Cream was assigned and became solely responsible for the development of a cleaning and maintenance chemical supply division. . . .

In 1965, on the death of the principal of Silfen and the taking of control by his widow, Cream was named executive vice-president and general manager of plaintiff corporation for a term of 12 years. The written agreement between the parties provided for a base salary of $26,000 plus 25% of the aggregate net profits. The corporations reserved the right to discharge Cream if the aggregate net profits in any one year failed to exceed $35,000.

On November 17, 1967, Cream was discharged purportedly because of a decline of net profits. Cream, however, urges that he was discharged in order to make room for the new husband of the widow, the former Mrs. Silfen. Thirteen days after his discharge he set up Real Estate Maintenance Chemical Specialty Corporation and engaged in the me business as plaintiffs except limited to building owners and building managers. About three months later, in March, 1968, plaintiffs brought this action to enjoin defendants' solicitation of plaintiffs' customers. The complaint alleged that defendants had been soliciting plaintiffs' customers, that Cream had made copies of plaintiffs' secret and confidential customer files, and was using such information in his solicitation. Cream admits that of a list of 1,100 customers submitted by plaintiffs defendants had solicited 47. . . .

The court, in reversing the lower court judgment in favor of plaintiffs, noted that "plaintiffs did not attempt to sustain their allegation that Cream had made copies of plaintiffs' secret and confidential files, or used the recorded detail in those files with respect to each customer's 'profile.' The solicitation of plaintiffs' customers was at most the product of casual memory, or, as defendant would have the court believe, coincidence. If there has been a physical taking or studied copying, the court may in a proper case enjoin solicitation, not necessarily as a violation of a trade secret, but as an egregious breach of trust and confidence while in plaintiffs' service." The New York Court of Appeals concluded:

Generally, where the customers are readily ascertainable outside the employer's business as prospective users or consumers of the employer's services or products, trade secret protection will not attach and courts will not enjoin the employee from soliciting his employer's customers. . . . Conversely, where the customers are not known in the trade or are discoverable only by extraordinary efforts courts have not hesitated to protect customer lists and files as trade secrets. This is especially so where the customers' patronage had been secured by years of effort and advertising effected by the expenditure of substantial time and money. . . .

The customers solicited by defendants, as apparently found by the trial court, are openly engaged in business in advertised locations and their names and addresses may readily be found by those engaged in the trade. . . .

In the absence of express agreement to that effect between the parties, or a demonstration that a customer list has the several attributes of a trade secret, courts, without more, should not enjoin an ex-employee from engaging in fair and open competition with his former employer. The limiting effects upon the former employee with respect to his ability to earn a living are marked and obvious. . . .

In concluding, it may be stated expressly what was earlier implied, namely, that if defendants had been shown to have appropriated by copying, studied memory, or by some other manner which does not now come to mind, the detailed information in the customer files there would be a case quite different from this. The record shows no such appropriation with respect to a single customer, let alone many customers to an extent barring reliance on casual memory. Instead, it shows that defendants solicited 47 of the 1,100 customers submitted on a list prepared by plaintiffs from its confidential files. The point is that in the circumstances described names of customers alone involved no trade secret and there was no wrongful conduct by defendants. If trade secrets there were, they consisted of the data in carefully secured and segregated files.

In summary, it should be observed that an employee may be given confidential trade secrets[7] by the employer, and in such a case the employee may not disclose such knowledge to others. It is immaterial that the contract of employment did not expressly prohibit such conduct by the employee. But employees are not under a duty to refrain from divulging general information of the particular business in which they are employed. Nor are employees under a duty not to divulge the information of a particular business when the relation between the employer and employee is not considered confidential nor fiduciary in nature. Mere knowledge or skill obtained through experience are not in themselves trade secrets, and consequently employees may use the fruits of their labors in subsequent employment or in working for themselves.

Inventions of an employee belong to the employee in the absence of an express or implied agreement to the contrary, even though the employee uses the time and property of the employer in the discovery or invention, unless the employee has been employed for the express purpose of inventing things or processes. The employer has the burden of proving that the employer is entitled to the invention or process discovered by the employee in the course of employment. In United States v. Dubilier Condenser Corp.[8] the U.S. Supreme Court ruled that the inventions of the employee belong to the employer when the employee is employed to secure certain results from experiments to be conducted in the course of employment. The rationale is that there is a trust relationship or an implied agreement by the employee to make an assignment of the invention to the employer.

Restrictive, noncompetitive covenants[9] have greatly altered professional sports. The "free-ing" of professional athletes from team monopolies has, however, engendered many undesirable features such as the business agent. In Walters v. Harmon,[10] for example, the New York court refused to stay arbitration of a fee dispute in which a National Football League player sought to declare invalid an agreement with two business agents signed before the player was eligible to do so. The two business agents contended that the agreement with Ronald Harmon (who was a star player at the University of Iowa before becoming a first-round draft pick of the Buffalo Bills professional team) was not part of the NFL contract that precluded the signing of the agency agreement before Harmon signed a four-year, $1.4 million contract with the Buffalo Bills. The agents sought the customary 10 percent fee. The court observed that the case touched upon "a pernicious practice encouraging young college athletes to enter into deceptive agreements which are post-dated so they can continue to play college football." The agency contract signed in March 1985 while Harmon was at the University of Iowa is a violation of NFL rules as well as the rules of the National Collegiate Athletic Association prohibiting such agreements until the conclusion of college football eligibility.

NOTES

1. —A.2d—(N.J., June 22, 1988).
2. Citing Solari Industries, Inc. v. Malady, 55 N.J. 571 (1970) and Whitmyer Bros. v. Doyle, 58 N.J. 25 (1971).
3. —N.Y.S.2d—(New York County, April 19, 1988).
4. 16 Conn. App. 619 (October 4, 1988).
5. —S.W.2d—(Tex., July 15, 1988).
6. 278 N.E.2d 636 (N.Y. 1972).
7. See Warren Freedman, The Business Tort of Fraud and Misrepresentation (1988) at chapter 7.
8. 289 U.S. 178 (1932).
9. See Warren Freedman, Professional Sports and Antitrust (1987).
10. 516 N.Y.S.2d 874 (New York County, 1987).

11

Some Observations on Union Employees

Protection of union employees not only from employers but from their own unions has been the subject of countless lawsuits over the years. The U.S. Supreme Court on June 6, 1988, in Lingle v. Norge[1] ruled that union employees have a right to sue their employer over a dismissal, even though their contract of employment provides for a specific union grievance procedure. Here plaintiff Lingle, an assembly line worker, filed a compensation claim under Illinois law for a wrist injury she allegedly received at work. The company fired her within a week, stating that her compensation claim was fraudulent. She then filed a grievance complaint under the terms of her union contract, alleging that she was fired without cause. She won reinstatement of her job and back pay, and then she sued the employer for damages. The federal district court dismissed her suit on the grounds that the dispute should be handled under the union contract. But the highest court reversed, stating that she could file suit against the employer under Illinois law that prohibits retaliatory firing of employees.

States may provide greater safeguards to employees than those provided in labor management contracts as long as courts are not forced to interpret provisions of the collective bargaining agreements. A railroad employee is not entitled to representation by his own union at an employer's disciplinary hearing if a different union is the official collective bargaining agent for employees, according to the highest court.[2] The federal Railway Labor Act does not include "a right to minority union participation in company-level grievance and disciplinary proceedings."

At the state level, under the New York Taylor Law (which provides for termination of public employees engaged in a strike, inter alia) the New York court observed in New York City Health and Hospitals Corporation v. Local

2507 of District Council 37 of the American Federation of State, County and Municipal Employees[3] that the defendants sought the reinstatement of all provisional emergency medical service employees terminated by plaintiff employer after a "sickout" that violated a temporary restraining order. The defendants argued that,pursuant to both the New York Taylor Law and their constitutional rights, such employees were entitled to a hearing before they could be discharged. The plaintiff employer responded with the argument that the discharges were legally permissible because probationary and provisional employees are not protected by civil service status. But the court decided that the employees were entitled to a hearing in order to determine whether they had a valid excuse for failing to report on the day of the "sickout." The court even went a step further and urged the plaintiff employer to "give serious consideration to the immediate rehiring of any . . . person" with such valid excuse. The court said:

Courts in this state have in the following cases granted hearings to discharged, provisional or probationary employees who were stigmatized as a result of the nature of the charges causing their dismissal or non-appointment: Ranus v.Blum, 96 AD2d 1144 (4th Dept. 1983) mental instability; Salvatore v. Nassai, 81 AD2d 1012 (4th Dept. 1981) dishonesty; Horowitz v. Roche, 70 AD2d 854 (1st Dept. 1979) incompetence of only applicant to pass competitive examination; Perry v. Blair,49 AD 309 (4th Dept.) probationary patrolman charged with rape and sexual molestation; Reeves v. Golar, 45 AD2d 163 (1st Dept. 1974) narcotic addiction; Stearns v. Gilchrist, 84 Misc. 2d 519 (Sup. Ct., Orange Co. 1976) psychologically unfit; Mengione v. New York City Off-Track Betting Corp., 83 Misc. 2d 105 (Sup. Ct, N.Y. Co. 1974) misconduct involving public funds.

Although here the names of the discharged employees have not been publicly disseminated, it would seem that a discharge for violation of the prohibitions of the Taylor Law does stigmatize, and that as a result of the enormous publicity given to the alleged sickout, there has been sufficient publication to find that a "liberty interest" has been affected. . . . Since constitutional rights are involved, plaintiffs are hereby directed to grant any discharged provisional employee or any employee whose probationary period was extended, a hearing to determine whether such employee had a valid excuse for not being present at work on March 4, 1988. Any employee who makes a hearing shall request it of the Health and Hospitals Corporation within 30 days from the date hereof. Such hearings shall be held in an expeditious manner by said plaintiff.

It should be noted that, under the federal Food Stamp Act, as amended in 1981, the federal government may limit a family's eligibility for food stamps when a family member is on strike, according to the highest court in Lyng v. UAW,[4] where the court found that the act represented a rational effort by Congress to remain neutral in labor disputes. Families already receiving food stamps when a family member goes on strike are not dropped from the food stamp program but they are barred from receiving additional food stamps despite the loss of income.

Where the employee is disgruntled with his or her union for one reason or another, the employee can exercise many rights. For example, under the National Labor Relations Act a union, over the objections of dues-paying, non-member employees, may not spend funds collected from them on activities unrelated to collective bargaining; in Communications Workers of America v. Beck[5] the U.S. Supreme Court found that Congress was concerned with the dues and the rights of union members as well as with the dues and rights of nonunion members. Ordinarily, courts are reluctant to authorize judicial interference in the internal affairs of unions,[6] but where a violation of law has occurred the courts will interfere in union affairs. The interference is undertaken with due deference to the remedies available within the union.[7]

One of the prolific areas of litigation is the election process within the union. The Labor Management Reporting and Disclosure Act, or LMRDA,[8] for example, has been in the forefront of such litigation; one of the prime requisites is that the complaining union member must exhaust union remedies before the courts or the government will step into the fray. Employers obviously cannot interfere with union elections, but questioning an employee about his or her union sympathies during a union election campaign is not a per se violation of the National Labor Relations Act.[9] But in Springs Motel Co.[10] the board found that a supervisor's repeated and systematic interrogation of two employees following company-sponsored meetings violated the act. Indeed, employers should be particularly careful about what is said in interchanges with groups of union employees but remember that stricter standards apply only when the employer talks with truly uncommitted employees.[11]

In summary, employees have the right "to engage in concerted activities for the purpose of collective bargaining or for other mutual aid and protection." This provision of Section 7 of the National Labor Relations Act gives employees the right to choose a bargaining representative, i.e., a union, or represent their own interests by collective action.[12] Nonunion employees have the same rights as union employees! Under Section 8(a)(1) of the act it is an "unfair labor practice" to "interfere with, restrain or coerce employees in the exercise of the rights guaranteed in Section 7."

NOTES

1. 108 S.Ct.1877 (1988).
2. See Landers v. National Railroad Passenger Corp., 56 U.S.L.W. 4355 (1988).
3. 526 N.Y.S.2d 999 (New York County,April 13, 1988). According to the court,

although the Taylor Law does not differentiate between employees protected by civil service status on the one hand, and provisional and probationary employees on the other, there is nothing therein that would lead the court to believe that it grants to the latter any greater rights to continued public employment than would be possessed by them absent such law. Although the Taylor Law eliminated the automatic termination of employment for a strike against a public employer, it did not prohibit government from dealing with its provisional employees in the manner provided by other provisions of law. Thus, in determining whether the discharged provisional employees have any remedy, it is necessary to look to other provisions of law.

In Board of Regents v. Roth, 408 U.S. 564 (1972), it was stated that where "a person's good name, reputation, honor, or integrity is at stake because of what government is doing to him, notice and an opportunity to be heard are essential," and that a like result would ensue if "in declining to re-employ the respondent, (it) imposed on him a stigma or other disability that foreclosed his freedom to take advantage of other employment opportunities." (p. 573) . . .

Even though the court is limited in fashioning relief for any provisional employee unjustly discharged, probationary employees have greater rights as any determination to dismiss an employee with such status is subject to being attacked as arbitrary and capricious. Wilborn v. Starr, 58 AD 2d 785 (1st Dept. 1977). In that case the court found that the discharge of certain employees followed "baseless judgments" concerning their work, and the lower court's three month extension of their probationary period was found to be "an improvident exercise of discretion."

Thus, if any probationary employee is found to have had a valid reason for not being at work on March 4, the 60 day extension of his or her probationary period would be in bad faith and arbitrary and capricious, and is to be rescinded.

4. 56 U.S.L.W. 4268 (1988).

5. 56 U.S.L.W. 4857 (1988).

6. See Trail v. International Brotherhood of Teamsters, 542 F.2d 961 (6th Cir. 1976).

7. See Hodgson v. Local 6799 of United Steelworkers, 403 U.S. 333 (1971).

8. 29 U.S.C. 481(a) et seq.

9. Note Hotel Employees and Restaurant Employees Local 11 v. NLRB, 760 F.2d 1006 (9th Cir. 1985).

10. 280 NLRB 33 (1986).

11. See N.L.J. 24 (October 10, 1988).

12. 29 U.S.C. 15 et seq.

12

Immigration of Employees and Responsibility of Employers

Workers from outside the United States have been a boon to certain industries but a headache to other industries where they have sought employment. Congress somewhat recognized the overall problem in enacting the Immigration Reform and Control Act of 1986,[1] which places the burden of policing immigration laws on private industry by requiring employers to hire only those persons authorized to work in the United States.[2] The legislation affects employers in three ways: (1) fines up to $10,000 and jail sentences can be imposed on employers that knowingly hire undocumented aliens; (2) every employer must verify and maintain records on the immigration and citizenship status of each prospective employee, even if the applicant for employment is a U.S. citizen; and (3) the antidiscrimination provisions prohibit all but the smallest employers from discriminating in hiring or firing on the basis of an individual's national origin or status of citizenship.[3] In essence, the burden falls upon employers to police and enforce the act. Employers may lawfully continue to employ unauthorized aliens hired before November 6, 1986, however. Congress in enacting the new legislation does have the broad constitutional powers for "nationwide control and regulation of immigration and naturalization."[4]

Interestingly, the act prohibits employers from asking those seeking employment to post security or agree to indemnify the employer against liability for violating the act.[5] But employers may exact a bond against liability from an incorporated referral service. Full sanctions under the act went into effect on June 1, 1988.[6]

Among the many documents that employers must use to verify the status of applicants for employment are U.S. passport, certificate of U.S. citizenship issued by the Immigration and Naturalization Service, and alien registration receipt card.[7] Other necessary documents must show employment authorization, such as Social Security card, certificate of birth in any state, and U.S. citizen identification card.[8] Employers are required to file a Form I-9 certifying that they have examined the person's documents, that these documents appear to be genuine and relate to the applicant for employment, and that the person is authorized to work in the United States.[9]

Section 102 of the act prohibits discrimination in employment based on national origin or citizenship status, and complements the employer sanctions in the act. But aliens who are unauthorized are not protected from discrimination.[10]

The act preempts state and local employer sanctions laws,[11] yet in League of United Latin American Citizens v. Pasadena Independent School District[12] it would appear that local considerations dictated the result. Here four undocumented alien school janitors were fired for using false Social Security numbers, and the federal district court in Texas granted a preliminary injunction and ordered the school district to reinstate the janitors in their positions because they were "qualified for legalization and . . . intend to become citizens." The court opined that "a policy of terminating undocumented aliens for no reason other than they have given employers a false Social Security number constitutes an unfair immigration-related employment practice."

While there appears to be some overlapping of the antidiscrimination provisions of the act with Title VII of the Civil Rights Act of 1964, note that Title VII applies only to employers who have 15 or more employees.[13] The act here applies to all employers with between 4 and 14 employees for national origin discrimination, and to all employers of more than 3 employees for citizenship discrimination.

In summary, it is evident that employers can be penalized for knowingly hiring unauthorized workers on one hand, and for firing or refusing to hire authorized aliens on the other hand.[14]

NOTES

1. 8 U.S.C. 274A or 100 Stat. 3359 (1986).

2. See Sussman, Payson, and Herrin, "The Immigration Reform and Control Act", Trial Magazine 50 (July 1987).

3. See Roberts and Yale-Loehr, "Employers as Junior Immigration Inspectors: The Impact of the 1986 Immigration Reform and Control Act," Internat Lawyer 1013 (Fall 1987).

4. See Takahashi v. Fish and Game Commission, 68 S.Ct. 1138 (1948).

5. See § 274A(g)(1).

6. See § 274A(i).

7. See § 274A(b)(1)(B).

8. See § 274A(b)(1)(C).

9. Supra note 2 at p. 52.

10. Id. at 53.

11. See § 274A(h)(2).
12. 662 F. Supp. 443 (S.D. Tex. 1987).
13. See section 4.3.
14. Supra note 3 at p. 1052.

ADDENDUM

Updating Significant Issues in Employment Contract Law

A.1 AGE DISCRIMINATION (*See* pages 16, 43, 64–67)

While a substantial number of court decisions are unfavorable to the person or persons claiming age discrimination, as illustrated hereinafter, it is refreshing to read the decision of the Seventh U.S. Court of Appeals in Aman v. Federal Aviation Administration, —F2d— (7th Cir., September 12, 1988). Here, the court told the defendant federal agency that their age regulation for pilots (for flights including commercial flights carrying more than 30 passengers, the pilot must be less than 60 years of age) was wrong. The pilots successfully argued that experience improves performance, offsetting any deterioration in skill, and that pilots 60 and older who meet FAA medical and psychological standards are no more likely to cause accidents than younger pilots. The FAA was found not to have facts to support its rejection of the pilots' arguments. And in Montana v. First Federal S & L Association, —F2d— (2nd Cir., February 21, 1989) the court held that the bank worker established a prima facie case of age discrimination by setting forth specific facts raising a genuine issue as to whether the bank's reason for her termination was supported by facts.

On the other hand, the majority of claims of age discrimination have been refused: in Arnold v. U.S. Postal Service, —F2d— (DC Cir., December 20, 1988) the "senior-first rule" resulting in the mandatory transfer of older postal employees to chronically understaffed offices did not violate the Age Discrimination in Employment Act. In Silverman v. New York State Division of Human Rights, —NYS2d— (November 8, 1988), the New York court rejected the claim of a 66-year old applicant for a position with the City of New York; the applicant had sent in a hand-written resume devoid of educational and employment background, he was therefore properly passed over for the position according to the court. And in Ioele v. Alden Press, Inc., —NYS2d— (App Div., 1st Dept., January 19, 1989) the plaintiff, a commission sales representative, contended that "the corporate defendants undertook a series of acts calculated to force him to resign," to which the court responded:

"To succeed in his age discrimination claim, plaintiff must show that 'age was the determining factor' in Alden's alleged ill treatment of him, that ' "but for" his employer's motive to discriminate against him because of age, he would not have been discharged.'(*Pena v. Brattleboro Retreat*, 702 F2d 322, 323, quoting *Loeb v. Textron Inc.*, 600 F2d 1003, 1019.) As this record makes clear, plaintiff cannot meet his burden. The purported issues of fact relied upon by the motion court are irrelevant to whether Alden discriminated against him because of his age, and the proof offered in support of the claim that his resignation was, in fact, a constructive termination is fatally deficient. Accordingly, we grant summary judgment and dismiss the first two causes of action alleging age discrimination."

For an analysis of the question of damages for age discrimination, see Wallach and Marx, "Damages for Age Discrimination: Courts Split on 'Willfulness' Rule," NLJ (April 11, 1988), citing such recent cases as Cooper v. Asplundh Tree Expert Co., 836 F2d 1544 (10th Cir., 1988), Bethea v. Levi Strauss & Co., 827 F2d 355 (8th Cir., 1987), and Dreyer v. Arco Chemical Co., 801 F2d 651 (3rd Cir., 1986), cert den 107 S Ct 1348 (1987). In the latter case, the Third U.S. Court of Appeals stated that in order to recover liquidated damages, a plaintiff would have to show "additional evidence of outrageous conduct" by the employer. And in Gilliam v. Armtex Inc., 820 F2d 1387 (4th Cir., 1987), the Fourth U.S. Court of Appeals concluded that "the employer acted in bad faith or with knowledge that its action was so lacking in justification as to warrant a jury's characterization of its conduct as willful," therefore supporting plaintiff's claim for damages.

An unsupervised release of an employee's claim under the Age Discrimination in Employment Act (29 USC 621–634) is permissible according to the Eighth U.S. Court of Appeals in Lancaster v. Buerkle Buick Honda Co., 809 F2d 539 (8th Cir., 1987), cert den 107 S Ct 3212 (1987). The termination agreement could bar the employee's claim for age discrimination.

"Piggy-backing" in an ADEA claim was sanctioned by the Seventh U.S. Court of Appeals in Anderson v. Montgomery Ward & Co., 852 F2d 1008 (7th Cir., 1988) as long as the charge serving as its basis alleged class-wide age discrimination. The underlying purpose of ADEA's statutory scheme was to provide the employer with notice of the charges and to permit conciliation of matters by the Equal Employment Opportunity Commission. Indeed, the Third U.S. Court of Appeals in Hoffmann-LaRoche v. Sperling, —F2d— (3rd Cir., April 4, 1989) ruled that the federal district court had the authority to facilitate notice to members of an asserted class who have not yet filed consents to join the action based on age discrimination.

A.2 AIDS AND THE EMPLOYMENT CONTRACT (*See* pages 4–5, 89–90)

It is self-evident tht employers should develop a corporate policy on AIDS so as to deal with the issue of discrimination fairly and compassionately. Information is available from the American Foundation for AIDS Research, 40 West 57th St., New York, N.Y. 10019–4001.

A.3 ALIENS AND DISCRIMINATION

The Immigration Reform and Control Act of 1986 (Pub L 99–603, codified at 8 USC 1324 et seq) created a new category of discrimination, to wit: an unfair immigration-related employment practice dealing with hiring, recruiting, referring for a fee, or discharge of aliens. It is unlawful to base any employment decision on an alien's national origin, whether the alien was granted amnesty, legally admitted into the United States for permanent residence, or granted asylum or refugee status. Businesses with three or less employees are not subject to the Act. On the other hand, an employer may not knowingly hire an alien whose status does not permit employment.

A.4 ARBITRATION AND THE EMPLOYMENT CONTRACT (*See* page 61)

The arbitration clause in Sablosky v. Edward S. Gordon Co., —NYS2d— (February 21, 1989) was upheld by the New York Court of Appeals, despite the fact that the arbitration clause required one party to arbitrate all disputes but allowed the other party its choice of arbitrating or litigating the dispute. The highest New York court found the clause not invalid for lack of mutuality of remedy or obligation.

In DeSapio v. Josephthal and Co., —NYS2d— (New York County, April 6, 1989) the claim by a former vice president of a stock brokerage house that her employer was guilty of illegal discrimination by firing her from her job because she had been ill with breast cancer, must be arbitrated under the broad arbitration clauses of her employment contract. The arbitration clauses here were determined by the court to be governed by the Federal Arbitration Act (it should be noted that there is no federal law prohibiting discrimination based on a person's handicap or a history of cancer, according to the court):

Arbitration agreements are favored in law and are to be broadly construed (Coudert v. Paine, Webber, Jackson & Curtis, 705 F2d 78). Although arbitration is a favored and efficacious method of dispute resolution, the New York courts have fashioned a few narrow exceptions to that general rule when the issue involves a strong public policy 'amounting to gross illegality or its equivalent,' generally found in a 'readily identifiable source in the statutes or common-law principles . . . ' (Matter of Port Washington

Union Free School Dist. v. Port Washington Teachers Assn., 45 NY2d 411, 422). The public policy prohibiting arbitration bars 'in an absolute sense, particular matters being decided or certain relief being granted by an arbitrator' (Matter of Sprinzen [Nomberg], 46 NY2d 623, 631). The rationale for the public policy exception is the possibility of inconsistent decisions by arbitrators who are not bound by law and may rely on their own sense of equity on matters of important public concern resulting in adverse consequences for the public in general (Matter of Aimcee Wholesale Corp. [Tomar Prods.], 21 NY2d 621). A claim of sex discrimination is an issue which has been found to be a matter for the courts and not arbitration (Matter of Wertheim & Co. v. Halpert, 65 AD2d 724, affd 48 NY2d 681).

Notwithstanding the existence of state policy exempting some matters such as discrimination claims from arbitration, defendants maintain that federal law requires arbitration of this dispute. Plaintiff's agreement to arbitrate is governed by the Federal Arbitration Act (9 USC § 1 et seq.) because her employment involved transactions in commerce. . . . The broad arbitration agreement involved here (see, Flanagan v. Prudential-Bache Sec., supra) does not exclude statutory claims. Since plaintiff's discrimination claim arises out of the termination of her employment, it is encompassed by the arbitration agreement (see, Steck v. Smith Barney, Harris Upham & Co., 661 F Supp 543). The question, then, is whether there are external legal constraints which preclude arbitration of plaintiff's discrimination claim.

In enacting the Federal Arbitration Act, Congress 'withdrew the power of the states to require a judicial forum for the resolution of claims which the contracting parties agreed to resolve by arbitration' (Southland Corp. v. Keating, supra, at 10). The rigorous enforcement of arbitration agreements mandated by the Act is not to be limited or constrained by state law (id., at 11, 13). Therefore, it is federal and not state law which must provide the 'legal constraints,' if any, to enforcement of this arbitration agreement. . . ."

In Queens Park Realty Corp. v. Bevona, —NYS2d— (Queens County, November 15, 1988) the employer moved to stay the union's demand for arbitration of claims for alleged underpayment of wages. Since the union contract of employment had expired, the arbitration clauses, according to the employer, also expired. But the New York court disagreed, holding that a labor dispute that arises during the life of an arbitration provision remains subject to arbitration, even after the labor agreement has expired:

"it is well settled that the duty to arbitrate a dispute arising during the term of a collective bargaining agreement survives the contract. (Nolde Brothers, Inc. v. Local No. 358, Bakery & Confectionary Workers Union, AFL-CIO, 430 US 243; Matter of Dickenson, 84 AD2d 872; Matter of County of Orange v. Faculty Assn. of Orange County Community College, 77 AD2d 894; Matter of Bd. of Educ. v. Pearl River Teachers' Assn., 71 AD2d 654.) Here, there is no question that the dispute arose during the term of the Agreement and that petitioner's obligation under the arbitration clause survives the expiration date of the contract.

Petitioner further asserts that the Union waived its right to arbitrate because one year has elapsed since the court order permitting respondent to refile the grievance pursuant to the Agreement. In this case, the order did not specify any time period for the refiling of the grievance, thus it is deemed that the Union was required to act within a reasonable time. It cannot be said that the Union failed to act within a reasonable time, particularly in view of the subsequent NLRB proceedings. A party will not be deemed to have waived his right to arbitration unless active participation in litigation or other conduct inconsistent with an intent to reserve any issues for arbitration is demonstrated. (Faberge Intl. Inc. v. DiPino, 109 AD2d 235.) While a great lapse of time has been construed as a waiver (cf., Matter of Buchanan v. Rogers, 9 AD2d 1010), no such facts are presented here."

A.5 DISCRIMINATION GENERALLY (See pages 6, 12, 21, 55–86, 87–96)

The U.S. Supreme Court in Price Waterhouse v. Hopkins, —S Ct— (May 1, 1989) ruled that an employer, not the discriminated employee, has the legal burden of proving that its refusal to hire or promote someone is based on legitimate and discriminatory reasons. The defendant accounting firm had failed to promote a woman into partnership. The court rejected the employer's contention that she should be required to prove that it was sexual discrimination and not legitimate judgments on her managerial ability that cost her the partnership position. The highest court opined that evidence that she was judged by her male supervisors on the basis of stereotyped notions of appropriate female appearance and behavior can establish the existence of illegal discrimination. The 6–3 majority of the court, however, ruled that the defendant employer has to show only by a preponderance of the evidence that its reasons for denying the partnership were legitimate, for example, the employer's reasons were "more likely than not" legitimate. See also New York Times (May 2, 1989) at A.1 and A.17.

In Peter P.K. (The Port Authority of New York), NYS2d (New York County, November 8, 1988) the applicant's inability to obtain employment as a police officer was found to have resulted from his failure to pass the required psychological examination. The court declared that

"This court may only overturn the decision of an agency if it is not based on substantial evidence or is arbitrary and capricious (Pell v. Board of Education, 34 NY2d 222 [1974]; John Doe v. Thomas A. Coughlin, III, 71 NY2d 48 [1987]; Muzio v. Thomas A. Coughlin, III, 136 AD2d 640 [2d Dept., 1988]).

For a decision to reach this level it must be one that no reasonable mind could reach (Buck v. New York State Liquors Authority, 186 NYS2d 684, aff'd 8 AD2d 851 [2d Dept., 1959]).

The decision to disqualify petitioner clearly does not meet that standard since two independent psychological examinations found the petitioner unfit to serve as a police officer (see, Resp. Exhs. "7," "9," and "10" and "11"). Although petitioner also submits a separate report that he was psychologically fit to serve as a police officer (see Pet. Reply Affirmation, dated April 26, 1988) it is not for this court to choose between

diverse professional opinions (McCabe v. Haberman, 33 AD2d 547 [1st Dept. 1969];
Palozzola v. Nadel, 83 AD2d 539 [1st Dept., 1981]). Therefore, based upon those
findings respondent's decision to disqualify petitioner are not arbitrary, capricious, unreasonable nor an abuse of discretion."

The New York Court of Appeals in Matter of Deas v. Levitt —NE2d—
(New York, May 9, 1989) set the stage:

"Petitioner, seeking a promotion in the competitive classification of the Civil Service,
took the required examination and achieved the third highest score. His certification was
delayed, however, because he was found to be medically unqualified. After administrative proceedings, the disqualification was reversed but the eligible list on which his
name appeared expired before the Department of Personnel certified him. He instituted
this proceeding to compel establishment of a special eligibility list, claiming that this is
the appropriate remedy under our decision in *Matter of Mena v. D'Ambrose* (44 NY2d
428) and that is warranted by the due process clauses of the State and Federal Constitutions.

There should be a reversal. Before being entitled to placement on a special eligible
list for a civil service position, an applicant must bring a proceeding, before the list
expires, successfully challenging the validity of the list itself. Because petitioner does
not challenge the validity of the eligible list as being contrary to the merit and fitness
requirements of the State Constitution (Art V, §6), he has no right to the relief requested. This conclusion does not violate due process of law under either the Federal
or State Constitutions; nor is distinguishing between applicants who attack the constitutional validity of the list and those that allege only that they were otherwise eligible
arbitrary and capricious. Accordingly, the order of the Appellate Division should be
reversed and the judgment of Supreme Court dismissing the petition should be reinstated."

A.6   EMOTIONAL DISTRESS AND EMPLOYMENT

In Hartman v. R. P. McCoy Apparel, Ltd., —NYS2d— (App Div., 2nd
Dept., December 19, 1988) the plaintiff alleged that she was induced to leave
a permanent position with a large retail store by assurances of a promising
future working for defendant employer. Her employment was then terminated
five weeks later, causing her "extreme emotional distress and damaging her
reputation as a retail manager." Her employment-at-will, however, precluded
any emotional distress claim: "Accepting all of the plaintiff's allegations as
true, the defendant's conduct is far from being ' "so outrageous in character,
and so extreme in degree, as to go beyond all possible bounds of decency, and
to be regarded as atrocious and utterly intolerable in a civilized community" '
(Fischer v. Maloney, 43 NY2d 553, 557, quoting from Restatement [Second]
of Torts §46[1], comment [d])." However, in Carroll v. Tennessee Valley
Authority, —F Supp— (DC, 1988) the court sanctioned an intentional infliction
of emotional distress claim where the employer failed to respond to plaintiff's
requests for a smoke-free environment!

A.7   EMPLOYEE AS AN INDEPENDENT CONTRACTOR

See generally Simon, "Distinguishing Employees from Independent Contractors: Lessons from the California Experience," 14 Employee Relations L J 569 (Spring 1989), citing, inter alia, Borello & Sons Inc. v. State Dept of Industrial Relations, 242 Cal Rptr 554 (1987) to the effect that share farmers working for the plaintiff corporation were independent contractors and not employees. Therefore, the plaintiff corporation was not required to pay workers' compensation insurance on behalf of the share farmers. See also Truesdale v. Workers' Compensation Appeals Board, 235 Cal Rptr 754 (1987) holding that the injured cosmetologist was an employee of the beauty salon where he worked. In a more complicated set of facts, in Rinaldi v. Workers' Compensation Appeals Board, 244 Cal Rptr 637 (1988) the California court determined that the general contractor was required to pay workers' compensation benefits to the injured worker of the subcontractor who had willfully misrepresented its status as an independent contractor; the subcontractor had no workers' compensation insurance and no license to operate as a subcontractor.

A.8   EMPLOYER CLAIMS AGAINST EMPLOYEES (*See* pages 9–36)

Employers generally demand loyalty and honesty from their employees, and disparagement of employer by the employee may be actionable, as illustrated in Mandelblatt v. Devon Stores, Inc., 521 NYS2d 672 (1987). Here a consultant involved in a contractual dispute with his employer disparaged the employer's business and financial condition in meeting with prospective buyers of the employer. The New York appellate court found that his behavior could support the employer's counterclaims for breach of fiduciary duty as well as interference with prospective advantageous trade relations. The court found that the employee's malice existed in the disparaging statements made after the employee's contractual demands had been rejected by the employer: "It therefore appears that this was a retaliatory action, prompted by malice and intended solely to damage appellants with whom respondent had a confidential, fiduciary relationship." See generally Kandel, "Enforcing Employee Duties: Employer Claims Against Disloyal, Dishonest, or Negligent Employees," 14 Employee Relations L. J. 617 (Spring 1989).

A.9   EMPLOYMENT-AT-WILL (*See* pages 13–16)

It is abundantly clear that employment-at-will ordinarily gives the employer the right to hire and fire employees at the employer's discretion. See 30 AARP New Bulletin (January 1989) at 6–7. However, workers are increasingly attacking this age-old concept in court and often winning substantial awards in damages (an average of $150,000 in California). At least 28 states are said to have enacted "public policy" employee protection statutes by defining "good cause" as the basis for firing an employee. In Springer v. Weeks and Leo Co., —NW2d— (Iowa, September 21, 1988) the court narrowed the powers of the employer by declaring that the female employee who was fired after making a workers' compensation claim was deemed by the Iowa court to have suffered "tortious interference" with her contract for employment-at-will: "It is the public policy of this State that an employee's right to seek compensation which is granted by law for work-related injuries should not be interfered with regardless of the terms of the contract of hire." See A.B.A.J. (January 1989) at 81–83.

In the state of New York it is still settled law that, absent an agreement establishing a fixed duration, an employment relationship is presumed to be a hiring-at-will, terminable at any time by either party; see Sabetay v. Sterling Drug Inc., 514 NYS2d 209, 506 NE2d 919 (1987). See generally Baer, "Employment at Will in New York—An Update," NYLJ (November 22, 1988) at 3 and 4, delineating the three typical challenges to employment-at-will: (1) challenges alleging that a plaintiff's discharge constitutes a breach of an express or implied promise to terminate only for cause; (2) challenges alleging that the discharge violates an important public policy; and (3) challenges alleging that the discharge violates an implied obligation to deal fairly and in good faith. See Warren Freedman, *Richards On Insurance* (6th ed., 1989) at Chapter 8 thereof. It wowuld appear that a plaintiff who cannot cite a provision in an employment contract or a company manual that expressly states that employees will be terminated only for just cause or solely for some other specified reason, fails to state a valid cause of action in New York. In Brown v. General Development Corp., NYS2d (Nassau County, November 9, 1988) the at-will employee could not sustain the wrongful discharge action. The employee was hired by defendant as a manager-trainee and within two years he was demoted, reassigned, and finally terminated due to "lack of production." The New York court declared:

"it is well established that New York law does not recognize a claim for wrongful discharge of an at-will employee. (Murphy v. American Home Products, 58 N.Y. 2d 293.) Absent an agreement establishing a fixed duration, an employment relationship is presumed to be a hiring at will, terminable at any time by either party. (Sabetay v. Sterling Drug, 69 N.Y. 2d 329.) Here, the two employment agreements signed by plaintiff essentially provide that plaintiff's employment could be cancelled at any time by either plaintiff or defendant upon written notice to the other. Under these circumstances plaintiff was an at-will employee, and his claim for wrongful discharge must be rejected for failure to state a cause of action. Furthermore, plaintiff's second cause of action for punitive damages based on the alleged wrongful discharge must fail as well.

This court recognizes that an at-will employee may be lawfully discharged for any reason or for no reason, but not for a statutorily impermissible reason (State Division of Human Rights v. Sheriff, 71 N.Y. 2d 623, 630), and that discrimination in employment on the basis of race is statutorily barred (Executive Law §296 (1) [a]. However,

bare allegations that certain conduct is racially motivated are insufficient to raise a genuine triable issue. The opponent of a summary judgment motion must law bare its affirmative proof to demonstrate the existence of genuine triable issues, and reliance upon mere conclusory or unsubstantiated allegations is insufficient.
(Zuckerman v. City of New York, 49 N.Y. 2d 557; Corcoran Group, Inc., v. Morris, 107 A.D. 2d 622, affd., 64 N.Y. 2d 1034.) Under all of the circumstances of this case, this court is compelled to conclude that defendant is entitled to summary judgment dismissing plaintiff's sixth cause of action. As a result, the seventh cause of action for punitive damages due to the alleged racial discrimination must likewise fail.''

And in Roberts v. Jaguar Gold Products Corp., —NYS2d— (New York County, November 25, 1988) the at-will discharge doctrine was upheld, but the court found that the discharged employee nevertheless had a cause of action for the 1% incentive pay: "The complaint, however, states a cause of action with aspect to the alleged breach of the parties' incentive arrangement. Regardless of plaintiff's discharge, pursuant to the incentive arrangement provision of the parties' agreement, defendant's letter states plaintiff is 'to receive 1 percent of net sales of Jaguar Zodiac watches exceeding $3,000,000 in the calendar year of 1985.' ''

In the State of New Jersey the employment-at-will doctrine also holds sway, except where the termination breaches an express or implied promise to terminate for cause only, as illustrated in Shebar v. Sanyo Business Systems Corp., 544 A2d 377 (N.J., 1988), or where the termination contravenes an important public policy, as seen in Pierce v. Ortho Pharmaceutical Corp., 417 A2d 505 (N.J., 1980).

A.10 DRUG–TESTING IN THE WORKPLACE (*See* pages 7, 22–26)

In April 1989 the U.S. Supreme Court rendered a 5–4 decision approving the right of the U.S. Customs Service to impose mandatory urine tests to check for drug or alcoholic abuse in employees seeking drug-enforcement positions. In National Treasury Employees Union v. Von Raab, —S Ct— (1989) the highest court found that such testing did not violate the Fourth Amendment rights of privacy even when there was no evidence in advance of individual drug or alcohol abuse. According to the majority, the federal government "has a compelling interest in ensuring that front-line personnel are physically fit and have unimpeachable integrity and judgment."

The Drug-Free Workplace Act of 1988 (Pub L 100–690, signed into law by President Reagan on November 18, 1988) imposes on federal contractors the duty to maintain a workplace that is free of illegal drugs. Effective March 18, 1989, the Act provides that no person shall be considered a "responsible contractor" as defined in Section 4(a) of the Office of Federal Procurement Policy Act (41 USC 401 et seq) for the purpose of being awarded a contract for procurement of any property or services of a value of $25,000 or more, or a grant in any amount from any federal agency, unless the contractor certifies to the contracting agency that it will provide a drug-free workplace. See generally Silbergeld, "Federal Contractors Must Keep Work Place Free of Illegal Drugs," NLJ (January 16, 1989) at 18–19. Interestingly, the Federal Rehabilitation Act (29 USC 793 and 794) which protects handicapped persons from discrimination by most federal contractors and in federally funded programs, does not extend protection to any person who is an alcoholic or drug abuser whose current use of alcohol or drugs prevents him or her from performing the duties of a job or whose employment would directly threaten the property or safety of others. See Burka v. New York City Transit Authority, 680 F Supp 590 (SDNY, 1988).

In the State of Connecticut under Public Act No. 87–551 (1987) no employer may determine an employee's eligibility for promotion, additional compensation, transfer, termination, disciplinary, or other adverse personnel action solely on the basis of a positive urinanalysis drug test unless the employer gave the test using a reliable methodology which produced a positive test, a second urinanalysis test confirmed the first test result, and the third test used a gas chromatography and mass spectrometry methodology that had been determined by the State to be a reliable or more reliable test and had confirmed the results.

A.11 HANDICAPPED EMPLOYEES

See generally Sido and King, "Monetary Remedies Under the Education for All Handicapped Children Act: Toward a New Civil Rights Act?" 33 Tort & Ins L J (Summer 1988) at 711–743.

In the 1985 case of DeLa Torres v. Bolger, 610 F Supp 593 (ND Texas, 1985) the plaintiff employee was terminated on his 30-day evaluation report as "unsatisfactory." Apparently his supervisors at the U.S. Postal Service predicted that he "would not make it" because he was left-handed! His handicap of not being right-handed was, however, not recognized by the court because he did not have a physical or mental impairment which substantially limited one or more major life activities such as walking, seeing, hearing, speaking, working, etc. Yet 10 percent of the population is left-handed. See Case & Comment (September–October 1988) at 22. Cf. School Board of Nassau County v. Arline, 107 S Ct 1123 (1987).

A.12 INSURANCE COVERAGES AND EMPLOYMENT

In Cutwell Beef Co. v. Hartford Insurance Co., NYS2d (New York County, November 25, 1988) the employer who was burglarized filed a claim with defendant insurers for $12,500. The insurer refused payment on the ground of fraud because the proof for $173 of the amount was bogus; it had been "manufactured" by an employee without approval of plaintiff employer. The court opined that the doctrine of respondent superior barred plaintiff's recovery, even though the sum was relatively immaterial, but the employee's fraud was not immaterial, according to the court:

"I appreciate that the result to which I am tending is harsh, and I have struggled to find a decent formula to avoid it, but unsuccessfully. The result accords with unbroken authority at the highest level; Litke v. Travelers Ins. Co., 36 N.Y.2d 998; Saks & Co. v. Continental Ins. Co., 23 N.Y.2d 161; Seawide Fish Market, Inc. v. N.Y. Property Ins. Underwriting Assn., 111 A.D.2d 137; see Deitsch Textiles, Inc. v. N.Y. Property Ins. Underwriting Assn., 62 N.Y.2d 999; see Jonari Mgt. Corp. v. St. Paul Fire & Marine Ins. Co., 58 N.Y.2d 408. The result also accords with logic and sound public policy. Anything else would be an invitation to insured claimants to falsify with impunity in hopes of avoiding detection. The criminal law is an inadequate barrier to this kind of conduct."

See generally Peer and Mallen, "Insurance Coverage of Employment Discrimination and Wrongful Termination Actions," Defense Counsel J (October 1987) at 464–481.

A.13   JOB REFERENCES (*See* pages 133–34)

In Aaron v. R. H. Macy & Co., —F Supp— (SDNY, 1989) the federal district court threw out a suit by a disgruntled former employee who argued that the defendant retailer had broken a settlement agreement with a poor "job reference" given to a potential employer. According to the court, the potential employer had contacted another former employee of defendant retailer for a "job reference," and the latter's "job reference" could not be considered a recommendation or "job reference" by the defendant retailer.

A.14   NEGLIGENT HIRING (*See* pages 11–13)

The employer's tort risk begins when an applicant first approaches the employer in pursuit of a position, although negligent hiring actions have traditionally been the province of third parties who have been injured at the hands of the unfit employee. See generally Blakley, "Employer-Employee Relations: Employment Torts Come of Age; Increasing Risks of Liability for Employers and Their Insurers," 24 Tort & Ins L J (Winter 1989) at 268 et seq. To establish liability for negligent hiring the plaintiff must prove that the employee who caused the injury was unfit for his or her employment; secondly, plaintiff must prove that the employer's hiring or retention of the employee was the proximate cause of the injury to the plaintiff; and thirdly, plaintiff must prove that the employer knew or should have known that the employee was unfit. See Branch, Negligent Hiring Practice Manual (1988).

A.15   POLYGRAPH PROTECTION (*See* pages 45–48)

The Employee Polygraph Protection Act of 1988 (Pub L 100–347), effective December 27, 1988, bans the use of the polygraph for pre-employment screening or random testing by most private sector employers and significantly restricts use of polygraph tests in investigations. It is believed that the Act will curtail 85 percent of current polygraph usage, according to Waks, Brewster and Prager, "Investigating Workplace Wrongdoing Under Employee Polygraph Protection Act," NYLJ (November 15, 1988) at 1 and 6, and NYLJ (November 16, 1988) at 3. The Act provides exemption for the federal government, State, and local governments, although governments are subject to all constitutional restraints, as delineated in Texas State Employees Union v. Texas Dept. of Mental Health, 746 SW2d 203 (Texas, 1987). Where the polygraph is administered, it must be administered properly and carefully, as seen in Johnson v. Delchamps Inc., 846 F2d 1003 (5th Cir., 1988).

There appear to be about 28 states that lack their own statutes on polygraph testing according to New York Times (December 28, 1988) at A13. The complexity of lie detectors and polygraphs makes reliability difficult to gauge; see Hartford Courant (February 2, 1989) at F1. In Anderson v. City of Philadelphia, 845 F2d 1216 (3rd Cir., 1988) the court reversed the trial court's holding that use of the polygraph violated the due process and equal protection clauses of the U.S. Constitution; the Third U.S. Court of Appeals found that the use of the test for pre-employment screening was legitimate and not in violation of constitutional rights. Even polygraph testing on existing employees was approved in Zaccardi v. Zale Corp., 856 F2d 1473 (10th Cir., 1988). An at-will employee in Grynberg v. Alexander's Inc., 519 NYS2d 838 (1987) found that after he failed a polygraph test, he was not entitled to recover damages for injury to his reputation on a defamation theory! See generally Brown and Ream, "Polygraph Examinations for Employees," For the Defense (May 1989) at 2–6, which concluded: "Polygraph testing has been relied on for many years by employers as a means of deciding whether to hire a particular job applicant, as well as an investigative tool in instances of suspected employee dishonesty. But increasing state regulation of its use, and the sweeping federal Employee Polygraph Protection Act of 1988, make polygraphs less appealing. While no cases have yet interpreted the new federal law, its impact will almost certainly be to reduce the use of what, admittedly, has been a somewhat unreliable piece of machinery in the employment setting."

A.16   PREEMPTION (*See* pages 101–103)

A State-law based retaliatory discharge claim was not preempted by the Federal Labor Management Relations Act, according to the U.S. Supreme Court in Lingle v. Norge Division of Magic Chef Inc., 108 S Ct 1877 (1988), unless resolution of the State claim requires interpretation of a collective bargaining agreement (which it did not here). The State tort claim requires only findings of fact as to whether the employee was discharged and whether the discharge was motivated by a retaliatory reason. In Schultz v. National Coalition of Hispanic Mental Health and Human Services Organizations, 678 F Supp 936 (DC, 1988) the court concluded that "neither the plain language of ERISA nor its legislative history supports displacement of State employment law to the extent implied by defendants." Indeed, state laws of general application with only an incidental effect on ERISA plans fall outside the preemption provision, Mackey v. Lanier Collections Agency and Service Inc., 108 S Ct 2182 (1988). See generally Golden and Burkett, "ERISA Preemption of Damages in Wrongful Discharge Cases," Trial Magazine (December 1988) at 57 et seq.

A.17   PRIVATE CLUB DISCRIMINATORY PRACTICES

Discrimination by so-called private clubs is one of the most pervasive and entrenched forms of discrimination that employees with minority backgrounds have to face. The Anti-Defamation League of B'Nai B'rith has been the leader in this fight, and its Model Legislation Concerning Discrimination by Private Clubs (1989) is set forth in Exhibit 1.

A.18   PROPERTY OWNERSHIP IN WORK-FOR-HIRE SITUATIONS

"Work-for-hire" is defined in Section 102 of the Copyright Act of 1976 as work prepared by an employee within the scope of employment, or work specifically ordered or commissioned "within one of nine enumerated categories if the parties expressly agree in a written instrument signed by them that the work shall be considered a work made for hire." According to Raysman and Brown, the crucial question is how to determine who is an employee for copyright ownership purposes, as discussed in their article "Conflicting Standards in Work-for-Hire Situations," NYLJ (May 10, 1989) at 3 and 6. This article cites Dumas v. Gommerman, 865 F2d 1093 (9th Cir., 1989) for the "actual employee" test, and Aldon Accessories Ltd. v. Spiegel Inc., 738 F2d 548 (2nd Cir., 1984) for the "actual control" test. A third test, the "agency test," is described in Baster Seal Society v. Playboy Enterprises, 815 F2d 323 (5th Cir., 1987). It would appear that where signed assignments of copyrights are obtained, the various tests are immaterial.

A.19   PUNITIVE DAMAGES AND EMPLOYMENT (*See* pages 22, 48–50)

The availability of punitive damages in contract-based employment litigation is seen in Foley v. Interactive Data Corp., 765 P2d 373 (Cal., 1988) where the California Supreme Court reviewed plaintiff's allegation that his employer ter-

Exhibit 1
Model Legislation Concerning Discrimination by Private Clubs

I. General Prohibitions Against Discrimination by Clubs or Organizations

Sec. 1. *Findings and Purpose.*

After a public hearing and receipt of testimony, the [legislative body] finds and declares that:

A. Discriminatory practices of certain clubs or organizations where business is frequently conducted and personal contacts valuable for business purposes, employment and professional advancement are formed are a significant barrier to the advancement of women and minorities in business and professional opportunities in the State of [. . . . . . .].

B. Business activity most frequently occurs in clubs or organizations which have more than four hundred members and which provide regular meal services facilitating the conduct of such business.

C. Employers often pay their employee's membership dues and expenses at such clubs or organizations because the employees' activities at said clubs or organizations serve to develop and enhance the employer's business. Such clubs or organizations also rent their facilities for use as conference rooms for business meetings attended by non-members.

D. Clubs or organizations where the above practices occur provide benefits to business entities and persons other than members and thus are not in fact "distinctly private" in their nature.

E. The State of[. . . . . . .] has a compelling interest in eradicating discrimination based on sex, race, creed, color, religion, ancestry, national origin, actual or perceived sexual orientation, or disability in order to assure all of its citizens a fair and equal opportunity to participate in business and professional opportunites in [State]. Conduct and practices by clubs and organizations which exclude persons from entry, consideration for membership, or the full advantages and privileges of such membership on these bases are discriminatory and unacceptable, and are injurious to the body politic, the business community and the State of [. . . . . . .].

F. It has been a fundamental policy of [state] to combat discrimination and to ensure that all people, regardless of their sex, race, creed, color, religion, ancestry, national origin, actual or perceived sexual orientation, or disability, are treated equally, and that the state does not, in any manner, whether direct or indirect, foster or support discriminatory behavior.

G. While the [legislative body] recognizes the interest in private association asserted by club members, it finds that this interest does not overcome the public interest in equal opportunity. It is not the [legislative body]'s purpose to dictate the manner in which certain private clubs conduct their activities or select their members, except insofar as is necessary to ensure that clubs do not automatically exclude persons from consideration for membership or unreasonably prevent enjoyment of club accommodations and facilities on account of invidious discrimination. Furthermore, it is not the [legislative body]'s purpose to interfere in club activities or subject club operations to scrutiny beyond what is necessary in good faith to enforce this Article.

Sec. 2. *Definitions*

A. For purpose of this Article, a club or organization (hereinafter "club") which is not "distinctly private" refers to any organization, institution, club or place of accommodation which:

    a. Has membership of whatever kind totalling 400* or more; *and*
    b. Provides regular meal service; *and*

---

*A small municipality which seeks to pass this ordinance may wish to lower the membership figure.

c. Regularly accepts payments: (1) from non-members for expenses incurred at the club; or (2) from non-members in the furtherance of trade or business.

B. "Furtherance of trade or business" as used in this Article shall mean: 1) payment made by or on behalf of a trade, business or professional organization; 2) payment made by an individual from an account which the individual uses primarily for trade, business or professional purposes; 3) payment made by an individual who is reimbursed for the payment by the individual's employer or by a trade, business or professional organization, or other payment made in connection with an individual's trade, business, or profession, including entertaining clients or business associates, holding meetings or other business related events; or 4) payment made by an individual which is deducted from the individual's federal or state tax returns as a business expense.

C. "Commercial Agreement" as used in this Article includes, but is not limited, to a contract for the sale or lease of real or personal property, or a contract for services or the use of facilities.

Sec. 3. *Prohibited Practices by Clubs Which are Not Distinctly Private*

A. It shall be unlawful for a club which is not distinctly private to deny to any person entry, use of its facilities or membership, or to unreasonably prevent the full enjoyment of said club on the basis of a person's sex, race, creed, color, religion, ancestry, national origin, actual or perceived sexual orientation, or disability.

B. The determination that an entity is not "distinctly private" shall be made on an individual basis by the [state civil rights commission] in accordance with [the applicable provisions regarding their hearing procedures].

C. Any finding that an institution, association, club or other entity possesses the characteristics which render it a public accommodation under this section shall create a rebuttable presumption that it is a public accommodation. The [state civil rights commission] shall make a determination that an entity is a public accommodation if the entity fails to rebut that presumption.

Sec. 4. *Prohibited Practices: Government Meetings at Discriminatory Clubs*

A. No [state] official, employee or agent shall sponsor, organize, attend or participate in any meeting or other activity, the purpose of which is related to [state] business, in any establishment or facility which does not afford full membership rights and privileges to any person because of sex, race, creed, color, religion, ancestry, national origin, actual or perceived sexual orientation, or disability. This provision shall not apply to [state] officials, employees or agents acting in the course of ongoing law enforcement, code enforcement or other required investigations and inspections.

B. No [state] funds shall be expended in connection with any meeting or other activity held at any establishment or facility which does not afford full membership rights and privileges to any person because of sex, race, creed, color, religion, ancestry, national origin, actual or perceived sexual orientation, or disability. This provision shall not apply to [state] funds expended during the course of ongoing law enforcement, code enforcement or other required investigations and inspections.

C. No [state] official, employee or agent shall be reimbursed for any dues or any other expense incurred at an establishment or facility which does not afford full membership rights and privileges to any person because of sex, race, creed, color, religion, ancestry, national origin, actual or perceived sexual orientation, or disability. This provision shall not apply to expenditures incurred by [state] officials, employees or agents acting in the course of ongoing law enforcement, code enforcement or other required investigations and inspections.

D. For the purposes of this section, a public official is a person who holds any elected or appointed position in the [state].

Sec. 5. *Prohibited Practices: Government Contracts With Discriminatory Clubs*

A. No [state] official, employee or agent shall enter into any form of commercial agreement with a club which denies to any person entry, use of facilities or membership, or unreasonably prevents the full enjoyment of said club on the basis of sex, race, creed, color, religion, ancestry, national origin, actual or perceived sexual orientation, or disability.

B. Prior to entering into a commercial agreement with [state], a club must file a statement, verified by the president or chief executive officer of the club, that it is in full compliance with Section 5(A) of this Article.

C. Nothing in this Section shall be construed in a manner which will deprive any club of police protection, fire protection or other essential service necessary for public health or safety.

Sec. 6. *Enforcement and Penalties*

A. Civil Action. The State of [. . . . . .] or any person who is discriminated against in violation of this Article may enforce the provisions of this Article by means of a civil action. Any person who violates any of the provisions of this Article shall be liable to that person for the actual damages and such amount as may be determined by a jury or a court sitting without a jury, but in no case less than two hundred fifty dollars ($250), and such attorney's fees and court costs as may be determined by the court in addition thereto.

B. Injunction. Any persons who commit an act or engage in any pattern and practice of discrimination in violation of this Article may be enjoined therefrom by any court of competent jurisdiction. An action for injunction under this subsection may be brought by any person who is discriminated against in violation of this Article, by the State of [. . . . . .], or by any person or entity which will fairly and adequately represent the interests of the protected class.

C. Non-Exclusive Remedies and Penalties. Nothing in this Article shall preclude any person from seeking any other remedies, penalties or procedures provided by law.

Sec. 7. *Criminal Penalties*.

Notwithstanding any provisions of this code to the contrary, no criminal penalties shall attach for any violation of the provisions of this Article.

Sec. 8. *Severability*.

If any part or provision of this Article, or the application thereof to any person or circumstance, is held invalid, the remainder of this Article, including the application of such part or provision to other persons or circumstances, shall not be affected thereby and shall continue in force.

II. Prohibition Against Discrimination by Clubs Licensed to Sell Alcoholic Beverages

Sec. 1. *Findings and Purpose:*

The [legislative body] finds and declares that:

A. The State of [. . . . . .] has the authority to grant licenses to sell alcoholic beverages to clubs.

B. Such alcoholic beverage licenses are issued to serve the public and in such a manner as to protect the common good and, to that end, to provide an adequate number of places at which the public may obtain alcoholic beverages.

C. There is a compelling governmental interest in the State of [. . . . . .] that such licenses are issued only to serve the public need in a manner to protect the common good and that such licenses are not unduly limited with regard to public access.

Sec. 2. *Prohibition Against Discrimination*

A. No club licensed for the sale of alcoholic beverages to members and guests pursuant to [state ABC law] may deny to any person entry, use of facilities or membership, or unreasonably prevent the full enjoyment of said club on the basis of any person's sex, race, creed, color, religion, ancestry, national origin, actual or perceived sexual orientation, or disability.

B. The [state liquor licensing authority] shall not issue or renew a liquor license for the benefit of a club unless that club files a statement with the [state liquor licensing authority], verified by its president or chief executive officer, setting forth that it does not discriminate on the basis of sex, race, creed, color, religion, ancestry, national origin, actual or perceived sexual orientation, or disability.

Sec. 3. *Enforcement and Penalties*

A. The intentional filing of a false or misleading statement under this statute shall be a [misdemeanor] pursuant to [state statute].

B. A club found to be discriminatory under Section 2(A) of this Article shall be subject to fines up to [dollar amount] and shall lose its license 30 days after a final determination is made.

III. General Exemption from all Sections of the Statute

Nothing in this Article shall be construed to prohibit a religious organization or any organization operating solely for religious, charitable, educational or social welfare purposes, from restricting membership or facilities to persons of the same religious faith, where necessary to promote the religious principles under which it was established and is currently maintained. This exemption shall apply only to organizations whose primary purpose is to serve members of a particular religion.

minated his employment because he informed a company official that a newly hired supervisor was being investigated by the FBI for embezzling from his former employer. The court rejected the claim for punitive damages on the grounds of the need for "predictability of the consequences of actions related to the employment contract." In short, any breach of an implied contract of good faith and fair dealing would be addressed by contract remedies and not by tort remedies as punitive damages. In Purdy v. Consumers Distributors Co., 648 F Supp 980 (SDNY, 1986) the federal district court for the Southern District of New York rejected a punitive damages claim in a private employment dispute, unless the employee can show that the conduct complained about was not an isolated private wrong but rather a morally culpable course of conduct designed at injuring the public generally. In Vance v. Southern Bell Telephone and Telegraph Co., —F2d— (11th Cir., January 23, 1989) an award of $2.5 million in punitive damages was vacated because it was "outside the realm of reasonableness." To the same effect is Levinson v. Prentice Hall, —F2d— (3rd Cir., February 14, 1989).

See generally Korotkin, "Damages in Wrongful Termination Cases," A.B.A.J. (May 1989) at 84 et seq, concluding that the size of some damage awards are not the product of caprice but of calculation.

A.20   RELIGIOUS DISCRIMINATION AND HARASSMENT
(See **pages 69–72)**

Employers must accommodate their employees' needs to observe religious holidays according to the U.S. Supreme Court in Ansonia Board of Education v. Philbrook, 107 S Ct 367 (1986). Employers do not have to grant all the time off with pay; unpaid leave is a reasonable accommodation. The employer's burden is significant, as illustrated in Lake v. B. F. Goodrich Co., 837 F2d 449 (11th Cir., 1988), cert den 109 S Ct 76 (1988). Here a Seventh Day Adventist was scheduled by his employer to work a 7-day week and was terminated when part of his shift went uncovered. The court found that the employer had made "no real effort, certainly not a good faith effort, to find an accommodation" for the employee. In short, the employer had "failed to understand that the company had the burden to accommodate religious observances" and "could have accommodated the employee's religious belief without undue hardship." Note EEOC v. Ithaca Industries Inc., 849 F2d 116 (4th Cir., 1988), cert den 109 S Ct 306 (1988) where the employer failed to make a specific effort to accommodate the employee, and EEOC v. Townley, 859 F2d 610 (9th Cir., 1988) where the court opined that "a claim of undue hardship cannot be supported by merely conceivable or hypothetical hardships; instead, it must be supported by proof of 'actual imposition on co-workers' of disruption of work routine. . . . " See generally Berman, "Employers and Sabbath Observers—Another View," NYLJ (January 19, 1989) at 2.

The contrary view is espoused in Edelman, "Responsibilities of an Employer to a Sabbath Observer," NYLJ (January 4, 1989) at 1 and 2, citing, inter alia, Section 296(10)(b) of the New York Executive Law which provides that "no person shall be required to remain at his place of employment during the day . . . that, as a requirement of his religion, he observes as his Sabbath." The Edelman article concludes that most cases have found for the employer. In Eversley v. M Bank Dallas, 843 F2d 172 (5th Cir., 1988) the court found that the employer had made reasonable efforts to find other employment for a Sabbath observer, even though an alternative job was at lesser pay; the employer was under no obligation to set up schedules which were uneconomical or inconvenient, and was under no obligation to require a co-employee to switch with the Sabbath observer.

A.21   REVERSE DISCRIMINATION (*See* pages 55–86, 87–96)

In recent years the validity of "affirmative action" plans has been questioned on the grounds of promoting "reverse discrimination." Yet the general principle that preferential hiring may be appropriate to end discriminatory employment practices or the effects of those practices has been reaffirmed by the U.S. Supreme Court in United States v. Paradise, 107 S Ct 1053 (1987). Nevertheless, to the extent that an employer stays with strict quotas based on race or sex or other discriminatory criteria, the employer's remedial purpose for its plan of operation will continuously be questioned. See Spencer, "When Preferential Hiring Becomes Reverse Discrimination," 14 Employee Relations L J (Spring 1989) at 513 et seq.

A.22   SEXUAL HARASSMENT AND DISCRIMINATION (*See* pages 56, 72–75)

Sexual harassment is discrimination under State and federal law. Sexual harassment consists of verbal and/or physical contact of a sexual nature or with sexual overtones by a supervisor or co-worker with direct employment consequences, plus subtle forms of the same conduct, as delineated by the U.S. Supreme Court in Meritor Savings Bank v. Vinson, 106 S Ct 2399 (1986).

The highest court held that sexual harassment constituted discrimination under Title VII of the Civil Rights Act of 1964 because such conduct created "a hostile or abusive work environment." Indeed, a man's joke can be unwelcome to a female employee and constitute sexual advances; if repeated continuously, there would be a hostile environment and outright discrimination. Note that an employer is liable for the acts of its supervisors or agents regardless of whether the acts were authorized or forbidden by the employer, and regardless of whether the employer knew or should have known of the acts. But the employer is not strictly liable, and common defenses are acceptable, as stated in the Meritor Savings Bank case, supra. But where to draw the line between legally permitted interaction between the sexes in the workplace and conduct amounting to unlawful sexual harassment is difficult. See Hall v. Gus Construction Co. Inc., 842 F2d 1010 (8th Cir., 1988) on the issue of the employer taking prompt and effective remedial action to address the problem of sexual harassment once the employer knows or should have known of such illegal conduct.

In SUNY College of Environmental Science and Forestry v. State Division of Human Rights, —NYS2d— (App Div., 4th Dept., November 15, 1988) the court awarded a woman who was sexually harassed 11 years ago by her "affirmative action" supervisor at the college was awarded more than $100,000, since the college "encouraged, condoned and approved" the supervisor's conduct by failing to adequately respond to her complaint. The court found that the "persistent daily sexual harassment" clearly caused her great emotional anguish resulting in "significant physical manifestations" such as hives and other similar ailments.

In Huddleston v. Roger Dean Chevrolet Co., 845 F2d 900 (11th Cir., 1988) the federal appellate court held that an employer could be liable where its delegation of authority enabled the supervisor to engage in sexually harassing conduct, regardless of whether the employer knew of the offending conduct. See generally Wallach and Marx, "Courts Draw the Liability Line on Work Place Sex Harassment," NLJ (February 13, 1989) at 21 and 22. Also, note Levine, "Providing Service—or Aiding and Abetting Discrimination?" 14 Employee Relations L J (Spring 1989) at 607 et seq. citing, inter alia, Colorado Civil Rights Commission v. Travelers Insurance Co., P2d (Colo., July 19, 1988) where the Colorado Supreme Court found that a provision in a group health insurance excluding coverage of normal pregnancy expenses constituted discrimination on the basis of sex.

A.23 "WHISTLE-BLOWING" AND THE EMPLOYMENT CONTRACT (*See* pages 3, 9, 42–45)

There are many federal and state statutes protecting employees who "whistle-blow" from discharge or termination. But in Ewing v. NLRB, —F2d— (2nd Cir., November 2, 1988) the Second U.S. Court of Appeals dismissed an action by an employee who was discharged for allegedly filing a complaint over workplace safety standards. The defendant's dismissal of the action was based on its determination that individual invocation of a statutory employment right did not constitute "concerted activity" under the National Industrial Recovery Act of 1933! Even the court was somewhat reluctant to deprive the employee of employment protection: "The Board's conclusion that a single employee's invocation of a statutory employment right is not 'concerted activity' is not, in our view, preferable. . . . Were we considering the question de novo, we might have considered the opposite view more in keeping with the spirit and purpose of the NIRA. . . . As it stands, the NLRB's interpretation . . . would allow management to discharge or otherwise discipline an individual worker for exercising statutory employment rights."

A.24 WRONGFUL DISCHARGES (*See* pages 2–3, 37–54)

Wrongful dismissal or wrongful discharge has been a lucrative field for both the terminated employee and his attorney, as illustrated by Williams v. Hall, F Supp (ED Ky., June 10, 1988) where a $25 million settlement was achieved. Two former vice presidents of Ashland Oil Co., the nation's largest independent petroleum refiner and marketer and distributor of industrial chemical products, were fired when they refused to follow the company defense in proceedings before the SEC and the IRS. The six-week trial brought an award to one plaintiff of more than $7.5 million in compensatory damages, tripled to $23.2 million, and $500,000 in punitive damages, plus $1.25 million in punitive damages against two named executives, plus attorneys fees and court costs; when combined with the other successful plaintiff, the cumulative total of damages exceeded $70 million. See 32 ATLA L Rep (April 1989) at 104–106.

But on December 29, 1988 in Foley v. Interactive Data Corp., 765 P2d 373 (Cal., 1988) the California Supreme Court limited damages to the contractual measure and not to the tortious measure of damages, despite the tortious breach of the implied covenant of good faith and fair dealing in the context of employment contract termination. According to the court, the relationship between employee and employer is "fundamentally contractual" and therefore damages are not measured by a tortious injury standard. See NLJ (January 16, 1989) at 3 and 22. According to the court: "contractual remedies should remain the sole available relief for breaches of implied covenant of good faith and fair dealing in the employment context. . . . [Employers] should not be deprived of discretion to dismiss an employee by the fear that doing so will give rise to potential tort recovery in every case." See New York Times (December 30, 1988) at D1 and D4; A.B.A.J. (March 1989) at 20 and 22, citing the California case of Moradi-Shalal v. Fireman's Fund Insurance Co., 758 P2d 58 (Cal., 1988) as justification for the Foley case; and Estreicher and Robbins, "A California Ruling on Damages Marks a Victory for Both Sides," NLJ (April 10, 1989) at 20 and 21, in which the authors opined that "the ultimate arena in which wrongful discharge litigation will be shaped is the State legislature."

In the Connecticut case of Louis M. Sileo v. Gulf & Western Inc., 15 CLT 21 (Conn Super, May 22, 1989) the plaintiff's wrongful discharge claim sanctioned claims for emotional distress, injury to reputation and lost wages, as well as punitive damages limited to costs of litigation plus attorneys' fees, less taxable costs.

Index to Cases

Subject Index

About the Author

WARREN FREEDMAN, member of the New York, Connecticut, Federal, and U.S. Supreme Court bars, was formerly Liability Counsel and Assistant Secretary for Bristol-Myers Co. Mr. Freedman presently serves as State Trial Referee, or Acting Judge, for the Connecticut Superior Court in Hartford, CT. Among his previous books are *Foreign Plaintiffs in Products Liability Actions, Frivolous Lawsuits and Frivolous Defenses, Federal Statutes on Environmental Protection, The Right of Privacy in the Computer Age, The Tort of Discovery Abuse,* and *The Constitutional Right to a Speedy and Fair Criminal Trial,* all published by Quorum Books.